To Jeff's children, Paris and Miles, and
to Elizabeth's emerging adults, Nate and Will

———————————

Published simultaneously in Canada by Thomas Allen & Son Limited.

Library of Congress Cataloging-in-Publication Data is available.

ISBN 978-0-7611-6241-4

Design by Sarah Smith
Jacket design by Raquel Jaramillo
Front jacket photo by Kamenetskiy Konstantin/Shutterstock
Elizabeth Fishel photo © Lisa Keating Photography

Workman books are available at special discounts when purchased in bulk for premiums and sales promotions as well as for fund-raising or educational use. Special editions or book excerpts also can be created to specification. For details, contact the Special Sales Director at the address below, or send an email to specialmarkets@workman.com.

Workman Publishing Co., Inc.
225 Varick Street
New York, NY 10014-4381
workman.com

WORKMAN is a registered trademark of Workman Publishing Co., Inc.

Printed in the United States of America
First printing May 2013

10 9 8 7 6 5 4 3 2 1

WHEN WILL MY GROWN-UP KID GROW UP?

Loving and Understanding Your Emerging Adult

JEFFREY JENSEN ARNETT, Ph.D.

and ELIZABETH FISHEL

WORKMAN PUBLISHING

NEW YORK

CONTENTS

INTRODUCTION

Why This Book (and Why We're Writing It Together)

Elizabeth

When my sons, Nate and Will, left for college on the other side of the country, I thought my child-raising days were over. No more family dinners, carpools, or weekends spent cheering at soccer games. But with their first phone calls home ("Should I take Economics 1 or Modern Poetry?" "How do you make lasagna?" "Do I have to separate lights and darks?") and the hundreds of email exchanges that followed, I realized that I was not quite out of business yet.

This new stage of parenting was not as daily or hands-on as before (and it was often virtual), but the boys and I still had a vital relationship. During the college years and beyond, they would disappear for a while, then check in. They would want help making this decision or that. They would come home for vacations or after they graduated. They would have money woes, or need financial advice (or, more likely, a bailout). They would fall in love (fewer calls), then out of love (more moral support). They would look for jobs, not find them, then find them, and leave them. They would travel to the other side of the world but Skype to stay connected. And then they would come home again, if only for a while, to retrench before embarking on the next phase of their lives.

Although we were relieved that our sons remained part of the family even as they launched themselves into the world, my husband and I were often confused about how to be good parents at this stage. When the boys were little, all it took was an extra-large pepperoni pizza and a bunch of Jim Carrey videos to make them happy. Now nothing was that uncomplicated. Their moods were as variable as their tastes in rap artists, blue jeans, and sushi. They could be fabulous company, full of humor and insights. But they could easily drift off to another planet, distracted or zoned out on their cell phones, checking email or surfing the Web for answers to life's big questions (or at least for their fantasy football scores). Their uncertainty about their life paths in turn stirred up our uncertainty about them. We often huddled behind closed doors and wondered, "Are they all right? Will they land on their feet? Is there something we should be doing to help them along?"

At dinner parties we compared notes with friends who had kids the same age. Most were similarly bewildered by their 20-somethings. Some were seriously concerned. One friend's daughter had opted out of college; without a circle of peers around, she was lonely and depressed. Another's son had changed his college major so many times that his parents wondered if he would ever graduate. Still another friend's son was living through a violent revolution in a far-off country and hadn't communicated in weeks. And another mother bemoaned her daughter's unemployed, live-in boyfriend and her son's choice to be a "manny" while writing his Great American Novel. "I could choose such perfect partners for them and such wonderful careers, if they'd just ask," she said with a sigh, only half joking. As if.

We also heard the anguish from parents in our circle who were coping with life-and-death issues and desperate to know how to cope with grown children's lives gone haywire: drug addiction, suicide attempts, bipolar illness with frightening outbursts of mania. The twenties are the years when certain mental health issues first become apparent, and the parents grappling with those problems were the most shaken and the most in need of support.

As we fretted about our kids there was one more topic that newly empty-nested parents discussed with equal passion: our own lives and how they, too, were suddenly full of uncertainty and flux. Raising kids had provided pleasure and meaning and structure for eighteen years or more, and now everything was up for grabs. Our marriages and friendships. Our finances and work lives. Our newly quiet households. What we did for fun. "I feel as if I've been at the center of the best party for twenty-five years," one friend said after the last of her three sons left home. "And now it's over." It seemed ironic that we parents were asking ourselves the very same question our kids were asking themselves: "What do we do with the rest of our lives?"

How my friends and I wished we had a guidebook to turn to! We had consulted Dr. Spock, T. Berry Brazelton, and *What to Expect the First Year* when the kids were young. Now we needed a parenting book that would not only steer us through our children's twenties but also shed light on our own lives.

Jeff

I began interviewing young people in their twenties during the early 1990s, when I was just beyond that age myself and a developmental psychologist and junior professor at the University of Missouri. It seemed to me that my experience of the years between 20 and 30 didn't fit any of the theories I had learned in psychology. It certainly wasn't "adolescence," even "late adolescence." Adolescence is defined by puberty, going to middle school and high school, and having a daily life structured by the demands of school and family.

It didn't seem like full-fledged adulthood, either. I thought of adulthood as a time of settling into grown-up commitments like marriage and parenthood, and that is not what my twenties had been about. I wanted to see what others' experience of those years was like. I found that for most of the people I interviewed it was a time of exceptional freedom, flux, and uncertainty, as it had been for me. Before long I became convinced that the period from the late teens through the twenties was now a new life stage, neither "adolescence" nor "adulthood" but something in between and unprecedented. To fit these young people's sense of being on the way to adulthood but not there yet, I decided to call the new stage "emerging adulthood."

Comparing today's emerging adults to their parents and grandparents at the same age, I was struck by how much had changed. In the past fifty years a revolution had occurred. People used to enter full-time work, marriage, and parenthood around age 20. Now it's really true that "30 is the new 20." Young people marry and become parents much later than in the past, and they stay in college longer and are more likely to go to graduate school. Premarital sex and cohabitation have become typical (if not entirely accepted), so that it is no longer necessary to get married to have regular sex. The rate of marriage is down and the number of unmarried women having children is up. The lives of young women have changed beyond recognition. More women than men are getting college degrees, and they now have their own career ambitions. Rather than looking for a husband to support them, most women will be financially independent—or supporting their husbands and families.

From the beginning, the relationships between emerging adults and their parents was one of the areas that fascinated me most. Having studied adolescence for years, I knew it as a time of high conflict between parents and children. In contrast, emerging adults spoke of their parents with love and respect. They got along better with their parents in part because they went out of their way to avoid conflict, editing their conversations with parents to sidestep anything that might stir up trouble. But the shift was more positive than that. Emerging adults seemed to like and understand their parents far more than adolescents did. They were less egocentric than adolescents, and more able to see life from their parents' point of view. Many of them were horrified at how they had treated their parents just a few years before, and were eager to make it up to them.

Elizabeth

Although I'd spent all of my career writing books and articles about family life, being a parent to our 20-something sons took me by surprise. This decade was turning out to be even more of a challenge than the toddler or teen years. When to step in, when to step aside? Where to take a stand, where to give way? How to be involved but not intrusive, caring but not overwhelming, open about what we believed but not dogmatic? And how to help when grown children did not seem to be thriving at all?

When I first encountered Jeff's work on emerging adulthood, I felt that I'd finally found an explanation and a framework to help me understand this rocky new emotional terrain. Jeff had interviewed hundreds of 18- to 29-year-olds all over the country about exactly the topics that I was up against with my sons: the twists and turns through college; finding love and looking for meaningful work; spiritual questions; and the nature of our relationship with one another.

I found Jeff's research at exactly the right time, too. Nate was just graduating from college and beginning to make his way into the world; Will was starting college and a new life three thousand miles away. Their worlds were filled with dreams and opportunities, as well as indecision, drama, and occasional chaos. Jeff's road map gave me hope and confidence: Being in constant flux is what emerging adults do, and understanding that reality immediately helped me relax as a parent.

When we met and decided to collaborate I felt we could create together exactly the guidebook I had dreamed of having. And with my sons—and eight nieces and nephews—still working their way through their twenties, I knew I would not run out of personal material.

Jeff

I've spoken to hundreds of parents about emerging adulthood in the past decade, and nearly every time parents approach me afterward and thank me for helping them understand where their children are at. Many of them have children who are struggling to find a place in the world, and just knowing what is normal comes as a great relief. They are comforted to know that it is common for 18- to 29-year-olds to have a period of years when the way forward is uncertain. And they find hope when they hear that nearly all emerging adults settle into the stable commitments of adulthood by their late twenties or early thirties.

I have thought often of writing a book for parents, knowing how enlightening and reassuring so many parents find the idea of this new life stage of emerging adulthood. Still, I hesitated. As a parent of 13-year-old twins, I know that I would prefer to take parenting advice about 13-year-olds from someone who has been the parent of a 13-year-old. I was reluctant to give advice to parents of emerging adults, even though I know a lot about how these young people view life and their goals, hopes, and fears.

When I met Elizabeth, I felt I had found the ideal collaborator. She is the mother of two children currently going through their twenties, so she's right in the middle of all the topics we are writing about in this book. As a bonus, she is an accomplished writer and is knowledgeable about psychological development throughout the life span.

Now, after three years of working together doing in-depth interviews and an extensive survey with hundreds of parents around the country, we hope we've written a book that will serve as a helpful guide to parents as their children make their way through this fascinating, eventful, sometimes confusing and exasperating, often wonderful time of life.

We would sum up our message this way. Years ago, Dr. Spock counseled new parents, "Trust yourself. You know more than you think you do." This time, trust yourself *and* your children. They may careen or falter or dash forward only to fall back. But eventually, nearly all of them will find their way. We offer this book to help you find your way along with them.

1

The Zigzagging Road
to Adulthood

When I was 22, I was engaged. At 23, I was married.
We worked six days a week and banked every single penny
to buy a house. My son spends every penny he gets.

MOTHER OF A SON, 22

They sometimes seem like a new breed, the young people of the twenty-first century. In many ways they are following a much longer road to adulthood than their parents and grandparents did, and it's one filled with false starts and U-turns that may puzzle the older generations. Not so long ago, adulthood arrived right after the teen years. By age 20 or 21 most young people had finished their education and started working. They were married or about to be married, and were new parents or planning for parenthood. Their adult lives were basically set, and they had a clear road map for what the decades to come would be like.

Now, at age 20, adulthood is still a long distance away, barely visible way out there on the horizon, with a vast, uncharted territory to cross before it is reached.

Consider some of the changes that have affected the lives of young people over the past half century.

• In 1960, the median marriage age in the United States was just 20 for women and 22 for men; today it's 27 for women and 29 for men, and still rising. In Canada and Europe it is even higher.

• The entry to parenthood has followed a parallel path to marriage, with the average age moving from the early twenties to the late twenties, and for many even to the early thirties. The birthrate has declined steeply in the United States, from 3.5 children per woman in 1960 to 2.0 in 2010. Similar declines have taken place in Canada and Europe.

• In 1960 only 33 percent of young people attended college, and most of them were men; today, 70 percent of high school graduates enter college the next year, and most of them are women. It now takes an average of five to six years to obtain a "four-year degree." All over the world, more young people are obtaining more education than ever before.

• Young Americans no longer settle into stable work shortly after high school. They change jobs an average of seven times from age 20 to 29. Most don't find a long-term job until their late twenties or beyond. This, too, is an international pattern.

One key reason for all these changes is economic. As the economy shifted from manufacturing to information, technology, and services, more education and training were required to fill the new jobs. Longer education and training led in turn to later marriage and parenthood. However, it's not only the economics of young people's lives that have changed in the past fifty years, but a wide range of attitudes, values, and expectations. Three upheavals shook America—and much of the world—in the 1960s and '70s and shaped the society we know today: the Sexual Revolution, the Women's Movement, and the Youth Movement.

Premarital sex used to be scandalous, and for young women risky, because of pregnancy fears, and disgraceful, if they were found out. Now, although their elders sometimes disapprove, for young people who have grown up in the aftermath of the Sexual Revolution with the freedom provided by contraception and the possibility of legal abortion, premarital sex is widely considered a normal part of a loving relationship. Similarly, cohabitation used to be "living in sin." Now it's normal, and

most young people view it as an important precautionary or prepara-
tory step before marriage, a way to get to know each other and make
sure they're compatible.

Young women's possibilities for adult life used to be mostly limited
to wife and mother; if they had a career—nurse, teacher, or secretary
were the main options—it ended with the birth of their first child. Now,
in the aftermath of the Women's Movement, few young women see their
gender as an obstacle to any future they might choose. They are as likely
as young men to be enrolled in medical school, law school, or graduate
business school. Rather than relying on men to support them, and hence
striving to find husbands as soon as possible, they want to have incomes
of their own. Most still plan to be wives and mothers, but they have career
goals as well, and they would prefer to wait for marriage and motherhood
until they have made substantial progress toward those goals.

Most subtle of all—but perhaps most important—the meaning and
desirability of adulthood itself have changed. For the young people of
fifty years ago, becoming an adult was an attractive prospect, a sign of
status and achievement. They could hardly wait to get there, and within
a few years after high school, most did. They had the new marriage, the
new baby, the starter house, the lawn, the car in the driveway. Today,
in the aftermath of the Youth Movement of the 1960s, young people
have much more mixed feelings about reaching adulthood. The value of
youth has risen, and the desirability of adulthood has dropped accordingly. Today's young people expect to reach adulthood eventually, and
they expect to enjoy their adult lives, but most are in no hurry to get
there. In their late teens and early twenties they are wary of the stability it represents, because in their eyes, along with stability comes stagnation. They prefer to spend the early part of their twenties unfettered,
having experiences that won't be open to them once the mantle of adult
responsibilities settles on their shoulders.

Put all these changes together, and the result is that young people
are no longer jumping from adolescence in their teens to a settled entry
to adulthood in their early twenties. Instead, there is a new life stage in
between adolescence and young adulthood. Jeff has studied this period
extensively and helped define it, giving it the name *emerging adulthood*

in 2000, and by now the term is widely used by researchers in psychology and other social sciences.

It's not just the social scientists who have noticed that the road to adulthood is different today. Many parents can't help but notice how different the twenties have become since they were young. "I do think times have changed," reflects a mother we interviewed in her early fifties. "For us you went to school, you met someone, you got married." In contrast, her son is now 21 and seems in no hurry to commit to adult responsibilities. "He's very young for his age," she says. "I had a plan, but he's just 'whatever.'"

So if we can all agree the twenties have changed, what are they like now? What is going on in the lives of these grown-up kids? And how should parents respond? What can parents do to help their children navigate this exciting but sometimes perilous decade? What options do parents have if they see their children floundering rather than flourishing in the face of the many challenges of emerging adulthood?

This book is devoted to answering these questions. A new life stage for young people requires a new guidebook for parents, and we aim to provide that here. We explore how life has changed for 20-somethings today in every sphere: in college and after they graduate, falling in love and thinking about marriage, finding first jobs and getting established in careers, managing money and answering questions about faith. We look at what happens when young people experience bumps or serious roadblocks on the way to adulthood. And we examine the evolving relationship between you and your emerging adults—and how your own life changes just as theirs does.

The book is based on over two decades of Jeff's research and interviews with emerging adults, as well as ninety new in-depth interviews done by Jeff and Elizabeth with a diverse group of parents and emerging adults. (We have changed the names of all the parents and 18- to-29-year-olds we interviewed, as well as occasional details to protect their privacy. We refer to them by first name only. We refer to ourselves by our first names as well, but we use full names for the other experts we consulted.)

We also present insights from a 2012 national survey of over a thousand 18- to 29-year-olds, the Clark University Poll of Emerging Adults (CUPEA), which was directed by Jeff, who has been a professor of psychology at Clark since 2005. In addition, we draw on the thoughtful responses from over four hundred parents all over the country to a survey we conducted online. Finally, we have incorporated the latest research by others who study emerging adults, as well as the advice of experts in psychology, education, career counseling, and financial planning who work closely with this age group. We combine the latest research, thoughtful guidance, and illustrative examples from real lives so that you will find valuable take-aways for your own families in these stories.

The results of all this research are complex—if only the challenges of parenting the emerging adult could be reduced to a simple piece of advice like "burp after feeding"—but you'll see that there is one theme that we'll come back to time and again: how to *step back while staying connected.* The stepping back part is perhaps the more obvious of the two. By the time children reach age 18, parents have had a lot of practice at it. They stepped back a little the first time they dropped their child off at daycare or preschool, a little more on the first day of primary school, and steadily more with the first sleepover, the first date, and the first time driving the car alone. As their children pass through the late teens and twenties, most parents are happy to step back further, and they take satisfaction in seeing their children make decisions and rise to the challenges of education, work, and long-term love.

> I remember finishing school and having my first job right after. A lot of it was boring. And I remember thinking, Oh my God, I went to all this trouble to get this education, and now I don't like it! I didn't think about other options. I'm not the only one who has had that experience; that's why middle-aged adults advise their children to take their time. The parents have often asked themselves, Did I really make the right decisions? Did I really explore my options?
>
> **MOTHER OF A SON, 25**

However, most parents also want to stay connected to their grown-up kids. Today's parents have cultivated close relationships with their children since the kids were very young. More than previous generations, they wanted to be not just parents but close friends to their children, with less of the parent-child hierarchy that they had experienced with their own parents. For the most part, they succeeded, and when their children grow up and begin to build their own adult lives, most parents want to stay emotionally close and keep the connection strong, while also giving emerging adults room to grow and stand on their own.

Connected is good—except when it isn't. During their children's twenties parents are likely to face—perhaps multiple times—the tricky question of how involved they should be in their emerging adults' choices and when it is wisest to step aside. All parents need to find their own comfort zone, but we'll provide guidance, examples, and some dos and don'ts from our research with families going through this stage of life.

And one other important thing: This is a book not only about emerging adults' development but about *parents'* development, too. A longer

---

Q: *I have three kids in their late teens and early twenties, and all of them seem to have big dreams—be a movie director, create the latest technological sensation, own a restaurant—and no apparent strategy for reaching them. When does optimism become delusion?*

A: It's a pretty fine line! And it can be hard to tell the difference, especially with emerging adults. Their high hopes can be unsettling to their parents, who know the likely fate of youthful dreams, but it's best to see optimism as a psychological resource that allows them to keep getting up again after they get knocked down, as most of them will in the course of their twenties. At least they have goals; perhaps the strategies will follow. Most of them will have to adjust their dreams a bit—opening a restaurant is a notoriously tricky business—but hey, some of them may actually have the talent and spirit to make those dreams come true. You may yet be dining at your son's or daughter's café.

---

road to adulthood for children means changes not just in their lives but also in their parents' lives. While their children are emerging, parents may find that they are reemerging. During their children's twenties, they finally have a chance to take a second look at their own lives and reassess not only their parenting role but their love lives, their jobs, their finances, and their dreams for the rest of their lives.

Yet the continuing needs of their grown-up kids may surprise parents and disrupt the process of turning toward their own lives and their own development. Parents may find themselves on duty longer than they expected, as daily hands-on parenting turns out to stretch past the 18 years they originally signed up for—perhaps 20 or 25 years or more. They may have to shoulder the financial support for their children for more years than they had planned, resulting in delays and disruptions in their own plans for retirement, for travel, or simply for achieving financial stability and security. Their health and energy may not be as good as it used to be when they chased after toddlers. They may also be pushed and pulled between their grown children's requests, both emotional and financial, and their aging parents, who also require more support and attention as the years go on. Yes, they may cherish their ties with both older and younger generations. But they may also feel impatience or frustration as that inner voice grows more insistent, asking, "When will I have time for my own life?" We'll explore these complicated questions of midlife development in Chapter 2, "Your Parallel Journey," and thereafter we'll discuss emerging adults' development and parents' development together in each chapter.

Let's begin by meeting some of the young people we interviewed whose lives illustrate the characteristics of emerging adulthood and the phases of this new life stage:

• Jake, age 21, is living in his parents' basement while working three jobs. He also attends community college, where he is studying criminal justice, and he sees more education to come. But he would like to be able to afford to move out on his own soon. Living at home makes him more dependent on his parents than he would like to be, and leads them to treat him more like a child than an adult. Though his mom is crazy about him, his dropped wet towels and pigsty of a room are making her crazy in a different way.

• Kendra, age 21, married at 19 and divorced a year later. Now she is living with a new boyfriend, but they fight frequently. She is talking about moving back in with her mother, but her mother, who is enjoying being free of daily parenting duties, is not so excited about the idea. Kendra is working as a checkout clerk at Target but making only minimum wage; it is clearly a job that is leading nowhere. She is thinking about going back to school, but to study what, and with what money?

• Ted, age 23, made it through college despite many emotional crises. But in his first year of graduate school, he seemed to lose interest, first in his studies and then in everything else. He was eventually diagnosed with major depression. He had to drop out of school, get professional help, and start medication.

• Susan, age 26, works for a nonprofit organization promoting environmental issues. It is work she enjoys and hopes to do for a long time to come. Her love life is less settled than her career. She's never had a serious boyfriend, and this missing piece causes her some anxiety, especially now that her friends are starting to pair up and get married. Yet she is also enjoying the freedom of being unattached in her twenties: "I can sleep over at a friend's on a Tuesday night and it's my decision."

• Malcolm, age 26, just returned from Afghanistan after serving in the Navy and is in transition. He's thirty credits shy of completing his B.A., has already been married and divorced, and has two small kids. His mom worries about his psychological problems (depression and anxiety) and his overdependence on violent video games and porn, which began while he was stationed abroad.

• Alexandra, age 27, lives in a big city, where she is an assistant editor at a magazine. Her job is demanding, often requiring evenings and weekends as a publishing deadline approaches, but she loves it. She lives with three friends, and on evenings when she is not working they are often in bars or clubs . . . and often drinking a bit too much. Her boyfriend of six months wants her to move in with him and is dropping hints about marriage. But she has lived with two other boyfriends, and it was painful and complicated to move out. Plus, she is not sure she loves him, and she's not sure she wants to give up her fun with her friends and all the other possible guys that might be out there.

• Karl, age 28, moved back in with his parents about a year ago. His parents describe him as having "no girlfriend, no job, no friends, and no motivation or ambition." He spends most of his nights drinking and playing video games, and most of his days sleeping. When he works, it's part-time, and only enough to pay his bills. His parents think he's depressed, but he refuses their offers to pay for a therapist.

• Simon, age 29, had two longish relationships in his earlier twenties that didn't work out, and has had a bunch of odd jobs to support himself. But a couple of years ago, he entered a graduate teaching program, and now he's found his calling as a third grade teacher in an inner-city school. Around the same time, he met his soul mate, a young woman with a career in television production, and they just became engaged.

The Five Features of Emerging Adulthood

With all this diversity, is there any way to make sense of the 18-to-29 age period? In the course of twenty years of research, Jeff has identified five features that describe this new life stage of emerging adulthood. The five features don't apply to all emerging adults, but they ring true for most of them.

1. *Identity explorations.* The emerging adult years are a time of exploring the big identity questions: Who am I? What do I really want out of life? And how do I fit into the world around me? To answer these questions, emerging adults try out various possible futures in love and work. These explorations can be exciting and motivating, and they can also be unsettling and overwhelming—both for the young people in question and for their parents. Sometimes exploring looks a lot like wandering, floundering, or even a failure to *grow up, for Pete's* *sake,* in the eyes of exasperated parents. But for the most part, sorting through the varied choices that are becoming available to them helps emerging adults learn more about who they are and how they want to shape their adult lives.

2. *Instability.* Emerging adults may change college majors, jobs, living situations, and love partners with dizzying frequency. Parents sometimes wonder if their children will ever settle on something, *anything,* but in nearly all cases the instability of emerging adulthood is a temporary but necessary part of identity explorations. Remember, parents, almost everyone has a more stable life by their thirties than they did in their twenties.

3. *Self-focus.* Most emerging adults are not selfish, although they're often accused of this. Just compare them to what they were like as teenagers, and you'll probably agree they are more considerate of others than teens are, and better at taking other people's perspectives. However, emerging adulthood is a time of intense self-focus, in the sense that your grown kids are focusing on their own lives, especially on how to get the education or training to qualify for a good job and then how to find one. They have to be self-focused, in order to make their way into a competitive adult world, and they're free to be self-focused, because most have fewer daily responsibilities or obligations to others than they'll ever have again. Emerging adults may seem selfish to parents when they don't return calls or "click reply" as soon as parents would like—and sometimes they are—but their self-focus doesn't mean they don't love their parents. It's all part of learning to stand alone as a self-sufficient person—an important goal in the emerging adult years.

4. *Feeling in-between.* Emerging adults don't feel like children or teenagers anymore, but most of them don't feel entirely adult, either. Instead, they feel in-between, on the way to adulthood but not there yet. And they have mixed feelings about the destination. Adulthood appeals to them for the stability it offers, and the rewards of marriage, children, and (they hope) a good job, but it also looks frighteningly predictable. Parents should recognize the ambivalence their children may have about adult responsibilities. Still, it's OK to expect that emerging adults will take on some adult duties, such as handling their finances responsibly, making (and keeping) their own appointments, and contributing an adult share of household work if they have moved back home. They are capable of far more than what many parents often ask of them.

5. *Sense of possibilities.* Emerging adulthood is a time of remarkably high hopes for almost everyone, even if life is currently not going all that well (and often it's not). Most are not entirely content with life as it is, but they believe they are on the way to better times. In the national CUPEA survey, a remarkable 90 percent of emerging adults agreed that "I am confident that eventually I will get what I want out of life." No matter how dismal their love lives, most young people believe that eventually they'll find a "soul mate." No matter how dreary their current job, most believe they'll someday be doing work they love and that pays well. Parents may worry that their children expect too much, but they should realize that emerging adults are quite good at modifying their ideals once they test them in real life. There's no need to remind them that their bubble is bound to burst. They'll find that out soon enough, on their own.

Launching, Exploring, and Landing

E merging adulthood covers the years between 18 and 29, and a lot happens during those years. Loving and losing love and finding it again; deciding on a direction in work and then realizing it's a dead end and forging ahead with a new focus; having memorable adventures (including some they may wish to forget); moving out of their parents' house, then sometimes moving back in again, and eventually setting up their own home. Most people are in a much different place by their late twenties than they were at age 18, so we have defined three phases within emerging adulthood: launching, exploring, and landing. The age ranges here are approximate, of course, but most people travel through all three phases to some degree.

Launching: ages 18 to 22. This is the entry phase of emerging adult-hood, when there are important strides toward independence but still a lot of reliance on Mom and Dad. To begin with, few 18- to 22-year-olds are capable of entirely supporting themselves financially. Either they are in college and not working or working only part-time, or they are in the workplace full-time but in a job that is not adequate to support independent living. Emotionally, too, they still need a lot of support when they hit bumps on the road to the life they envision, as nearly all of them do. The launching phase is also the time when most grown kids first leave home, either to go to college or to live on their own. Some 18-year-olds leave home and never look back, keeping in touch with parents only occasionally thereafter. But most 18- to 22-year-olds will want frequent contact with their parents, by phone, text, Facebook, Skype, or what-ever the latest technological marvel is, and if they're close enough they'll come home often for a good meal and some loving care. Gradually, over the course of the launching period, they learn to stand more on their own and they feel more comfortable about living independently.

Exploring: ages 22 to 26. By this phase most emerging adults have shaken off the insecurity and uncertainty of the launching phase. They have learned important lessons about making their own decisions and taking responsibility for themselves. They feel more confident in their ability to live on their own, and most have gained either the college cre-dentials or the work experience to get a job where they can make enough to support themselves—although many will still need to make the occa-sional cash withdrawal from the Bank of Mom and Dad, especially when the overall economy is rocky.

They get more serious during this phase about exploring work options and deciding what they really want to do—and trying to match that with the reality of what is actually available to them. Parents may be surprised (and dismayed) to find that going to college was just a preliminary step in this process. Many 22- to 26-year-olds entering the workplace will end up doing something that has little relation to what they learned in college, and parents may despair about the not-so-small fortune they spent to enable their children to get a college degree. However, having the college degree makes a huge difference in getting a good job, even if the connection to the actual work is not evident at first. Some young people in this phase decide to return to school in order to get further education now that they have a better idea of who they are and what field interests them most.

In love, too, the exploring period is a time for getting more serious. The days of college "hookups" are past. Hookups still take place, of course, but most 22- to 26-year-olds are looking for something more intimate and enduring. They are now searching for a "soul mate," that special person who seems just right for them and makes the prospect of marriage seem welcoming and delightful.

Landing: ages 26 to 29. During the last years of their twenties, most emerging adults make the important choices that will form the structure of their adult lives in love and work. Most are either married or cohabiting by this time, and most of those who are not are hoping to do so before they reach the Age 30 Deadline, the age many have long had in mind as the outer limit of when they want to be married. The majority of grown-up kids in their late twenties have finished their education and are committed to a long-term career path. Most importantly, they are ready to make major decisions and take full responsibility for their lives.

Although the launching, exploring, and landing phases describe the typical sequence of development during emerging adulthood, you've probably observed that there is a lot of variability in the timing of each phase. Some emerging adults go straight from launching to landing and skip right over the exploring phase, because they know from early on just what kind of work they want to do or perhaps because they found their soul mate early. Others have a longer exploring period than usual and don't really land until some time in their thirties. For emerging adults and their parents, these variations sometimes make it difficult to tell what is "normal" and what might be cause for concern. Be patient; we'll have lots to say about that later.

The Upside of a Later Entry to Adulthood

Have you noticed how scornfully many people talk about emerging adults? There are so many negative stereotypes, particularly among adults in their fifties, sixties, and beyond: Young people are lazy, they're selfish, they're worse than ever (and certainly worse than their parents' generation was at the same age). None of these stereotypes is true: They're not lazy, they're mostly working at crummy jobs for low pay or combining work and school; they're not selfish, they're remarkably generous and tolerant, as we'll see; and it's not true they're worse than ever. On the contrary, rates of alcohol abuse, crime, teen pregnancy, and automobile fatalities have all declined dramatically in the past 20 years.

Maybe one reason for the negative stereotypes of emerging adults is *fear*—the fear of parents and other adults that this generation of young people will not be up to the challenges and responsibilities of adulthood, not now, not ever. They see their grown kids undecided about which path to take, or declaring a path decisively and then abandoning it abruptly a few months later, and they worry, "Geez, won't this kid *ever* get it together?" Parents are usually ready to focus again on their own lives after a 20-year hiatus devoted to parenting, and they feel their patience (and their wallets) being exhausted as yet another year passes

---

Q: *My nephew, age 25, has been unemployed for about six months. Recently he had a chance for a job, but he turned it down, saying it was "not really what I want to do." How do I make his parents see that the kid's just lazy?*

A: Well, the kid may indeed just be lazy, but that conclusion would be a bit hasty on the basis of turning down a crummy job after six months of unemployment. There are advantages to being employed, even at a crummy job, such as, well, making money. But there are disadvantages, too. It would mean that he would have less time to look for a job that would be more appealing and that might have a more promising future. It would mean less time, too, for getting education and training to prepare for a better job. So don't assume he's lazy because he didn't take the job. Eventually he might have to take a job, any job, just to support himself. But right now, if his parents are supportive, and with no one else depending on him economically, it might be wisest for him to focus on striving for a job that really engages him and that he could use to build a future.

---

and their emerging adult is still emerging, still on the way to an ever-receding adulthood.

Knowing about the new life stage of emerging adulthood can reassure parents that the indecisiveness and instability they see in their children are not permanent traits but part of a temporary and transitional state that is entirely normal. Eventually nearly everyone does emerge into a more mature and stable young adulthood, usually by about age 30, with a more or less steady occupational path and a commitment to a life partner. Thirty may be later than parents originally expected, and later than they really prefer, but at least it's not forever. Unless there is some kind of major obstacle, such as a physical disability, a severe mental illness, or drug or alcohol abuse, young people almost always succeed in building a reasonably stable and satisfying adult life for themselves. It's not guaranteed, but it's highly likely.

But parents have more reasons to embrace this new life stage of emerging adulthood than simply knowing that it ends eventually. There is a lot of good news to tell about the years from 18 to 29 and how they help set the foundation for a happy and successful adult life. Just as the months of crawling prepare babies for a firmer footing when they finally get up and walk, so do the exploring, unstable, fall-down-and-get-back-up emerging adulthood years prepare a young person for the tasks of adulthood.

Perhaps most importantly, the extended years of emerging adulthood enhance the likelihood that young people will make good choices in love and work. The 28-year-old is a lot better prepared to choose a marriage partner than the 18- or 22-year-old is, having had far more years of experience with relationships and having gained far more cognitive and emotional maturity. The 28-year-old can also make a wiser decision about a career path than the 18- or 22-year-old would, having established a much clearer identity, that is, a much better sense of his or her abilities, goals, and opportunities. Sometimes 18- or 22-year-olds are unusually mature and can make wise choices in love and work even at this young age, but overall the prospect of choosing well is enhanced by waiting until at least the late twenties.

Experiencing emerging adulthood also makes young people better parents, eventually. Marriage is challenging, and building a career is challenging, but—as all parents know—there is nothing quite so formidably challenging as caring for a child. Your needs simply can't come first anymore when there is a child who literally will not survive without the love, care, and resources parents provide. Especially in their early years, children stretch us to the limit of our physical endurance, our stress tolerance, and our financial resources. There is no doubt that the 28-year-old is better prepared for these demands than the 18- or 22-year-old is. Again, some people who become parents in their late teens or early twenties fill that role remarkably well, but overall, young people will be better parents if they wait until their late twenties or early thirties to take on guiding a new generation.

> Our daughter realizes that she is clearly later than we were in entering adulthood. This has caused her a great deal of stress. She feels that because we were married and independent at 20, she should be as well.
>
> **FATHER OF A DAUGHTER, 23**

Another reason for parents to celebrate this new life stage is that it gives their children a window of opportunity to have experiences they could not have had at younger ages and will not have the chance for once they've taken on enduring adult responsibilities—take a shot at that musical career, volunteer for a service project in a developing country, or just move to San Francisco or New York City for a year to hang out and have fun while waiting tables or working for a dog-walking service.

At first glance, parents may not see these episodes of adventure as cause for celebration. They may think to themselves, and may say to their grown-up kids: "You could be going to grad school, or doing an internship, or starting to make progress in a career, or . . . something!" As parents ourselves, we sympathize with these concerns, but we advise parents to take the long view. In the words of one of the parents in our survey, "Why not prolong youth? It's already so fleeting."

Adulthood will come soon enough, and once it does, youth never returns. We should admire emerging adults who are bold enough to take on a youthful, once-in-a-lifetime adventure, not scold them for postponing adulthood for a year or two. Life is long today, lucky for all of us. If today's 20-somethings are likely to live to be at least 80 or 90 years old, why rush into adulthood at 18, 22, or even 25? Making the most of the freedom of emerging adulthood while it lasts will make for fewer middle-age regrets.

Emerging adulthood should also be embraced as one last chance for parents and children to be close before the kids become true grown-ups, preoccupied with the demands of career building, spouses, and child care. True, there are things parents won't miss later on, like urgent text messages at 3 a.m., persistent needs for cash, and jarring announcements of a need to move back home. Not a few parents may find themselves thinking wryly on such occasions, "How can I miss you if you won't go away?"

But miss them you will. Baby boomer parents wanted to be closer to their children than they had been to their own parents, and for the most part, they succeeded. Most parents today can talk to their grown-up kids as friends, about topics they never would have dreamed of broaching with their own parents. The long transition of emerging adulthood allows parents to enjoy the fruits of all those strenuous child-raising years from infancy through adolescence. It won't be long until you are no longer receiving their 3 a.m. text messages; instead, you'll be wondering why they haven't answered the text you sent three days ago. They'll fall in love; they'll find a partner who will become that person they rely on for support and nurturance every day, instead of you. It happens to almost everyone. So, if you're still seeing a lot of your children in their twenties, enjoy this special closeness one last time, and try to create a foundation of love and mutual trust that will endure in the decades to come.

2

Your Parallel Journey

I think this is the best time of life, because you know
where you're going, you know what you want, you
make better decisions. It's wonderful! But I worry
about my kids' future and well-being.

MOTHER, AGE 48

O K, now that you know your kids may not be fully grown up until
about age 30, what about *you*? This is a book not just about your
kids' development, but about your development, too, as you enter a
new stage of life. (Contrary to popular belief, people *are* still developing in
their forties, fifties, and beyond.) During the years their children are passing through emerging adulthood, parents are also growing and changing
as they pass through midlife. Parents have their children at varying ages,
and when children are in their twenties parents may be anywhere from
their late thirties to their sixties, but most parents of emerging adults are
somewhere in their forties or fifties, the midlife decades.

The same societal changes that led to a new life stage of emerging
adulthood have also transformed midlife development. The Sexual
Revolution not only made premarital sex common among the young, it
also inspired people to believe that their sex lives were not necessarily
over once their reproductive years were done. In fact, having the house to
yourselves after the kids move away might even provoke a midlife libido

revival (although the reality turns out to be more complicated, as we'll see). The Women's Movement not only opened doors for young women, it also made many midlife women think of their post-child-rearing years not just as a time to spend more hours in their garden but as an opportunity to enter (or reenter) the workplace and pursue their long-delayed dreams. The Youth Movement enhanced the appeal of striving to look as young as possible for as long as possible. As the baby boomer pioneers of the Youth Movement have entered midlife, they have also entered fitness centers and paid more attention to their diets, in an effort to stave off

Generational Journeys

QUARTERLIFE

Major transition: Out of childhood and college

From structure to flux: College provided an anchor, a purpose, a friendship network, and a busy social calendar

Assessing choices: Work, relationships, an affordable place to live, finding new friends, how to spend free time, how to make a difference

Decisions: Feel limitless, open-ended

Finances: Can I afford to live on my own? How to pay off student debt? Should I buy a new or used car? How much credit card debt is OK?

Wisest approach: Accepting that questions and doubts are a natural part of this time of life

MIDLIFE

Major transition: End of daily, hands-on child raising

From structure to flux: For 18 years, parenting provided much of the same

Reassessing choices: Work, marriage and friendships, whether to stay in the same place or move somewhere smaller, what to do for fun, how to leave a mark

Decisions: They're reopened, but awareness that time remaining is shorter than life already lived makes the future feel more limited

Finances: When can I afford to retire? How to pay off kids' college loans, help support their twenties, and help aging parents as well? How much credit card debt is OK?

Wisest approach: Ditto

aging. Consequently, the midlife decades are healthier for most people than they were in the past.

Along with these favorable changes to midlife have come new challenges. Today's midlife adults are likely to live longer than their parents because of great advances in health care, but will they have enough savings to support themselves financially through a long retirement? Not all are storming the fitness centers, and those who may not have taken care of themselves physically or have simply been unlucky may be looking at years of health struggles in midlife and beyond. Then there are the multitasking stresses of being the Sandwich Generation: caring for aging parents while trying to steer grown-up kids toward building a happy life, while also beginning to create a revised life plan for themselves. In a nutshell: Midlife adults have choices to make—what kind of life do I want to have, and how can I get it?—that parallel the decisions being made by their children.

Still, as complicated as midlife development can be, it is not nearly so grim as it is often portrayed. We talk of a "midlife crisis" as if the forties and fifties inevitably bring disappointment and perhaps desperation, but for most people midlife has a lot more than despair to offer. Yes, physical aging is a reality that can't be avoided by age 50, but most people remain physically and mentally sound. Most people struggle in some ways, as they do in other stages of life, but for many people midlife is also a time of contentment in love and work, a time when life is at its best.

Midlife: A Mixed Portrait

Like emerging adulthood, midlife is a life stage with many variations and shadings of contentment and confusion, as these examples from our interviews illustrate:

• Sarah, age 55, is mom to a 27-year-old son and a 23-year-old daughter. She enjoys her job as an administrative assistant at a college, although she is starting to feel as if she is not learning much after twelve years and ought to consider making a change. She has been divorced for fifteen years and now lives with her daughter, who is finishing her last year in the college where Sarah works. Her son lives on the other side of the country and works in the adult film industry;

Sarah does not approve, so they rarely talk. A lot of Sarah's time is spent taking care of her aging parents. "It's a blessing they've lived so long"—she sighs—"but on the other hand there's always bad news."

• Patty, age 47, is the mother of three children: two sons, 21 and 19, and a daughter, 17. All her children still live at home. Her life is good in most ways. She's happily married to her husband of twenty-six years, an auto mechanic. "People make fun of me for being so mushy," she admits with a smile. She's less than thrilled with her job as a nurse, but likes her coworkers. Although she enjoys spending time with her kids, they are also the source of her greatest stress and concern, particularly her oldest son, who is not working or going to school and can't seem to be motivated to try either one. Patty is reluctant to risk a serious rift with him by forcing him to leave home and stand on his own. "Someday this, too, shall pass, and I want to have a relationship with him. I don't want to burn that bridge."

• Steve, age 58, is an electrical engineer for a large company. His two boys, 26 and 24, have both graduated from college and are pursuing careers in engineering, like their father. Steve is happy in his marriage, now in its thirtieth year, and happy with his boys, but his job has been nerve-racking lately after a change in leadership at his company. He fears he may be fired soon. Financial pressures are also weighing on Steve, because he and his wife just built an addition on their house, and he's wondering how they will pay for it now that he might be out of work. He takes refuge in his hobbies of making three-story birdhouses and restoring classic sports cars.

• Stephanie just turned 45, and her life in middle adulthood is in disarray. A year ago she left her husband of twenty-four years. Since then she has been adrift, with no stable place to live. "I've been staying with friends all year, and I've moved three times," she says. She has two sons, 23 and 19, and the trigger for her divorce was the departure of the younger son from home. Without him to anchor her life with her husband, she soon recognized the emptiness of their marriage and the depths of her unhappiness. Her husband was "very quick to anger, and I hate to fight, so I would just not fight. And that means you don't have a voice." Leaving him has made Stephanie's life chaotic, but there are bright spots, too, and hopes of happier days ahead. Her work as marketing director for an art museum is challenging and satisfying. And she is savoring her new freedom, even with all the disruption and strain that have come along with it. "To wake up in the morning and have my own thoughts, I enjoy that."

> The good part of life right now is that work is good, family life is good, seeing our kids being successful and advancing. But as the kids move away, that's hard. The family is not the same as it was.
>
> FATHER, AGE 51

• At 55, Roger is glum. Recently he made a big change, quitting a comfortable job as a computer technician to start a small business refurbishing computers. It has not been going well. "I haven't had a paycheck yet," he says with frustration. His love life is not going any better than his work. He and his first wife divorced fourteen years ago, and the bitterness of their split still lingers. He has been married to his second wife for ten years, but he describes that relationship in terms that are tepid at best. "It's OK. It's a partnership, but I wouldn't say we're soul mates." He has two children from his first marriage and three stepchildren, all in their twenties, and his relationships with all of them are problematic, especially with his stepchildren. His health is not great, either. He has arthritis in his hands and chronic pain in his hips, and he is concerned about being overweight. Yet not all is dark for Roger at midlife. He plays in a bluegrass band with several old friends, something he greatly enjoys. Reaching the point when the daily demands of parenthood have diminished seems to him to have opened up new horizons. "I only decided to start the business when my youngest turned 21," he notes. "My wife and I have been able to turn to our own lives."

So what kind of portrait of midlife do we get from these examples, and from research on midlife adults? The midlife years are both good and tough, in different proportions for different people, and in different areas of life. Marriages are renewed or broken, career paths rise as well as fall, bursts of vitality occur, and so do chronic health issues. Overall, though, research on midlife should be encouraging for people about to enter this life stage. Your body may not look like it once did or do the things it used to be able to do, but for most people contentment rises, in their love lives as well as their work lives.

The Midlife Marriage

A loving marriage is a key contributor to happiness in midlife, and research has some good news for couples who make it to their middle years with their marriage intact. Decades of studies have shown that marital satisfaction follows a U-shaped pattern: high in the first year of marriage (the "honeymoon" phase), declining in the second year, reaching its lowest point when partners are caring for young children, and remaining relatively low for years after—until midlife, when the kids finally grow up and marital satisfaction rises steeply and steadily thereafter to its highest level ever. In an American study involving over two thousand middle-aged adults, ages 40 to 59, nearly three-fourths described their marriage as "excellent" or "very good," and in our survey for this book the results were similar. Other studies have shown that midlife partners often describe their spouse as their "best friend," and most partners feel their spouse has become more interesting, not less, in the course of married life.

It's easy to understand why most marriages get better at midlife. By then most married partners have fewer stresses from the daily responsibilities of child care, and spend less time on household chores. Most also have greater financial resources and more leisure time to spend as a couple. Partners who have stayed together have grown comfortable with each other by midlife and share an easy familiarity. Many reach a state of what psychologist Robert Sternberg calls *companionate love,* in which passion may have ebbed but emotional intimacy and commitment are high.

The Midlife Divorce

Of course, not all marriages have such a happy ending. It's true that the happiest people in midlife are those who have a strong, harmonious marriage, but marriages that are not going well are a big drag on overall happiness. As psychologist Bella DePaulo explains in her book *Singled Out,* single persons may not be as content as happily married people, but they are far better off than those who are in troubled marriages. After an extensive review of research, DePaulo concludes that "when you compare unhappiness levels across groups, no one matches the unhappily married in misery—not divorced people, not widowed people, and not people who have always been single." For this reason, some people are willing to risk the trials of a midlife divorce in pursuit of greater happiness.

Most divorces take place within the first ten years of marriage, but about 25 percent of divorces in the United States and Canada occur after twenty or more years, often timed with children leaving the nest. It used to be that divorce after twenty-plus years together was rare, but in recent decades rates have risen sharply. A 2012 AARP study found that while the overall American divorce rate has declined since 1990, for those over 50 it has doubled. Among the reasons given: longer lives mean less willingness to spend post-parenting decades with an incompatible spouse; less social stigma about splitting up; more women working and some out-earning their spouses; and, of course, no longer staying together for the kids.

Sometimes child raising is the glue that holds a shaky marriage together—a buffer or diversion from marital tensions. In the movie *Failure to Launch,* a send-up of the lengthening road to adulthood, the most poignant moment in an otherwise silly farce turns on this point. The mother of the lingering-at-home hero confides to his girlfriend that she actually doesn't want her son to move out, because she's not sure if her husband "would still like me after all these years." Having her emerging adult son remain in his childhood room has postponed the moment of marital reckoning.

Yale psychologist Elizabeth Rubin sees many couples who are reevaluating their relationship at this post-parenting transition. Some couples are having difficulties because the kids have been their focus, and now they're looking at their own lives, including their marriage, and may not like what they see. For couples who have kept their bond strong and their spark alive, she adds, the departure of grown children can present a more positive opportunity and a renewal of passion: "The couples who have a good friendship, they're relieved when the kids go."

How does divorce in midlife differ from divorce at younger ages? One study by University of Washington marriage researcher John Gottman followed a sample of married couples over a fourteen-year period and charted the divorces that took place in young and middle adulthood. Divorces in young adulthood tended to be full of anger and conflict, with each partner bitterly blaming the other for the failure of the marriage. In contrast, midlife divorces were more often between couples whose love had gone cold. There was not a huge amount of warfare, but these partners no longer enjoyed each other's company and avoided being together.

Q: *My husband and I can't wait for our last 20-something to be out of the house for good, but I'm frankly nervous about it—won't it be TOO quiet with just the two of us? What will we talk about?*

A: Yes, it may seem too quiet for a while. A lot of parents revel in the energy and activity that kids and their friends bring into the household, and miss it when the kids move out. But there's usually an upside, too. What kinds of things did you do together and talk about before you had kids? It may be hard to remember by now, but talk to your husband and maybe you can revive some of those old pleasures. And you can look for new common ground, too. What kinds of things have you been wanting to do for the past twenty years but felt as if you could never fit in? Maybe you'll soon be skydiving or traveling to a Guatemalan rain forest together, but it doesn't have to be that daring and dramatic. It could be as simple a pleasure as taking a walk around the neighborhood every evening, or going out to brunch on a weekend morning. As long as there is still love and goodwill between you after all these years, you're likely to enjoy the new expanse of time that has now opened up.

Perhaps because there tends to be less conflict in midlife divorces, midlife adults weather the stress of divorce better than young adults, showing less of a decline in well-being and less risk of depression. However, in some ways midlife divorces are harder on women than on men. Women are more vulnerable financially, since many have given up years of employment when they were caring for young children. After a divorce they may find themselves having to reenter the work world in midlife without the skills and experience necessary to obtain a good job.

In an AARP study of over a thousand adults who divorced in their forties, fifties, or sixties, 44 percent of the women mentioned having financial problems, compared to only 11 percent of the men. Also, only one-third of women who divorce after age 40 remarry, whereas nearly all men remarry. Still, many women find their later-in-life divorce to be a welcome release from the daily unhappiness of their marriage, and some say it inspires greater self-reliance and personal growth.

Sex in Midlife, or Sex? In Midlife?

What about sex? Well, it would be nice to say that after the kids leave home, couples who are still together get frisky again and rediscover their sex life now that they don't have to worry about whether or not the kids might be listening in (or barging through the door). For some of the couples we interviewed, time and opportunity did indeed create a second honeymoon. One mom of three grown children puts it succinctly: "After the kids left, dinner table conversation lagged but our sex life improved."

Another mother recounts how after her two daughters departed for college, she and her husband "redefined our life as a couple that has been on hold for twenty-odd years." They were so enjoying the pleasure of each other's company that when their older daughter boomeranged home after college graduation for an indeterminate stay, they felt a bit like two teenagers caught in the act by parents who arrive home earlier than planned. Suddenly, the party was over as quickly as it had begun.

For midlife parents, having the house to themselves is certainly a fringe benefit of the empty nest that can be a catalyst to a love life long on hold. The freedom to get naked at a moment's notice seems to be a common fantasy among couples who are finally alone together. Linda

Lee Peterson describes her revived romantic rendezvous with her husband in the essay "Naked Parents in the Pool," and confesses casually, "No longer did I need to throw on a robe before I could pad down the hall from the bedroom to the laundry room to find clean underwear." Other activities, once happening behind closed doors, could now take place in the open. In *Failure to Launch,* after the grown son finally moves out, the liberated father is shown butt-naked, calmly feeding his fish in his newly created "naked room."

But, alas, it's not all nudity and roses for most midlife couples. In the MacArthur Foundation's national study of midlife, sexuality was the only area of life for which satisfaction headed inexorably downward from age 25 through 74, on average. In another national study of Americans, one-third of men and over one-half of women in their fifties reported having

---

Q: *I want to be around for my kids—and someday my grandkids—but I am feeling so old lately! My weight is skyrocketing, my blood pressure is up, and I just don't seem to have the energy I used to have. Is there anything I can do, or is this just what it's like to grow old?*

A: The aging of the body actually begins in the twenties, but midlife is when most people feel it for the first time. Everything you mentioned is pretty much par for the course: weight gain, decline in energy levels, and the appearance of chronic health issues like high blood pressure. But there is still plenty you can do. Now is the time to establish good health habits for the rest of your life, if you haven't already. It's all stuff you already know—don't overeat, choose healthy foods and avoid foods with excess fat and sugar, and get regular exercise—but now these habits are more important than ever. Everybody ages, but the pace of aging and the quality and length of your life in the decades to come depend a lot on diet and exercise. It helps to have an ally, so talk to your spouse, partner, good friend, or even one of your kids about embracing these changes together. With wise health habits, there's no reason why you shouldn't be around for many grandkids to come.

sex only a few times or less in the past year. Over one-third of American women in their forties and fifties report some kind of difficulty in sexual functioning, especially once they reach menopause, and about half of men report problems of erectile dysfunction by age 60.

On the other hand, the MacArthur study also found that sex matters less by midlife to most people. Specifically, sexual satisfaction contributes less to overall life satisfaction in midlife and beyond than it does at younger ages. Marriage quality, financial security, and relations with children are all more important to general happiness at midlife. Also, effective remedies are now available for the most common sexual problems—for women, creams and gels to increase lubrication after menopause, and for men, Viagra and other medications for erectile dysfunction.

Sex may be less frequent and less important in midlife than it was earlier, but it can still be a source of pleasure. You don't have to look like you did at 25 in order to enjoy sex at 50 (or 60 or later), and you don't have to have the same level of lust as you did back then, either. For couples who have been together a long time, the emotional part of sex can improve with age, as their marital happiness rises and their love and trust deepens. With the years couples can also benefit from knowing each other's bodies so well, including what each person enjoys most (and doesn't enjoy). And it really is nice not to have to worry about the kids overhearing that enjoyment.

The Midlife Job

Sex may be losing steam for most people in midlife, but satisfaction with work is usually rising. However, there is a lot of variation here, too. Most people may be reaching the peak of their job satisfaction, but some may be losing their jobs, changing paths, retiring early, or reentering the job market after a long period devoted to caring for children and running a household.

Job Gains, Job Losses

A variety of studies have found that job satisfaction peaks in middle adulthood for most people, particularly in their fifties, in a wide range of occupations, from business executives to maintenance staff. Pay often increases with age, but the satisfactions of work in midlife have less to do with pay and promotions and more with enjoyment of the work itself. After many years in an occupation, people develop more *expertise*; they get better at what they do, and there is satisfaction in doing a job well. They develop social expertise, too; they get better at working with other people. They tend to be more patient than younger workers are, and more tolerant of others' personality quirks.

Midlife often means gaining more authority in the work environment and more involvement in making the decisions that influence how the job is done. Gail, 49, began working as a volunteer for a local government agency ten years ago, helping with summer programs for children. Volunteering led to being hired, and recently the agency expanded her responsibilities and authority, and increased her salary. Now she trains volunteers to help families prepare their children for the entry to primary school. Gail is thinking of going back to school part-time so that she can bolster her credentials and advance even further.

Another way to achieve greater work satisfaction is to lower your goals and expectations, and that's what happens in midlife for many. Rather than striving for the highest achievements, and perhaps being frustrated at not reaching them, they tend to realize they have risen about as high as they are likely to go in their profession, and they accept their achievements, however far-reaching or modest they might be. For most, the result of this dream-adjustment is not disappointment or despair but relief. They no longer measure their worth by how far up the ladder they have climbed. Instead, they take satisfaction in what they have accomplished, and they enjoy their work more, now that they are no longer grasping for more status and recognition. Many also turn more attention to finding enjoyment outside of work, in relationships and recreation.

Changing Paths

For some, midlife is a time for career adjustment. Sometimes these changes take place in pursuit of new challenges and opportunities. Larry, now 60, took over his father's hardware store when he was just 23 years old. It was a successful business for him, as it had been for his father, "but I never loved it," he says now. "I had the belief that I don't own the business, the business owns me." So at age 48 he decided to sell the store and start a new life as a financial consultant. The work is demanding and the hours are long, but now he says, "I love what I do." He could afford to retire but he plans to work as long as he is physically able to because he enjoys the work so much.

Other midlife adults quit their jobs because they become disillusioned, frustrated, and tired—in short, burned out. People who quit because of burnout complain of being overwhelmed by their work; they are often in helping professions such as teaching, health care, or social services, where the emotional demands are intense. By midlife they may feel they have done all they can do, and they may no longer get as much satisfaction from the work as they once did. Of course, being dissatisfied may not be a sufficient reason for midlife adults to quit a job. Emerging adults have no one depending on them, but by midlife most people have a spouse or partner, grown kids, and perhaps grandchildren and elderly parents, all of whom may require financial support. Midlife adults also have more "stuff" than emerging adults do—a house, a car, a retirement plan—and may not be able to walk away from the job that pays for their stuff, even if they dread going to work each day.

Q: *My kids keep asking me for advice about their careers, and I feel so ill equipped to help them. I'm having enough work troubles of my own! How honest should I be about my own struggles when they ask me for help?*

A: One of the main changes in parent-child relations when kids reach their twenties is that there is less of a divide, with parents on high and children down below, and more of a relationship between two adults, closer to a friendship. So, yes, be honest with them about your frustrations and uncertainties regarding work. They will probably be pleased that you trust them enough to be open with them. Maybe they will learn something from hearing about the issues that confront you and how you are dealing with them; maybe they'll even have insights that you'll find helpful.

Midlife adults who are laid off or fired face an especially difficult situation. Despite their abundant expertise, midlife adults stay unemployed longer than younger adults. Midlife workers require higher wages than younger workers, and employers may not see a long-term future for them. They may lack the information technology skills that are second nature to younger workers and a key part of the modern workplace. When midlife workers do find a new job after being unemployed, it tends to have lower status and lower pay than the job they lost. Given these bleak circumstances, it is not surprising that people who become unemployed in middle adulthood experience more disruption to their functioning than younger adults do, including declines in both mental and physical health.

> I wanted to be so much further at my age, and give my children so much more. But I believe I have time—if I continue to get my education and get some experience, I'll be able to do something great and get financially rewarded, too. But first I've got to see the children graduate from college.
>
> MOTHER, AGE 49

Although unemployment hits them hard, usually midlife adults have more to draw on than younger workers do. "Two of the key factors in surviving job loss are social support and financial support," observes David Blustein, a professor at Boston College and author of *The Psychology of Working*. "People who lose their jobs in midlife are more likely than younger people to have stable relationships and financial reserves." Nevertheless, years of interviewing adults across the economic spectrum have led Blustein to conclude that "losing a job at any point in life is devastating."

New Horizons

Some leave the workforce voluntarily in midlife, retiring early. Once their children have left home, and especially once the children have graduated from college and taken that financial burden with them, midlife parents may look to retire if they can afford to do so, especially if they are not particularly satisfied with their jobs. But these days retirement, especially early retirement, does not usually mean moving to a condo in Florida and sitting around in sandals and Bermuda shorts waiting for the early bird buffet to open. On the contrary, an early retirement can be a way of freeing up time to do more community service, or to initiate a more fulfilling "encore career" without having to worry about how much it pays.

For example, George, 54, the father of two sons in their midtwenties, has spent decades building up a small business that sells dietary supplements and other health products. The business has been a success, and he enjoys the work, more or less. Nevertheless, he is in the process of retiring from the business, as soon as he can arrange to sell it. But retirement, for him, won't mean kicking back and taking it easy. Instead he'll turn his energies to what he'd really like to do, "things that are more soulful." In the course of working in the health field he became fascinated with Chinese medicine, and his goal in his post-retirement career will be to help bring knowledge of Chinese medicine to the Western world.

Some women who have devoted most of their adult lives to bringing up their kids are now reentering the workforce after a long hiatus. Ella, 51, the mother of two college students, worked as a doctor in an emergency room for years, specializing in pediatric cases. However, when her children entered middle school, she decided to quit to be a full-time mom. As they reached the threshold of adolescence, Ella says, "I decided I was only going to have seven or eight years left with them, and I would have lots of years of doctoring afterward." Now that her kids are off to college, Ella is planning to return to medicine soon, although with some mixed feelings. "It's tough work, very stressful," she says, "but I loved doing it."

Midlife Stresses

Contrary to popular stereotypes, the "midlife crisis" is mostly mythical. Some people do make dramatic changes in midlife, such as a major career switch or leaving a spouse for a younger lover, but these cases are noticeable precisely because they are rare. Nor is midlife a time of exceptional tension or angst. Surveys of overall well-being across the life span consistently report that life satisfaction bottoms out in the early forties, just as midlife begins, but turns around and heads upward throughout midlife and onward into late adulthood. The most stressful time of life is not midlife but young adulthood, the thirties, when people feel the pinch of multiple demanding roles—caring for young children and struggling to make career progress, feeling a lot of financial pressure, and oh, by the way, trying to keep their marriage alive, too. In midlife these strains usually abate as children grow up and become more (if not entirely) independent, careers progress, and financial status rises.

Although experiencing midlife as a "crisis" is unusual, midlife is often a time of reevaluation and reassessment, particularly after grown kids are launched and parents look ahead to their post-parenting phase. Midlife adults, like their 20-somethings, often find themselves questioning their roles in love, work, friendship, and community, and reexamining their living situations and spiritual paths. And midlife does have distinctive stresses of its own. In our survey, 22 percent of participants rated their overall life stress as "high," 53 percent "moderate," and 25 percent "low."

Work is at the top of the stress list. Even for people who have a good job in midlife and enjoy their work, pressure often comes as part of the package. Having more author-

The Top Sources of Stress in Midlife

Work: 55%

Financial situation: 51%

Relationship(s) with children: 37%

Relationship with spouse/partner: 31%

Caring for elderly parents: 29%

Relationships with other family members: 28%

Physical health issues: 24%

ity and responsibility may be gratifying, but it also means more demands and more accountability when things go wrong. Having more expertise may be satisfying, but it may also mean that workloads increase. Nevertheless, views of work in midlife are largely positive, overall. In our

Q: *My elderly parents still need my attention. My 20-something kids still need my attention. My wife wants my attention, too. I sometimes feel pulled in so many different directions that I feel trapped, and I'm tempted to chuck it all and run away.*

A: Don't run away, but don't suffer in silence either. It's great when time and freedom open up in midlife, but sometimes they don't, as in your case. You're overwhelmed, so something needs to change. First and foremost, talk to your wife, tell her how you feel, and see if you can work together to take the pressure off. You'll probably find that she's feeling it, too, and you'll both feel a lot better if you're communicating and working together. Brainstorm about what steps you can take: Can you get outside help, even part-time, for your parents? Would they consider assisted living? Can your 20-something kids take on more responsibility for themselves—and maybe even help out with your parents? The pressures involve the whole family, and the solutions may as well.

---

survey, 82 percent rated their work satisfaction as "excellent" or "good," even as work was also the most commonly mentioned source of stress.

After work, finances come next as a midlife stressor. How could that be, if most people are better off financially at midlife than they were earlier in adulthood? Unfortunately, being better off does not necessarily mean being stable or flush. Some are struggling because a business or a job is not going well. Others are employed in a job that does not pay well enough to save for the future.

Not surprisingly, the midlife adults who struggle the most financially are those who find themselves out of work. However, even many people who are in a relatively high income bracket mention financial issues and uncertainty as a major source of concern. They face formidable tuition bills when their children attend college, as the costs of a college education rise faster than salaries every year and reach mind-boggling levels at the most elite schools. Most must do some serious rethinking about retirement planning. Many made their long-term plans for retirement years ago, assuming a modest return on investment. But the ups and downs of the stock market over the past decade have not allowed them to get ahead, and now they've had to revise their retirement plans, usually by planning to work for longer. Today, over one-third of 65- to 69-year-old Americans are still in the labor force, and the proportion is rising.

Caring for elderly parents is another common source of stress in midlife. Most people in their forties and fifties have at least one elderly parent who requires care and assistance occasionally or even daily. Just as their kids grow up and become more independent, their parents reach late adulthood and become more dependent. Midlife adults may find themselves having to visit elderly parents frequently to provide help or just to check and see if they're all right. Financial stresses may be deepened by the necessity of providing for aging parents who did not save enough for their later years or whose savings were drained by medical expenses. Midlife adults may also have to cut back on their own work hours in order to accommodate the demands of taking care of their parents, reducing further their incomes and their ability to save for their own eventual retirement.

> This is not an easy time of life for me. I'm in limbo, trying to take care of my mom, who has had a brain tumor. Money is a big concern! I had to take a leave from work, and when I came back it was part-time. But I like being with my kids and my family.
>
> MOTHER, AGE 42

Midlife Joys

But, thankfully, most people at midlife have much to celebrate. Family relations top the list, with relationships with their grown children most enjoyable of all. Travel and holidays also rank high, reflecting the greater freedom and financial security of midlife adults after children leave home, which allows them to take trips they had imagined for years. For Ruth and her husband, an accountant, the period after their two sons left home became "a second honeymoon" of travel and treating themselves well. They took trips lasting two or three months to places they'd always imagined visiting—Italy, China, New York City. This freedom to enjoy themselves stood in high contrast to their sons' high school years, when they felt chained to the house, standing guard. "We didn't go anywhere when the boys were in high school, because they were so naughty," Ruth remembers. "When they went away, it was a huge relief. We felt we'd been sprung out of a trap!" Grown children's emergence can be parents' reemergence, and that long-awaited freedom is sweet.

Other nonwork interests also ranked high as a source of enjoyment in our survey. Many of the people we interviewed burst forth enthusiastically with a long and varied list of things that have brought them pleasure since their grown children moved on. They named everything from writing a memoir to speed skating to learning the tango to volunteering in an Ecuadoran village. For many midlife adults, there's a renaissance of self-discovery that comes with the gift of freed-up time. Many describe a feeling of release and rebirth that's almost giddy, like Miranda, a developmental psychologist and mother of two college-age daughters, who calls this awakening "delicious": "I feel nine again! I'm in that zone of my own pleasure. I can read a book, I'm reengaging with my work, doing what I like without being interrupted to stop a fight or make a meal." Iris, a lawyer in a large metropolitan firm, has a female partner who travels often for work, so Iris was always the primary caretaker for their two children, both recent college grads. She recalls that when her kids were young and she wasn't with them, she always had her eye on the clock, whether she

The Top Sources of Joy in Midlife

Relationships with children: 90%

Relationship with spouse/partner: 71%

Travel/holidays: 70%

Other nonwork interests: 68% (friends, church, exercise, gardening)

Work: 57%

Relationships with other family members: 48%

Pets: 45%

was at work or somewhere else. But "all that falls away when kids go to college," she says, and now her time is pleasantly her own. "You go back to your own rhythm of life before you had children: reading a book at night, seeing a movie midweek, going to the gym, gardening."

The Midlife Parent

Now that we've charted the midlife journey, how does it pertain to parenting? Understanding midlife development helps make sense of the delicate balance between stepping back and staying connected that is central to parenting grown-up kids. On the one hand, it's kind of liberating to let go. Raising children is often wonderful, but it's indisputably demanding, for many years. Young children are delightful but exhausting little creatures, always in need of something—their next meal, a Band-Aid for a boo-boo, or a ride to soccer practice. Adolescents can do more for themselves, but they are needy and exhausting in their own ways, as they learn to navigate the complexities of love and friendship and begin trying to figure out who they are and how they fit into the world. Emerging adults need a lot less from their parents, and usually they want a lot less, too. They begin to make decisions for themselves and take on more of their own responsibilities.

So for parents navigating midlife as their children go through emerging adulthood, stepping back can be a relief in many ways. As children move from launching to exploring to landing, their demands on their parents' time, money, and emotional reserves gradually diminish. "Their freedom is my freedom," as one of the mothers we interviewed put it. At last parents get to turn their attention back to their own lives and focus on their own goals and dreams.

Of course, this pretty picture assumes that all is going well in the lives of their emerging adults. Sometimes that's true, but there is often something or other to deal with in the lives of near-grown children: a financial or love crisis, a lost job, a college flunk-out, a physical or mental health problem. And so on. For most midlife adults the challenges, duties, and stresses of parenting are not entirely over, as we will see in the chapters to come.

3

From Parent and Child to (Something Like) Friends

I always felt a parent shouldn't be a friend,
but now I think it's okay.

MOTHER OF SONS, 25 AND 22

I t's a seismic shift for parents, their grown child's transition to adulthood—exciting and unnerving, like the first time a toddler stands upright or a teenager takes over the wheel. A child's transformation to adult may sneak up in baby steps: a home-from-college son's unprompted offer to make a dish for dinner or schlep relatives back from the airport, or a 20-something daughter's unexpected (and smart!) piece of advice given to a parent. The change may also become known in a sudden, shocking flash of recognition: The son or daughter confiding about career plans across the table, whipping up brunch in a first apartment, or introducing parents to a beloved partner is no longer the child who's been lovingly shepherded for eighteen years or more but a near-grown person with an independent life.

For Deirdre, that wake-up moment came on a cross-country trip to celebrate Mother's Day with her 25-year-old son, Nick; her husband; and their high school daughter, 17. Two years earlier Nick had left behind the known territory of the East Coast where he had grown up and gone to college. He had made himself over in San Francisco with an apartment, a job at an ad agency, and a girlfriend soon to finish business school and move in with him. As the family puppy-dogged after Nick up and down the Bay Area hills, he pointed out his office, his gym, his favorite burrito place, and where he grabbed an espresso on the way to work. Finally, Deirdre got it: "He had a life," she says.

Her response to this news surprised her. Pride, of course: "You raise them to leave you, and he's been good at leaving." But there was something unfamiliar, too, an uncertainty, as if the person she knew like none other had suddenly turned into a stranger: "Sometimes it's as if the adult he's become has swallowed the old Nick." Nevertheless, it didn't take long for pleasure to get the better of doubt and for the whole family to embrace the new normal. "I like the kind of human he's become," she says, beaming.

Shifting Boundaries

If families survived the foot-stomping tantrums of early childhood, the homework-hassling school years, and the cold-shouldering or fiery outbursts of adolescence, this life stage may feel like the Promised Land. Sons and daughters are morphing into people parents would like as friends. For most parents this friendship is a long-dreamed-of state, but some, encountering setbacks along the way, may also wonder how to get there and, dear Lord, when.

Here's some good news: The cultural sea change is in your favor. By the early twenty-first century, the hostile generation gap of the sixties and seventies has been left far behind in the ash can of history, and today, it's a kinder, gentler separation. Over the past thirty years, there's been a major cultural shift toward a shared universe between parents and children. By their twenties, most of today's grown kids consider themselves allies of their parents, not combatants. Many parents we interviewed also remarked that their grown children were light-years more open with them than they'd been with their parents.

One catalyst to the friendship between parents and their grown kids is the child-centered lifestyle of so many of today's families. Many parents and children have been joined at the hip since the get-go: from babies

> I'm really enjoying my children as people now, and I'm not always asking myself, "Am I doing a good job as a parent?" I'm letting go of some of the responsibility and control and just watching them unfold. I'll continue to advise for the rest of my life, but it's lovely to step back and say, "Wow, you're really doing it!"
>
> MOTHER OF TWIN DAUGHTERS, 18

in the family bed to Mommy and Me gym classes, from mother/daughter book groups to weekends devoted to kids' sports events, from crafting college applications together to multiple texts a day when kids get to campus. Why would parents want to stop now? Most cherish the rapport that builds through their children's twenties and do everything they can to nurture it—staying available, involved, and open to midnight phone calls and unburdening heart-to-hearts even when they may sigh or cringe at the occasional oversharing.

But still, as the British say, mind the gap—the generation gap, that is. Just as with any relationship that is going through a redefinition, both parents and their emerging adults are looking for where to strike the new balance, the comfort zone between closeness and separation. "I'm trying to figure out how to be supportive, not intrusive," says family therapist Monica McGoldrick, 68, author of *The Expanded Family Life Cycle,* whose son is 25 and establishing himself in work, love, and a new locale. Even a professional like McGoldrick, who has spent a lifetime counseling families, admits that this balancing act is an art when it comes to her own son: "I want to stay connected but not be overly invested in his every move."

Whose Life Is It Anyway?

Much of the angst between parents and emerging adults stems from the tug-of-war over whose life it is. There is often a disconnect between parents who still want to shape their grown-up kids' future course and the kids determined to live their lives their own way. Who knows best, parents or their emerging adults? This mother of a 21-year-old daughter captures the push-pull: "Education or occupational choices aren't so much a question of conflict as it is my helping her to navigate and her not wanting to be intruded upon."

For loving parents, their grown children's trials and errors, futile dreams, dead-end roads, failed projects, or teary breakups can be anguishing. It can be wrenching to let go of the old parental omnipotence and not be able to fix everything or help make grown kids happy in a way that felt so easy when they were young, when a kiss on a skinned knee made it better. But these ups and downs are the very definition of the emerging adult stage, and coping with them will shape the resilient, self-sufficient people they will become. And beyond the many mishaps are the projects that do work out, the lasting relationships that are worth waiting for, and the confidence that comes from standing on their own feet.

A Parent Is Always a Parent

While the overall trend of 20-somethings and their parents from conflict to companionship is a welcome one for all concerned, there are still plenty of flash points during the emerging adult years. "These kids sure know how to pull your chain," says one mother with a sigh, hearing about her newly graduated son's motorcycle escapades along the hairpin roads of Laos. Bungee jumping, eating fried grasshoppers, wandering in strange cities—she needs to take many long, deep breaths before she reads his emails from the edge.

Despite the stronger, more adult-to-adult bond that's emerging, parents still report no dearth of strains and lingering concerns about their 20-somethings:

- The feeling that [my sons] don't have time for me anymore.

- It was always the school part. Now it's worrying about him making ends meet and what he's going to do with his life.

- Dealing with all the frequent changes in their lives. Also, I worry about my kids being able to afford a house! Real estate is so expensive.

- I want her to finish school and not get pregnant!

But those touchy issues—the ones that pull your particular chain—tend to change during the decade from the late teens to the late twenties. In the launching phase, a son or daughter may not want to go to college but has no backup plan; or maybe the child does go to college but struggles to separate and calls home five times a day . . . or parties excessively or flunks classes. In the exploring phase a more typical conflict would be over a work choice or a love interest: a son who can't hold a job and keeps asking for a bailout, a daughter who chooses a romantic partner her parents dislike. And in the landing phase, the thorniest issue is, well, not yet landing.

Throughout emerging adulthood, the transition from parent and child to friends may be disrupted by times when parents have to move more firmly back into their parental role. Just when you think you're dealing with an equal, you may be brought up short. The inner, irresponsible child may show up even in the guise of an otherwise graciously emerging adult. Young people's regressions are sure to cause parental frustration, as this mother of a 25-year-old describes: "The most challenging thing is my desire to have that friendship with her but still having to deal with areas of her life where she hasn't grown up, and still having to be that parent [who says], 'Why the hell haven't you paid that bill yet? It's got my name on it, too!' That's the stuff I hate. I don't like to have to argue with her."

Mixed Emotions

Whether emerging adults have stayed home or moved out, and whether family life growing up was smooth or rocky, relaxed or tense, their relationships with parents remain emotionally charged. Yes, the trend for most is toward a respectful friendship, but the bond may be colored by more complex shades. A stewpot of emotions still roils within grown kids, both positive and negative. Love—with roots all the way back to infancy and childhood. Gratitude—from a new perspective of understanding. Acceptance—as they relate to parents as one adult to another. And there are darker, more difficult emotions as well. Resentment— for how they believe their parents may have failed them in one way or another. Disillusionment—when they observe flaws that their parents have tried to hide. Wariness—as they try to keep parents from meddling in their lives. Even outright hatred—especially in the aftermath of parental divorce or abuse. A common pattern during the twenties decade is the ebb and flow of these conflicting emotions as young people grapple with their own identity issues and reflect on the role their parents play in who they are.

For their part, parents may become more willing to bend to accommodate their grown kids, but they, too, may have mixed feelings. Most know the potential is there for closeness and a more balanced relationship of equals, but potholes lurk along that road. Parents in our survey rank the issues that rankle them this way:

• Money: 48 percent (*I'm still waiting for him/her to become financially self-sufficient*)

• Occupational progress: 39 percent (*Will s/he ever get off the couch and find a job?*)

• Substance use or abuse: 36 percent (*I wish s/he partied less*)

• Educational progress: 27 percent (*It seems as if s/he's been in school forever*)

• Romantic life: 19 percent (*I think s/he could do better*)

• Sex life: 9 percent (*I prefer s/he not share a bed with a partner in our home when I am there*)

The degree of closeness between parents and their emerging adults can also be a source of tension. Perhaps a parent dreams of being a child's confidant, but the son or daughter wants to open up more space between them and regards parental attempts at intimacy as intrusive. This may be an issue especially during the exploring period, when emerging adults are intent on showing that they have learned to be self-sufficient.

On the young person's side, keeping a privacy buffer is a crucial part of defining a separate identity, building confidence in making decisions, and becoming autonomous. Parents who have cherished a close relationship with their children when younger may feel hurt if they sense them pulling away as 20-somethings. Suddenly grown kids are balking at coming home during their vacations or are no longer available for long chats on the phone. While it's natural to miss the kind of intimacy parents had when children were young, it helps to see their pulling back, their increased need for distance, even what one mother calls their "trajectory of secrecy," as appropriate for their life stage and not a personal affront.

Even among emerging adults who keep their parents in the loop, most master the art of editing. Presenting the slightly edited version of their lives lets them be in charge of what to share and what to keep to themselves. They learn to present an abridged version of certain down-and-dirty details so as not to set off parental alarm bells. The killer Sunday hangover, the lackluster job review, or the rising credit card debt may go unmentioned to spare parental anxieties, sidestep lectures, or protect tender feelings on both sides.

Meanwhile, parents should take it as a given that they don't know everything about their grown-up kids' lives. One young man we interviewed is still living at home with his folks, who put a high premium on saving money for the future. But he confesses in our interview that he "wants to enjoy himself now." To that end, he and his girlfriend bought expensive mountain bikes that they are hiding at the girlfriend's house. At 22, enjoying the rush of those early morning rides is a higher priority than squirreling away savings for a far-off future. Don't be too surprised if your grown son or daughter is stashing a similar secret in someone else's garage.

Sometimes the emotional imbalance tips the other way: The emerging adult needs and wants a lot of emotional support and companionship from parents, but parents feel they are ready to turn their focus back to their own lives and don't really want to be involved in daily parenting duties anymore. "I would like her to think about a problem more first before just calling for the solution," says one mother, 63, of her 27-year-old daughter. Or as another mother, 60, with a 23-year-old daughter, sums it up, "We both need our space to grow up!"

There's the heart of it, as this mother acknowledges: Her own growth curve and her daughter's are intertwined. The younger woman needs space to grow into herself, to know her own desires and talents. But her mother also needs room to grow into the next chapter of her life, to rediscover her own goals and dreams now that her parenting years are winding down.

Minding Your Manners

Creating a strong parent-child bond in emerging adulthood requires some gracious etiquette, marking again a careful balance between stepping back and staying connected. As your child progresses from launching to exploring to landing, emotional picket fences will become steadier, and the equilibrium between separate and overlapping territories will be more clearly established. For parents, this decade-long downshift means learning to let go and graciously relinquish eighteen years in the driver's seat. Holding too tightly to the old parental reins will only cause strain, and may well backfire. Restraint is the elusive virtue required of you, to keep from giving too much unwelcome advice or asking too many nosy questions.

You may bridle at all the tongue-biting that's become necessary as children make both smart and foolish decisions. After years of hands-on child raising, it's hard for many parents to step back and let their grown kids make their own mistakes. Both mothers and fathers suffer from the wanting-to-fix-its, as this doting, at times overly doting, father of three sons in their twenties admits: "When one of the boys is stumped, I want to jump in." Thankfully for family harmony, his wife usually holds him back and saves the boys from their dad's well-intentioned meddling. What may have been appropriate when the boys were little is no longer the right approach with grown sons.

As at any age, if parents jump in too quickly to unravel their children's dilemmas, they won't give those important problem-solving muscles a chance to develop. Instead, elders have to hope that the life lessons learned even the hard way will help their grown-up kids become stronger and more resilient adults.

What's especially painful is if a parent spies something potentially unpleasant on the horizon and a young person remains oblivious. A mother could see trouble ahead for her 27-year-old stepdaughter and her longtime boyfriend: He was clearly becoming not into her. But in this case, she kept her thoughts to herself: "Your kids' job is to move away, yours is to guide them. You can cling or you can launch them and be on the sidelines. You see the train wreck coming, but you're not on the train. You want to protect your kids from all harm, but instead you need to let them take steps themselves."

Not speaking up is most difficult when kids are doing something parents perceive as not in their best interests—from a dead-end relationship to a job that wastes their talents. One mother's son and daughter are almost 30, and though she realizes that it's not her role anymore to steer them clear of every snake in the grass, it still pains her when they dally with danger: "There's a whole category: I wish you wouldn't . . . drive in the rain, live in that crime-ridden neighborhood. . . ." No, the late-night worrying never totally ends, but at some point even the most devoted parent needs to trust and let go.

Q: *How can we know when to speak up about our 20-something's questionable behavior and when to turn the other cheek?*

A: There are still times during your kids' twenties when you do have to voice your concerns and get involved even if your grown kids don't want you to (and even if you aren't happy stepping in yourself). If you're wondering about whether or not to say something, ask yourself if the behavior that's bothering you is serious, dangerous, or simply unpleasant. Here's a for-instance: If your son hasn't shaved in a few days and looks rather scruffy and a family reunion is scheduled, well, that may not be pretty, but it's not life threatening. But if your daughter shows signs that she's smoking pot every day, that habit can be harmful. You need to address it directly with her.

When a lively social life with lots of partying veers into substance abuse, when a struggle with normal identity issues about "what to do with my life" becomes clinical depression, or a preoccupation with fitness turns into an eating disorder—parents need to step up, speak up, and be ready with resources for outside, professional help. (For more on these red flags, see Chapter 12, "When Things Go Wrong.")

Then again, this same woman is the first to admit that mother doesn't always know best. When her son reported awhile back that he was leaving his job at Lehman Brothers to try a new challenge, she told him in no uncertain terms he was making a major mistake. Hah. Lehman collapsed the next year.

Greater Distance = Fewer Hassles

That giant parental exhale as kids leave for college or places of their own is the collective relief (okay, often blurred by tears) as home life calms down and day-to-day conflict eases. Distance—whether provided by an apartment three blocks down the street or a dorm room three thousand miles away—is an efficient shock absorber. Absence does indeed make the heart grow fonder, and ignorance is in fact bliss. No more homework misplaced, curfews broken, rooms disordered, bottles of booze discovered, family cars brought home with no gas and a mysterious new dent—at least, not as far as you know. What parents don't know is less likely to hurt them, and many emerging adults control the flow of information by providing a sanitized version of their lives and by carefully scheduling visits—please, Mom and Dad, no drop-ins. (If and when kids move back in with parents, conflicts may once again spike, so that's the subject of Chapter 6, "The Boomerang Kid.")

When asked how the relationship has changed since their kids were age 15, three quarters of parents we polled said the relationship was better, and almost the same number said there was less conflict than in the more combative teenage years.

Typical comments: "OMG—way less conflict"; "When she was 15 it wasn't a pretty scene"; and "In her 15-year-old eyes I did nothing right." "You don't have to manage their lives as much as when they were teenagers," concludes one mother, whose three formerly high-maintenance adolescents have finally become more self-reliant in their twenties. "I didn't like driving them, micromanaging, it was more work. This is the time to reap the benefits."

From the young person's point of view, as well, absence makes the relationship easier, and proximity stirs up old ghosts. One 21-year-old college senior speaks for many of her peers about the benefits of turf

Q: *When my son and daughter were at college many miles from home, what I didn't know about their whereabouts couldn't upset me and cause me sleepless nights. But when they're living under our roof again, I get very anxious when they're out late at night. I usually can't fall asleep until they're both safely home . . . and sometimes that's not until 4 a.m.*

A: Some families may trust the universe enough to sleep soundly wherever their kids may roam, but for most mortals, it helps to set some rules and rituals. Many parents request that their 20-somethings call or text them if they're staying out past a predetermined time (say 1 a.m.) or overnight. This heads-up can spare parents a lot of anguish, especially if drinking and driving may be involved. Once home, decide on other non-verbal signs that will signify your 20-somethings have returned safely, like having them turn off the front-hall light or closing your bedroom door. Then if you wake in the middle of the night and see that the light's still on or the door's open, you can check your phone for a message or text.

boundaries and the culture shock of transitioning between her own college apartment and back to her childhood home for vacations: "I get along better with my mother when we're not living together. Distance helps. I'm very independent, and I work so I support myself. When I'm away at college it's like being an adult: I deal with doctor's appointments and living on my own. When I'm home, I feel like nothing's changed. [Laughs.] It's not rare for my mother to say, 'Are you dressed warm enough? Did you take care of this or that? Weren't you going to write that application?' The day she drives away after dropping me at school, I become an adult again."

For this mother and daughter, the pendulum is still swinging pretty widely between the daughter's growing ability to take care of herself and her mom's wanting to mother her. As her daughter is on the threshold of college graduation and launching her own life, this mom may need to start acknowledging how her child is turning into a competent young person, able to support herself and take care of her own stuff. That protective, maternal instinct may feel like one of those trick birthday candles that will never entirely blow out. But at this crossroads, it may be time to allow her daughter's independence to flourish. It takes patience—and faith—to give children room to grow into themselves.

Friends or Foes

Two roads diverge in the woods of the twenties, and both generations face a choice going forward into a shared adulthood: friends or foes? Once grown children turn 18, once they live on their own, and certainly once they stand on their own financial feet, you no longer have the authority you did when children were young, at home, and playing by Mom's and Dad's rules. Suddenly the relationship feels more up for grabs. It's no longer just a given, a habit, or a daily duty.

Mimi, 59, a divorced mother of an only child, faced this emotional turning point during parents' weekend with her college sophomore son, Max. Max wanted to major in music theory, and he spent most of his waking hours at college doing jazz dancing. She believed the job prospects for music theory grads were slim and also felt that dancing 24/7 was not the best use of his time—or her hard-earned tuition dollars. During parents' weekend, an argument flared up

Top 10 Things That Are Better Left Unsaid

10. When are you getting a haircut?

9. Are you really going out in that?

8. Do you think you're dressed warm enough?

7. Must you get that tattoo? That piercing?

6. Have you gained weight?

5. Is that dinner—six energy bars and a diet soda?

4. What do you see in him/her?

3. When are you moving back to (name your hometown) from Berkeley/Brooklyn/Timbuktu?

2. Have you set a date for the wedding?

1. How long must we wait for a grandchild?

between them, and she heard herself sputtering: "I'm not paying for a jazz dancing college!" She huffed off, feeling righteous. But minutes later, she had second thoughts: "I realized, I have a choice. I can be an ally or an adversary. I called Max on his cell and said, 'I'm going to be your ally. But you have to pay for [everything to do with jazz dancing]. Clothing, fees. Still, I'll be your cheerleader.'"

She also assured him that she'd pay his tuition whatever his major. She'd be his cheerleader in that department, too. Telling the story, she sighs and says, half to herself, "Will he ever learn to make money? Yes, eventually."

One of the toughest but most necessary lessons of parenting emerging adults is accepting that they'll follow their own dreams, even if you don't share those dreams or have doubts they'll come to fruition. But don't be the Cassandra in your grown children's lives, the first to tell them a harsh, unwelcome truth. Instead, let them navigate around the unforeseen obstacles lying ahead. Yes, they might derail or change course. Or they just might pleasantly surprise you by reaching their goals.

Parents Are People, Too

For eighteen years, you've been the givers in your relationship with your children, handing out not only food, shelter, and clothing but encouragement, congratulations, and praise. You've been avid fans and publicity directors for every milestone and accomplishment. But now, pride starts showing up in both directions, and respect sprouts from the other side. Although emerging adults may be self-focused, they tend to be considerably less egocentric than adolescents and much better at understanding another's perspective, especially their parents'. Now both generations are seeing each other with fresh eyes: parents begin to view their children as adults, and grown-up kids realize that their parents are real people with both charms and flaws, not the idealized—or demonized—figures of their earlier years.

Elizabeth watched on the sidelines as her sons' perspective on their dad gradually shifted. The summer before Nate headed off to college, he and Bob went on a weekend bike trip along the California coast. They bonded over pedaling the rugged terrain, the scenic beauty, and the stories shared. Years later, in a birthday toast to Bob, Nate referred to that trip as a turning point. "That was when I stopped thinking of Dad as the guy who made me breakfast every morning and started thinking of him as a person," Nate recalled.

For Elizabeth's younger son, Will, the *aha* moment came at the end of his junior year of college when the father-son power struggles of high school disappeared like old basketball shoes. In their place appeared a genuine admiration of his dad's global political knowledge, the way Bob can remember which nation had a coup and which had finally become a democracy. "How does he know so much and keep it all straight?" Will wondered out loud. It never gets old for a parent to receive a shout-out from a child, and appreciation like this helps advance the relationship to one between equals.

Appreciation is a word that came up often when we asked our survey respondents how their emerging adults perceive them differently now than when they were youngsters of 15. Typical comments were "Our daughter has more appreciation for what she was given," or "Our son has more understanding of what we tried to do with him and for him, what we demanded of him." In addition, many parents report that their grown children have a more nuanced sense now of their parents as complex people, gifted and flawed, giving and selfish, struggling just like their kids to do the best they can:

- "Things that seemed so black-and-white earlier are not, and she gets that."

- "She has made a certain peace with my faults and inconsistencies. She still sees them, but she is less inclined to have to name them, which is a grace."

- "Being seen more as a person is so important. As an adult, she can see my strengths and my limitations or struggles. I think it takes the pressure off her, realizing that while I have many areas of success, I also have my challenges, as all people do."

This newfound tolerance can be particularly healing if there were family stressors or crises in the past. One mother, who fought depression throughout her son's life and then tried to be honest about her failings when he was in his twenties, reflects, "I am forgiven for not being the best mother I could have been. You can't undo mistakes that have been made, but you can make the best of the present."

As the twenties unfold from launching to landing, child raising's one-way street becomes two-way, and reciprocity begins to replace "What have you done for me lately?" The interdependence that will grow through the adult years starts to take hold now as helping hands extend in both directions. As young people enter the exploring phase of emerging adulthood, they begin to face decisions in work and love that have also defined parents' lives. Instead of living in separate worlds, older and younger generations are now planted in the same one with parallel concerns: job stresses, financial problems, relationship blues, worries about friends.

A mother of two freshly employed 20-somethings notes the overlap and mutuality of their situations. She has just founded a new nonprofit; her son, 25, does business development for a young finance company, and her daughter, 22, works for a tech company. "We're all in start-ups," she

---

Q: *Two years ago, I was diagnosed with breast cancer. I'm a single mother, and my 20-year-old daughter took a semester off from college to help take care of me. Now, unfortunately, I've had a recurrence, and I'm concerned about asking for her help again.*

A: Your daughter has given you a loving gift of her time and attention, and you've undoubtedly benefited from her help during a difficult time. But she has also grown by lending you a hand and would most likely feel that she does not regret her choice. At the same time, she needs time and space to explore the possibilities for her own life like the rest of her age-mates. So, tell her honestly when you need her help, but also do your best to tap into whatever support network you have—friends, other family members, neighbors—so that your daughter does not feel overwhelmed with single-handed caretaking duties at such a young age.

observes, "so I can help them with their work lives and I also go to them." Her son worked on the logo design for her organization and fine-tuned a PowerPoint presentation she gave. Her daughter eyeballed the draft of her mother's latest article and offered her the kind of savvy feedback her mother used to give her on high school papers. Their parallel worlds create new and satisfying chances for reciprocity.

Half Launched—and Half Not

Still, don't be fooled by the self-confidence bursting into bravado of kids who've just flown the coop. And don't sign off too quickly in the launching years. Parents may yet be called up for active duty. It's not until the exploring years or even the landing phase that emerging adults become capable of standing on their own without parents to fall back on. Most launching-phase kids still want or need some hands-on, be-there-when-I-need-you parenting.

When they're happy, grown kids may go missing for days. But after the first botched test or broken heart, the calls or texts may ramp up. And if Mom or Dad is not available, ready to snap into action, don't be surprised if kids are a little annoyed. Sure, they want to live their own lives, but they're often not ready for their parents to move on to their own freedoms just yet.

Despite kids' big show of "I'm outta here," launching youth still value parents' opinions, moral support, approval, and contact more than they might let on. One mother of a 20-year-old son heard this first from a friend with children ten years older: "Talk to them. Tell them what you think. They will pretend not to hear you. They *always* hear you."

A mother of an 18-year-old found out that her son was listening even when he pretended not to be. She had gotten into the habit of phoning him from work at the same time every day. But he appeared to have "selective hearing" for her ringtone and would never pick up her calls. Then one day, stuff happened, and she skipped a call. Did she ever hear about it! "You don't care about me," wailed her young man. She reinstated the daily calls faster than you can say "Family Calling Plan."

Transitions in and out of college, apartments, or new jobs can be needy times, even in the lives of young people who are becoming increasingly

> It's the parent who needs to initiate the next call or redial the one that's cut short. Not just a couple of times, but a gazillion.
>
> **MOTHER OF FOUR DAUGHTERS, 24 TO 33**

self-reliant. Throughout childhood, many developmental leaps forward are preceded or accompanied by brief backslides to greater dependence, like a game-faced kindergartner who makes it through the first day of school and then falls apart at home. Emerging adulthood is also marked by its own swings from autonomy back to neediness and then forward to independence again.

Even on the brink of graduation from a college a few hours away, one 21-year-old surprised her mom with her need for motherly TLC. When this mother graduated from a women's college thirty years earlier, she'd borrowed the family station wagon for move-out day, piled it high with four years of gear, and happily driven herself and her roommate home. It was a girls' road trip before the concept was invented, and she figured her daughter would want the same experience. But this agenda didn't impress her daughter, as this mother recounts: "After I came for graduation, I offered her the family van to bring her stuff home with a friend. I thought it would be fun for them. But she laid into me for not offering to help, for asking her to make the transition alone. 'Even Dad asked about helping,' she said. I was so surprised!"

Parents' showing up to mark meaningful life events—graduations, performances, major birthdays—still matters to emerging adults, even if they may be too proud to ask for it.

Hanging Out Together

With kids off to college, moved out of the house—or back in—the emerging adult stage calls for finding new ways to connect, have fun, or just hang out together. When kids were young, family time happened inevitably. But now to hang out with their cooking-on-all-burners 20-somethings, parents need to get creative, even crafty (hard-to-get baseball tickets, anyone, or dinner at that great new restaurant?). And yes, some trends remain timeless: The older generation generally craves their kids' company more than the other way around. As Mel Brooks's 2000 Year Old Man lamented, "I have 42,000 children and not one of them comes to visit me!"

So how do families stay close at this stage? "Other families bike or ski. We eat together," is one mother's answer. Still, she admits to some tension as family dinners adjust into a new phase. When her older daughter came home from college for her first vacation, Mom put a lot of effort into making the elaborate meals her daughter had always enjoyed, steamy curries and tasty soups. But time after time, she didn't show up for these time-consuming meals, and her mother confesses, "I'd get pissed off." It took a blowup or two and then some artful negotiation for dinners to become more flexible. For her daughter's most recent home-from-college vacation, the family put five or six events on their calendars—most of them dinners around the family table or food-centric dates at favorite restaurants. This plan balanced the parents' need for structure with their daughter's desire to be in charge of her own time.

Many parents will go to great lengths to carve out occasions and activities that work for their grown-up kids. One gutsy, 64-year-old mother of three agile sons trained for marathons with the two younger ones, both fit and in their twenties. "My knees hurt, but I learned so much about them," she says. Jigsaw puzzles can work for the less athletic. Another mother of three sons ages 18 to 25 has her most intimate conversations with them while searching for this or that matching puzzle piece. "An oblique question is more likely to be answered than a direct one," she says about her low-key information-seeking missions, and she is always careful to keep her responses neutral. "I take what's offered, I'm never down their throats about anything, and I very rarely raise a subject they mentioned once in another conversation." Plus, she respects her guys' conversational styles. "They keep it short and sweet. A long discussion is sixty to ninety seconds."

One Size Doesn't Fit All

"One size fits all" is a dubious claim for socks and bathrobes. It doesn't work any better when it comes to calibrating a relationship with emerging offspring of different temperaments. Just as when the kids were young, successful parents adapt to fit the child. Rachel is the mother of four daughters who are now 24 to 33. When each of them left for college just five miles from home, Rachel had to get inventive about keeping in touch without overwhelming them. She came up with four different moves to suit her girls' various styles. Her oldest daughter, still a mama's girl, welcomed a weekly visit. She'd sit on the library steps eating her mother's Tupperwared leftovers and pour out her heart about boys she had crushes on, professors she admired or feared.

Rachel's second daughter needed her own space, and her sphere of privacy was more firmly defined, so Mom kept her distance, driving in to join her for a late-afternoon jog every couple of weeks. While keeping the focus on cardio health and tension-busting, Rachel also showed up to catch whatever confidences her daughter offered on the run. For her even more hands-off third daughter, she invented "drive-bys"—parking

Q: *Many of my friends complain that their kids never call them, but I have the opposite problem: My daughter contacts me too much. In the middle of a work day at my busy office, I might get twenty-five text messages from her. "What's your recipe for salad dressing?" "Do you have the phone number for a tailor?" "Have you seen my copy of* Fifty Shades of Grey*?" Help! How do I get her to unhook?*

A: If your child is the kind who wants too much advice and too much of your time, you'll need another kind of patience while self-reliance takes root and you can slowly step back. Of course it's nice to know that your daughter is thinking of you, but there's a time and a place for everything, and kerplunk in the middle of your workday is not the best time. It's not just young people who make the ground rules for friendship and communication with their parents during emerging adulthood. It's perfectly legit for you to set some expectations for your grown kids as well. If twenty-five texts are twenty-four too many, answer only the ones that seem urgent and encourage her to do her own problem solving. Both of you will come out ahead.

briefly in front of the girl's dorm, her station wagon stuffed with chicken soup and brownies. As she dropped off the meals on wheels, she'd wait for a few personal morsels to be dropped. And her gregarious youngest was most comfortable with restaurant dinners, plenty of other guests included; the lively table talk could be shared and cushioned by friends.

Just as you adjusted to your infants' variations in temperament and your young children's different signals, so with emerging adults: The dance between closeness and distance varies from child to child during their twenties, and you need to notice and learn from your children's cues when to reach out, when to step back, when to wait to be called.

We Can Work It Out

Many of the benefits parents reap at this stage are the results of 20-somethings' more sharply honed communication skills. Compared with their younger fly-off-the-handle and know-it-all selves, emerging adults are more likely to talk things over with their parents and peaceably process disagreements. Plus, they're increasingly able to see the other person's point of view. Their frontal cortex is ripening like fine wine, and that means improved judgment, less impulsivity, and a greater likelihood they'll think before they speak. Conversations become more nuanced as young people become sensitive to parents' signals and more skilled at reading between the lines.

In the best-case scenarios, a more even-keeled civility replaces teenagers' door-slamming or silent sulks. Now both sides can agree to disagree without causing World War III. Parents may find a recipe for dialing down the volume by listening (without interrupting) and then commenting in a neutral manner without hostility. If that's not possible, taking a time-out for both sides to calm down is as useful at this stage as it was when raising toddlers. "Sleeping on it" or letting heated emotions cool is as good a strategy for parents and their grown-up kids as for any couple or pair of friends.

For Bettina, her adopted son Jethro's increased maturity turned into a window of opportunity. She came along on several of his counseling sessions to work out some long-standing difficulties between them. "Even though he's 19 and six feet tall, he wanted me there," she says, surprised but pleased at the invitation. Jethro sought out therapy to face his own demons: low-boiling rage that often sputtered over the top, simmering sadness about his birth mother's abandonment. And Jethro and Bettina both wanted to learn how to head off explosions at home: "The counselor taught Jethro to say, 'Grapes' instead of 'You piss me off!'" Bettina can't even remember the word the counselor gave her—"Bananas?"—but she does recall learning to take a breath, get regulated, and address the situation more evenly rather than letting her emotions run wild.

The moment that made Bettina's years of hard times worthwhile happened when the therapist asked Jethro, "How do you see Bettina?" Jethro replied, "I see her as loving, kind, bold." Bettina's grateful response: "I waited nineteen years for that! You have to give them room to really express what's in their heart."

The Seesaw Between Parents and Friends

In emerging adulthood, family roles begin to realign with a growing sense in both generations that authority is becoming shared, not just top-down. In most families, these new green shoots of friendship are a good thing, promising a lifelong positive connection. But not all family dynamics are alike. In families where parents are involved and responsive but allow children their autonomy, the transformation from parent and child to friends has a good chance of taking hold during the emerging adult years. But in authoritarian families where parents have been controlling and overly punitive, this transition may come harder. Parents who have raised kids with a strict hand may be facing an attitude adjustment—or confrontations—as 20-somethings grow into their own decision-making and feel they've aged out of being told what to do.

Still, even when a good relationship blooms between parents and their grown kids, it may always be its own particular kind of friendship. No matter how simpatico the parents, it's hard to change eighteen years of habits overnight. You may still often be tempted to give unsolicited advice or do whatever you can to protect your kids, at whatever age, from harm. You may still jump in to correct their "Me and my friends are coming over" grammar or remind them to get car insurance.

More often than not, whatever sort of parent you've been or are becoming, emerging adults are the ones who set the boundaries and decide how close (or not) the relationship with parents will be. And emerging adults may sometimes be frustrating friends, the sort who don't return your calls, who cancel dates at the last minute, and text their buddies on their cell phones while dining with you. Forgiveness is the name of the game. As the Jewish proverb says, "To make a friend, close one eye. To keep a friend, close the other eye." Same goes for parents and their grown kids. But don't be afraid to set some ground rules, like no cell phones at the dinner table, or asking that they return a text from you that begins URGNT.

How to Be a Good Friend to Your Grown-up Kid

- Observe respectful boundaries; be available but don't pry.
- Listen more than you talk.
- Do what you both love together and intimacy will follow.
- Set ground rules for how to disagree.
- Be the first to forgive.
- Make room for the significant others in their lives.

Until children are emotionally and financially self-supporting, parents' lives are still entwined with theirs. "When will my grown-up kid grow up?" is a question that may have worried previous generations of parents. But it's especially challenging for this one.

4

Mom, R U Up?

I would like to see her in person more,
but have her call and text slightly less often.

MOTHER OF A DAUGHTER, 24

For eighteen years, parenting is hands-on and children are ever present. Parents birth them, bathe them, feed them, crawl on the floor playing with them, cheer them, giggle with them, comfort them, correct them, eyeball their homework, and carpool them. Then they're launched, and suddenly they become ... virtual. Though parents may dread being just another contact on their grown kids' Gmail list, staying in touch digitally can become a blessing in disguise.

How r u doing? Can u talk? What r u working on? When Elizabeth sees a tiny green light by Nate's and Will's names on her email screen, one click and they're in the room, two clicks and they're deep in conversation, never mind that they may be miles (or continents) away. She can pop them a reminder, a question about plans or logistics, or a "You arrive safely?" in one far-flung spot or another. And often there's an intimacy that might never happen in real life. Just recently, she and Will had a heart-to-heart Gchat about a key difference between her husband and her (conclusion: Dad's more "save the world," Mom's more "family-first").

Their family entered cyberspace when both boys crossed three time zones to attend college and arranging phone calls became trickier. As slightly homesick and unsettled freshmen, Nate and Will were eager emailers, and Elizabeth kept their in-box full. But their messages waned as their college lives took off, and she got used to clicking her motherly missives into a void of silence.

All that changed when Nate graduated from college and took a "wander year" through Southeast Asia. The family didn't see him face-to-face for nine months, but he left them a digital bread crumb trail they avidly followed. He and two buddies created their own website (HugeinAsia!), posted blogs, and produced online videos about their travels, two or three each week. If Elizabeth wanted to know if Nate had left Vietnam and arrived safely in Laos, whether his hair was short or long, or if he had a girlfriend, she didn't have to will the phone to ring with some static-crackly foreign update. She would simply track him online and reassure herself that he was having the adventure of a lifetime.

The following year Will spent his junior fall semester in South Africa, and he, too, left the family for cyberspace. He began telling tales on the blogosphere about his rural homestay, game-spotting treks, and thoughts on post-Mandela politics. Even though he was at the other end of the earth, Elizabeth knew their digital chats would bridge the distance. Compare this to her husband Bob's volunteer year in Uganda as a college student decades before the Internet, when letters to the States took three weeks and he never once phoned home.

Digital Natives vs. Digital Immigrants

Yes, it's a brave new world out there, and some parents are more at home in it than others. "I'm tech clueless and my son is tech savvy," admits one mother of a 19-year-old. This is one life skill where kids lead the way and parents follow, where advice moves up, not down, the generational ladder. And despite parents' very best intentions, in most families with 20-somethings there remains a digital divide.

On one side are most of today's emerging adults, the children born after 1980 who acquired their digital know-how as effortlessly as they learned to talk or walk. Today they live much of their lives online—they study, work, play, shop, pay bills and bank, listen to music, and meet people there. They read blogs instead of newspapers, download music instead of buying CDs, connect online before they meet in person, and text rather than phone to make a plan. These are "digital natives," so-called by writer and educator Marc Prensky.

On the other side, according to Prensky, are the "digital immigrants," those tech-clueless parents who learned to use email and social networks relatively late in life. Like anyone who takes on a new language as an adult, these immigrants of the older generation may always be a step behind, threatening to embarrass their fluent offspring with a mispro-nunciation or malapropism. Family therapist Sheri Glucoft Wong calls parents' communication disability "DSL"—Digital as a Second Language.

Although some boomers will aways feel more at home with hard copy and landlines, more and more are getting up to speed and enjoying the pleasures of connectivity. That's largely because one thing parents know for sure is that old-school methods won't do when it comes to maintaining their connection with their grown kids. So it's a huge motivator for parents to stay current in the widening wired world if it means keeping the conversation going with their kids.

Video telephones were once a futuristic promise at the 1964 World's Fair. Today, Skype, Google Hangouts, and many other forms of video-conferencing have become a marvelous virtual meeting ground for parents and their grown kids in faraway places. Hour-long video-conversations with a son taking a semester abroad in Australia or a daughter volunteering in a Zambian hospital make distances disappear and create the illusion that the missing child is briefly home again. Family events can be shared long-distance—Hanukkah candles lit at home and in a dorm room, Christmas presents opened together on two different coasts. At the end of a warm and lengthy video-chat between Jeff and his niece teaching in Ecuador, she said with a sigh, "I don't know what I'd do without Skype." Among 20-somethings in love in different cities, Skype has kept many long-distance relationships alive. Young couples on opposite coasts can still spend all evening in each other's bedrooms. Sort of.

Digital tools like Skype, vlogs, or blogs can also provide parents with a heads-up if things are not going so well. Once kids are posting in a public space, parents are able to monitor their highs and lows and snap into action if they spot a red flag. One 18-year-old headed to Europe after four emotionally rocky years of high school. His parents were unsure he would be able to sustain this on-the-road adventure but wanted to let him give it a try. His blog posts from abroad were an open journal for them, and they followed his updates carefully. When suddenly the posts turned from coherent travelogues into incomprehensible rants, his parents consulted with a therapist who warned them that their son could be heading for a manic break. They did what they needed to do to bring him home safely, avoid an international incident, and get him help in the form of counseling and medication.

Whether it's good news or bad, if you want to meet grown-up kids where they live, head to their screens. "Tonight I'm having a party," announces a young woman in a *New Yorker* cartoon, "so all my friends can come over and stare at their phones." In another cartoon, a young man hugs his computer: "I love my computer," he says. "All my friends live there." Even living in the same house, some parents have noticed that it's easier to get their 20-somethings' attention by texting, not talking.

Most twenty-first-century parents have figured out that leaving kids a voice mail and expecting a call back is whistling in the wind. ("Mailbox is full" . . . since 2005.) Email is slightly more effective but can still be stonewalled. If you want a quick answer from your kids, LRN 2 TEXT. Texting is so quick, easy, and uninflected, it's more note passing than writing, and like an all-night diner, it's always open for business. It can be done on the fly; in fact, it's the preferred medium for the on-the-fly generation—from class, from cars (unsafely), from parties, from restaurants in the middle of elaborate meals. One mother wondered why her 21-year-old son was madly texting as he surveyed a menu at a hot new bistro with the family. Eventually she realized he was texting the choices to his girlfriend, a foodie with confident tastes, so she could text back her suggestions for what to order.

Photo-sharing apps, like Instagram, a photo-posting service that's also a social network, have made many a dinner (or any other activity) a communal experience. Users can create a minute-to-minute scrapbook of their lives, posted for the world to see or in a private account. And that's just one example of today's latest digital inventions . . . or fads. By tomorrow, it may be supplanted by something we can't even imagine today.

Despite parents' best efforts, texting and photo-sharing still largely remain the playing field of the young. One mother of a college freshman proudly spent her hour-long subway commute hunting and pecking a long, loving text message to her son. His reply deflated her: "You text wrong."

Twenty-somethings Lauren Kaelin and Sophie Fraioli found their parents' misuse of texting and their random bloopers so common and hilarious that they started a website, *When Parents Text* ("small keypad, old hands"). Among the gems collected in their book of the same name:

The cat wants to know why she found condoms in your laundry.

Nerdy daughter, it is Saturday night. Please go out.

In Colorado. Am very sob. (short of breath)

clouds look like dancing bunnies, go look outside

FYI: Texting does not usually lead to heart-to-hearts between parents and grown kids. As one mother of a 19-year-old laments, "I would prefer a more 'connected'/mindful type of contact. It is the quality of contact that I would change, not the quantity." But monosyllables are what texting's all about.

The 24/7 Electronic Connector

In ancient, predigital times, when young people left for college and wider horizons, keeping in touch with family usually meant a dutiful Sunday phone call every week or two with both parents on the line at home, straining to hear. Sometimes sixties' or seventies' college kids went missing for days or weeks on end, merrily (or not so merrily) finding their way in the world, falling flat and getting up, staking out their own lives, making their declaration of independence. If they didn't want parents knowing about their misadventures, they simply didn't call, and parents had no recourse. They accepted the silence until their kids broke it.

Even as recently as fifteen years ago, when email was just starting to revolutionize global communication, a friend remarked that she had decided not to use it with her college freshman son in another city. She didn't think it was fair to be a constant, lurking presence in his dorm room. A child of the sixties, she'd studied Orwell's *1984* and was duly suspicious of Big Brother. Now she didn't want to turn into Big Mother. "He needs some space and some privacy to find himself," is how she described her policy.

How quaint that seems now, when parents and kids are linked by an electronic connector that never sleeps and keeps generations psychologically connected even as the physical space between them widens. Technological innovations have joined forces with social changes to create a communication explosion like never before between parents and emerging adults. As Purdue gerontology professor Lynn Fingerman reports from interviews with more than six hundred middle-aged parents, parent-child ties have changed in striking ways over the past few decades. Societal changes like smaller families and increased closeness between generations, plus technological advances like cell phones and Skype, have hugely increased the potential for intergenerational connectivity.

> We hear from our daughter less when she's happy/busy and sometimes the communication is just a quick text message. Phone calls usually happen only if there's some major disappointment, problem, or if she wants to vent or needs advice, and that is happening less.
>
> **MOTHER OF A DAUGHTER, 23**

Today parents can lob email messages back and forth all day with their college students or recent grads. They can Skype to see a dorm room or a first apartment, meet new roommates, or give a thumbs-up or -down on the choice of outfit for a first job interview. They can check in by cell phone while kids are walking across campus between classes or exchange texts when kids are bored in a lecture or losing focus at an office job. They can track their grown children on Facebook—if "friended," that is—or even without permission they can follow them on Twitter, Tumblr,

Pinterest, or Instagram, as well as read their kids' blog posts from across the globe. Surely all this communication is a boon to keeping the generations close.

But there are pitfalls, too, for the digital "tools that giveth also taketh away," says William Powers, author of *Hamlet's BlackBerry,* his critique of über connection in the Internet age. Parents' good-advice emails allow them to look over their grown kid's shoulders nonstop (*Don't forget to sign up for Professor So-and-So's seminar! Go to the health service for that cough!*). Children's night or day texted requests sometimes mean they don't have to figure things out for themselves (*How do I change my printer cartridge? What's the best cold medicine?*). Lurking on Facebook may give parents more information than they need to have (photos of that raucous Saturday night party a young reveler would rather forget by Monday). A grown child's blog post written in haste or to amuse friends can cause undue parental worry.

Across society, people of all ages are still catching up with the lightning-fast changes in communication of the past twenty years. It's a transitional time when everyone continues to adjust to the benefits and drawbacks of today's ramped-up connectivity. New tools, new formats, new apps are being created faster than the average user can keep up with them, and it's impossible to predict which are here to stay and which will be a flash in the pan, like Myspace, which 20-somethings fled as soon as it became too popular with high school kids. Today kids have earbuds stuck in their ears and fingers attached to their iPads. Tomorrow, who knows, but we all might wear Google goggles and have neural chips embedded in our brains!

But however the digital landscape changes, between parents and their emerging adults, the underlying issues will remain the same. Today's grown-up kids are becoming separate, autonomous adults amid this new landscape of ballooning social media and constant connection. Both the potential and the pitfalls play out during the dance of closeness and separation that marks the twenties' decade. The promise of closeness is greater than it's ever been before, but so are the dangers that result from relentless communication that can go over the top. Suddenly 24/7 entanglement can ensnare both generations in a web that's now worldwide.

As family therapist Wong puts it, for a parent who's tempted by a child's unlocked diary, "the Internet is one big, unlocked diary!" Let both sides beware. Parents of emerging adults need to take care that they're not overwhelming their launching children with a messaging blitz. Finding the right balance is an evolving decision for every family. It may be a good idea to discuss the issue directly with your grown kids: How much should we be in digital contact? How much is too much? What's the best way to reach you and get a reply?

Who Clicks First?

In a very twenty-first-century *New Yorker* cartoon, parents stand at their front door, waving and watching their daughter drive off to college, and voice the modern mantra, "Don't forget to click reply!"

Who clicks first when parents and grown children start living separate lives has become a key point of Internet etiquette. Thoughtful parents make careful, conscious decisions about how often they'll be the first to reach out and how much or how little communication is the right amount. Perhaps remembering their irregular contact with their own elders, most of today's parents of 20-somethings are relieved-verging-on-grateful that their kids want to stay as in touch as they do.

Digital contact ebbs and flows through the stormy weather and calmer zones of the twenties. There's often a barrage of calls, texts, and emails during the early launching years when kids first leave home and burst with hot-off-the-presses news or the need for a shoulder to cry on or a cash infusion. Newly arrived college students often still rely on parents' guidance in making decisions—what classes to take, how to resolve roommate disagreements or open a bank account. But as students get their bearings and build new networks, calls and emails usually drop off.

It's during the initial transition out of the home, to college or independent living, that how to stay connected becomes a sensitive issue. Many parents proceed with the caution of someone arranging a date with a shy prospect. Miranda, for example, recalls how delicately she raised the subject when she dropped off her older daughter, Grace, now 22, at a college across the country. "Grace is a gentle, sensitive person,"

> It's rare for me to initiate communication unless there is something transactional to be communicated, like where to meet for dinner. I tell my children it is not because I don't love them, am not thinking of them, etc. I just assume they'd like to be in control.
>
> MOTHER OF THREE SONS, 22 TO 28

her mother explains, so "it was more difficult for her to individuate." As they stood in Grace's dorm room, getting ready to hug good-bye, Miranda asked, "How much should I contact you? I don't want to be one of those helicopter parents." Grace's reply took the pressure off: "Just trust our relationship. If you feel like calling, call." Not every family is this attuned, but their organic connection might be something to strive for.

Communication during the twenties is a two-way street, and there's jockeying on both sides over what feels right, how much contact versus how much space. Young people want to proclaim their independence yet often need support and advice. Parents' better selves tell them they need to step back, yet multimedia make staying in constant contact so tempting. And, hey, parents left behind at home may crave a little notice, too. As teenagers, they may have sat by the phone willing a sweetheart to call; now they're checking their in-box or cell phone just as fervently to see if there's any news from grown kids on faraway campuses or in far-off cities.

Libby, the mother of a 20-year-old daughter, Pam, now a college junior, gives a measured description of how their connection shifted after Pam left home. Libby admits that she needed to hear from her daughter at least as much, if not more, than Pam needed news from home during her freshman year. At first, Libby's life was still defined by her daughter's, and she hungered to hear what Pam ate for dinner in the campus cafeteria, whom she sat next to in class, and what movie she saw on the weekend. But as Libby began to believe that Pam was indeed well launched, she started to get her own life back and let her daughter handle hers. As she became less invested in her daughter's every experience, she let Pam set the tempo between them: "When my daughter first left home, I wanted to be part of her college experience. As I 'matured,' I realized that I was ready to let it be *her* experience and not mine. I now wait for her to contact me, most of the time. I wonder if we help to prolong emerging adulthood by continuing to initiate daily contact. I just wonder . . ."

> **If we don't hear from him, we know he's doing well.**
> FATHER OF A SON, 22

Libby aptly describes how the maturation process in a family with emerging adults is double-headed. Mom is maturing into being a parent of a grown child, not a needy toddler or teenager, at the same time that her daughter is growing into her more independent self. Just as the mother of a toddler uses increasingly longer forays into the playground as a way to gauge how much separation her child can handle, so in a different way will a parent try to read the feelings of a grown child who is far from home. You want to be available when needed but also convey the message that you have faith that your grown kid can handle things and be OK. You also want to be clear that you're doing OK on your own, too, not crying by yourself in your kid's empty bedroom.

As launching-phase kids get established, you'll probably hear from them less. But contact may bump up again during the exploring phase, especially for grads who lose their college social ties and may lean more on their parents even as they start to build stand-alone lives. Mid-20-somethings may also feel less need to assert their independence and more comfortable drawing closer to their parents. "As my daughter [now 24] approached the latter part of college, she started calling me 'just because,' whereas earlier it was more based on need or problem solving," says one mother. "Since she graduated, we have lots of contact that is initiated easily by each of us."

> **We always know he's up to no good when we don't hear from him.**
> MOTHER OF A SON, 21

During the landing phase of the later twenties, communication may settle into a pattern typical of any close friendship where either side feels comfortable initiating contact and it's no big deal either way.

Long-Distance Ma-therapy

"Only connect," wrote E. M. Forster almost a hundred years ago, but he could have been talking to the lion's share of today's boomer parents. The vestigial parenting arm still wants to reach out even after kids have left the nest, and digital tools make long-distance parenting easier than it's ever been. The majority of parents in our survey reported sending at least ten emails a month to their faraway children, and some admitted to stuffing those in-boxes with twenty or thirty or even "hundreds" every month.

A 2005 survey of students at Middlebury College by psychology professor Barbara K. Hofer first put this story on the map. In focus groups with high school graduates the summer before their freshman year, most students looked forward to an exciting parent-free zone with contact home limited to one weekly call. But by the end of their first semester when polled again, the same students revealed they were in touch with parents an average of ten times per week. And most of these students, despite their earlier predictions, were happy with this frequent "iconnection." Today's college students, according to Hofer, often say, "'My parents are my best friends.' People would have seen that as aberrant a generation ago, as pathological." Today's college kids mostly don't mind keeping their parents close by toting them around campus via cell phones or laptops.

"Parenting by email," one mother calls the preferred strategy for imparting anything lengthy or dicey, words of wisdom or the occasional pep talk. "To stay healthy, happy, and keep an even keel, remember the daily four," was Elizabeth's "Welcome to College" email to both her sons when they first arrived on campus as freshmen. "Eat plenty of fruits and vegetables, take an exercise break, write in a journal or share feelings with friends, and make sure to do something fun every day that gives you pleasure."

Wisely used (but not overused) digital contact or even the old-fashioned phone extends the symbolic tie between parents and grown-up kids across large continents and rough times. During the initial year of her first really adult job far from home, Frances's daughter, Tina, who's 24, made daily midday calls to her mom, one nonprofit office worker to another. Tina refers to these private sessions as "Ma-therapy," and they became a lifeline to sanity. "I close my door at work and give her twenty minutes," Frances explains about their daily routine. "Tina kind of over-sold herself for this job and is now trying to live up to it," Frances says. "She has a lot of insecurity. With me she can vent about her bosses."

Parental advice may be welcome up to a point. But too much advice can backfire and undercut young people's ability to think for themselves. One college student describes her best friend's constant stream of calls with her dad. Admitting that she herself talks to her mother the least of anyone she knows—it can be three weeks between calls—this senior questions her girlfriend's perpetual electronic bond to her father: "To me it seems almost strange. She calls him before she gets to a class and then after. Sometimes she gets frustrated and hangs up but then she talks again. He gives her great advice . . . but is it impartial?"

From her more independent perspective, the cord of connectivity has been pulled too tight between her friend and her friend's father. Being constantly on call like that wouldn't work for her. But all families do the

---

Q: *Our college junior son is usually a good communicator, but occasionally he goes missing for a week or two, and we start fearing the worst. Should we leave him alone or is it OK for us to initiate contact if we're concerned about him?*

A: Most parents develop a second sense about when their grown children need encouragement and when they want to be left alone to puzzle things out on their own. Unmade or unanswered calls may just mean your son's life is happily full and his attention is elsewhere, but they can also be a sign of trouble brewing or a crisis that has deepened into despair. You have to make a sensible judgment about each child and each situation based on what you know about your child. If a longer than usual silence suggests that a child is having a hard time, or if a recent call home has been particularly emotional, it might be time to follow up with an email or text: "Send me a brief message to say you're OK" (or arrange a future call).

---

minuet of closeness and separation differently, and what may feel like overinvolvement to an outsider may seem natural within this particular family—and may work well for them.

Is There a Right Amount of Contact?

Many parents interpret their kids' alternating spikes of contact and silence like financial experts analyzing the stock market's rise and fall—and often with similarly conflicting opinions.

Most every parent of emerging adults has had the experience of getting a phone call from a child in great distress and losing a night's sleep fretting over the crisis . . . only to find that the child has forgotten about the drama two days later. "My daughter always calls when her world is falling apart," says one such mother, "but she neglects to call back an hour later when it's back together again." No parent should overlook an SOS call from a worried child, but don't push the panic button too soon, either.

Communication swings between closeness and distance during the delicate, demanding process of individuation for young people in their twenties, and parents are wise to read the messages shared but also to respect the pullbacks. One mother of a recent college grad was at first distressed that her daughter would phone only when she had something positive to report. But she came to understand that her daughter's need for psychic space was pivotal to these growing-up years: "[Our daughter] can't shake the sense that she must have good news to call. I'm not happy with that. But it's pride. She wants to show independence."

Sometimes little or spotty contact means a child is wrestling with decisions in private, and parents need to appreciate the budding self-reliance that gets stronger during the midtwenties' exploring years. At other times, loss of contact can indeed be a warning sign. Trust your instincts about your child and be ready to jump in if you feel something is seriously awry.

"I'm glad to support you, but really, you handle it."

Finding just the right method and amount of contact to make both generations comfortable can be a high-wire act. A wrong step in either direction can spell danger, particularly if parents want to spend more time connecting than their kids . . . or the reverse, which happens, too, when kids want more from parents than parents want to handle.

Once their kids have left home, some parents are plenty ready to sign off. They're not waiting for a phone to ring or a text to pop up and interrupt their newfound freedom at a concert or a movie—far from it. Some parents recall their hard-won distance from their parents during their twenties and feel ambivalent that their grown children still need constant reinforcement. For these parents, the treadmill of connectivity made possible by digital tools and the demands that come with it can be a burden or at least stir up awkwardly mixed feelings.

Meredith, 53, a university administrator and the mother of two daughters, Abby, 21, and Kim, 19, is one of the generation that left for college and never looked back. It's a point of pride that she supported herself and made every decision on her own. "My life circumstances are so different from my daughters'," she says. "My parents were very unaware. I went to a women's college on a full scholarship, worked through college and grad school, and always had two things going on (e.g., grad school and a job)."

Thinking that she had raised Abby and Kim to be as independent-minded as she was, Meredith has been surprised by their need to touch base frequently and a bit taken aback by their reliance on her opinions during college and afterward. When she attended college, she never remembers her parents calling her at all, and she called them only once a month. But her daughters seem to be in touch nonstop. Occasionally she's had to stifle her impatience when Kim emails a photo of a fancy new coat and asks her what she thinks of it and would she share the cost. Or when her daughter phones her from college upset because she got an A-minus instead of an A on a paper. Meredith has learned to reply as patiently as possible: "I'm glad to support you, but really, you handle it."

For parents like Meredith who feel inundated by texts, calls, and emails from their kids, know that the passage of time will most likely ease the number and frequency as kids develop a network of friends or a serious romantic partner to consult for help and advice. If you still feel you're drowning in their requests, consider setting some ground rules for contact—for instance, choose one or two nights per week for calls or suggest limiting texts to serious emergencies . . . not new coats or A-minuses. But keep in mind this paradox: Often if grown kids know they can lean on you if need be, and not be pushed away or belittled, they'll start gaining confidence and be less, not more, dependent.

"I was overinvested in my child."

When boundaries between the generations are too porous or fluid, parents and their grown children can become overly enmeshed, electronically as well as in other ways. The potential for endless connectivity can be an irresistible temptation for a parent who's excessively curious about a child's life and a child who can't say no. Melanie's story illustrates what happens when a parent wants and needs to have more contact with a far-from-home child than is good for them both.

Melanie, 61, swells with pride talking about the early career success of her daughter, Ariel, who's 24 and in her first postcollege job working for a women's health organization. "She is so lucky to have a job!" says Melanie. "She just went to a party with many of her college friends, and she was the only one with a 'real' job." But for a concerned mom, learning to sit back during this in-between stage while her daughter is finding her life path can be frustrating.

Ariel was Melanie's baby—her older brother is 29—and she was a self-confident but emotional and demanding child. When Ariel went off to college, Melanie had mixed feelings: "I was overinvested in my child, so it was pretty hard when she left. But she is extremely intense, and it was a huge relief not to have to deal with her on a daily basis." Ariel's college was far from home, and they saw each other face-to-face only a few times a year. But email kept them in more or less perpetual contact. Ariel got in the habit of sharing a steady parade of stories about her classes, her roommates, her love life, her hopes and fears.

At first Melanie was thrilled to be privy to these details—some of them quite intimate—but as the college years progressed, their intimacy began to make her increasingly uncomfortable. And she couldn't help but disapprove when her daughter shared tales of getting stoned or having fleeting relationships with men who seemed inappropriate.

Although Melanie had encouraged these email confessionals, soon they began veering into "too much information," and she wasn't sure how to disentangle.

Q: *Like many middle-aged friends from our generation, my wife and I are now on Facebook. We use it to catch up with people in our past, stay current with friends we do see but not that often, and put out word about professional projects or political issues. But here's my $64,000 question: Should we friend or not friend our own children and their friends or respond to their friends' requests to be Facebook friends with us?*

A: Although 18- to 34-year-olds comprise over half of Facebook's active users, more and more of their parents are joining this seductive global community—as of 2012, 45- to 65-year-olds made up 20 percent of Facebook users, and the number is climbing, with 45- to 54-year-olds one of Facebook's faster-growing segments, according to social media expert Jamie Turner.

The Facebook currency is "friends," those people to whom your Facebook page is linked. In theory there are privacy settings on Facebook that allow some friends to see more of a user's profile than others, and these concentric circles of familiarity could help transfer to cyberspace the staying-close-but-not-too-close balance between parents and emerging adults. But Facebook's privacy settings are often in flux. So observe the same etiquette about closeness versus distance in cyberspace that you do elsewhere.

For example, if you're Facebook friends with your kids, you might look at the photos they post . . . but refrain from leaving a trail of comments on their wall. Likewise, don't post anything potentially cringe-inducing about them on your page. And a word to the wise: If you become "friends" with their current girlfriend or boyfriend, then when a breakup occurs, that former lover will be able to track your child's new relationships in photos on your page. During these years of changing partners and tender feelings, that's something to think about before you click "accept."

Meanwhile Melanie sometimes couldn't help but overshare herself, and that tendency, too, strained the bond and the boundaries between them. Indeed, when we asked Melanie, "How much does your daughter rely on you for emotional support?" she turned the question around: "You should ask parents: How much do you rely on your *child* for emotional support?" In spite of a good marriage and wanting to be a caring, generous mother, she came to regret that she had leaned too heavily on her younger child.

By the time Ariel graduated from college and started her life a continent away from home, she and her mother had become so electronically engaged, so overly attached that, as her mother reports, they "didn't know where one of us stopped and the other started. We had to completely separate in order to figure this out." Their solution was radical and very twenty-first century: They went cold turkey for three months and stopped all communication, digital and otherwise. Melanie calls this effort to cut back "deliberate but not articulated." Meanwhile, Ariel continued to stay in touch with her father, who made sure that his wife knew that their daughter was alive and doing well.

A year later, Melanie assesses the benefits and strains of their trial separation this way: "It was important for Ariel to gain control of her own life. It was important for me to remember that she is in charge of her own life! It was painful, but we have reconnected with less blaming and neediness and more genuine caring and listening."

Now they're back in touch and have redefined their relationship with more comfortable distance and respectful boundaries (their contact can vary from a bunch of emails in one day to no communication for a week or two). Melanie feels fairly satisfied but wants to safeguard what they've achieved: "I would love it if Ariel would move back to our area, but I would still like to keep the new separateness that we have gained." Looking ahead to her own retirement in a year or so and concerned about her financial security, Melanie is happy that she and her daughter have a fiscal separation as well. But Melanie's relief that they've established a healthier connection these days is mingled with worries. For a mother-daughter pair who once shared everything, it's now the things unspoken that keep Melanie up at night: "We don't talk a lot about sex and drugs, but she uses pot regularly, and I'm not happy about that, and she knows it. She also has open relationships, which I'm not thrilled about."

Melanie admires her daughter in many ways—"She is young, smart, attractive"—but she worries that her daughter is wasting her twenties with men who are not worthy of her. Still, after overstepping the emotional turf lines between them and then having to take a giant step back, she's learned to respect her daughter's privacy. "I used to know more about her love life," she says, "but now I prefer not to know so much."

Clicking Hello

"Technology is us," say today's emerging adults. There's no doubt that interconnectivity defines the modern world, and if parents don't want to be left behind, they're wise to go along for the ride. To stay connected with their grown-up kids, parents will do well observing good boundaries in cyberspace as elsewhere and strive for that Goldilocks kind of balance, not too much communication, not too little, but just right for your particular family.

Now that Elizabeth's sons are both 20-somethings, she treads carefully between connection and distance, support and snooping. She doesn't lurk on Facebook, constantly text, or badger them multiple times a day for replies to emails. So an instant message initiated by one of them is especially sweet, like a surprise gift when it's not her birthday. One morning, for instance, she settled at her computer and found a Gchat message left over from late the night before: *"Mom, r u up?"* it read. She and her sons keep wildly different hours both online and off-line, but knowing they were thinking of her made her day.

Nothing is better than seeing children's faces across the breakfast table, but digital clicks close the gap in between.

5

The College Years

My daughter took five years to graduate, because she changed her major three times. She figures things out as she goes along. I'm supportive. I say, "However you do it is fine," but my husband never graduated from college and he told her, "You've got to make progress so you won't end up like me."

MOTHER OF A DAUGHTER, 24

"Off to college!" It's a familiar phrase in American life, and one tinged with a sentimental glow. It conjures images of throwing Frisbees on the quad; cheering for the football team on a crisp fall afternoon; stretching your mind to contain a wealth of new knowledge; and meeting the people who will become your best friends, including, perhaps, the love of your life.

The reality of college life is quite a bit different for most people, and not nearly so romantic: high rates of loneliness and depression, especially the first year; rampant alcohol abuse; out-of-control costs; and a dropout rate of about 50 percent. And less than half of college students even go "off to college," with most remaining at home or moving out but living off campus. Nevertheless, for most emerging adults the launching phase, ages 18 to 22, includes the pursuit of higher education. Emerging adulthood is the age of identity explorations, and the college environment is tailor-made for it. College is in many ways a practice field to try out being an adult: making independent choices; defining fields of interest (that might or might not lead to a future career); falling in and out of love; forming friendships that may (or may not) last a lifetime; pursuing passions and striving for success; and testing resilience by coping with uncertainty and disappointment.

It is a setting for trying on different personas and interests, and it often includes a series of starts and stops and changes of direction. When Elizabeth's son Nate started college, the dean sent a letter to all the freshman parents with a warning about the shifting winds ahead: The daughter parents thought was destined to be a doctor might return home in December having fallen in love with French literature; the son headed to be an engineer might find his way into music and math; a child's high school sweetheart who was practically part of the family might be replaced by a stranger with a nose ring or an unfamiliar background. Just knowing that these surprises might come with the college territory can take the edge off the shocks that lie ahead.

Q: *My husband and I have planned a seven-college tour with our son for this summer, but he says he doesn't want to go. In fact, he's warning that he'll refuse to leave the car! What do we do now?*

A: Our first reaction is "Grrrrrrrr," so we can imagine what your reaction must be. But try to avoid an angry response; it won't help. Have you tried talking to him about why he resists the idea? Perhaps he feels like you and your husband have taken over the process. Maybe you should ask him to lead the planning of the trip; if he won't, just let it go. There's really no point in forcing the experience on him if he's that resistant. You can learn a lot from each college's website and from parent websites like collegeconfidential.com, and save yourselves the costs (and headaches) of the trip. An alternative approach is to wait and see which colleges accept your son and visit just the top contenders in the spring.

For certain, there are changes and challenges in store for the whole family when grown-up kids apply to college and then head out the door. Nor is the transition to college an isolated event accomplished in one singular swoop when that fat letter of college acceptance arrives, or months later, when the family car packed with a student's possessions pulls up in front of a new dorm. Instead, as University of California, Berkeley counselor Gloria Saito points out, every step young people take—from listing potential colleges to deciding where to attend, from adjusting to a strange roommate to choosing a major—is a step toward their making independent decisions and toward parents letting go. "Parents have been preparing for this moment since their kids were toddlers," says Saito. "They've been encouraging their children to explore but also being an anchor for them." Yet now's *not* the moment to wave good-bye, close the door on the relationship, and let kids fend for themselves. Parents' advice and encouragement can be crucial during the off-to-college transition. It's a time to stay available, and offer support and guidance if asked, but without trying to control young people's choices.

How Involved Should Parents Be?

It's a big turning point, deciding where to go to college, and most parents understandably want to be involved. But *how* involved should parents be? How much is too much? This is an issue for which the ideal stepping back/staying connected balance is tricky to find and challenging to achieve.

Among parents in our survey, the overwhelming consensus is that parents should be supportive and provide counsel and information when needed, but emerging adults should be the ones who make the ultimate choice. Beware the "*We're* applying to college" syndrome that some over-eager and overanxious parents fall into. The student does the applying; the parents' best role is support staff.

Parents may certainly set the parameters of the decision. "Here's the limit of what we can afford," for example. Or "Yes, you can apply to an out-of-state school, but we won't be able to fly you home for vacations." But students will fare much better and be more motivated to succeed if their college choice is their own. "We have been there to support our son, not to tell him what to do," is the way one dad put it. "He's chosen his own path, and we are the fans in the background cheering him on."

Of course, it's a lot easier to be content with cheering from the grandstand when your favorite player is hitting home runs and rounding the bases with a wave and a smile. "We're amazed by his determination to become a doctor," one mom says proudly. "I am in awe of her," says another mom, speaking of her daughter's college success. "She is a star by all accounts." But if your would-be star is striking out, sitting on the bench, or not even showing up for the game, well, then it's harder to sit in the stands and say nothing. "I wish she liked school," a disappointed mother says with a sigh. "She lost interest in school after her first try at college even though she says she wants degrees." Another dad observes sardonically, "He wants to be a professional wrestler. Need I say more?"

So what can parents do? What if a talented student sells herself short by applying only to "Where-My-Boyfriend-Goes U" or a less-skilled student is wildly overreaching with his college choices and not applying to any "safe" schools where he is more likely to get in? This is one of the many areas of parenting grown-up kids where parents have to accept the hard truth that there are limits to what they can control. It's not primary school, where you could declare a rule that there would be no TV until homework was finished, or high school, where you could make holding a part-time job contingent on keeping their grades up. In emerging

> I kept bugging my daughter to apply to college during her senior year in high school, but she kept putting it off. Finally, I started making calls myself, pretending to be her. I started filling out her applications, all the basic, mind-numbing, time-consuming stuff. She did the creative part, she wrote her own essays. And it worked; she got in.
>
> **MOTHER OF A DAUGHTER, 20**

adulthood, the ultimate decision-making power in education is theirs, and they know it. "I have tried to be involved, but she resists," bemoans a mom. A dad recounts of his daughter, "She declined our offer to pay for four years of college and chose to move in with a boyfriend, work full-time, and attend college part-time. This is her seventh year of college."

This does not mean parents are without options. You can't make kids go to college if they'd prefer to pursue a career in professional wrestling, but high school students applying to college can benefit greatly from parents' assistance. Parents can help gather information and fill out financial aid forms. They can keep track of deadlines and give reminders as they approach. Most aspiring students are happy—grateful, even—to have parents provide support and companionship in the college application process, as long as parents don't try to take it over. Some families find it useful to limit discussion of the C-word—*college*—to one night a week, or encourage high school seniors to reserve one weekly block of time (say, Saturday afternoons) to work on college applications and essays so the process doesn't seep into family life like a toxic spill.

Even parents whose high school seniors really want to go to college and are full partners in the application process can find themselves getting stressed out. Many parents feel a lot of social pressure for their child not just to go to college but to go to the *very best* college. Because high school seniors apply to more colleges than ever, acceptance rates at many elite schools have plummeted to single digits—which spurs ambitious students and their parents to apply to even more schools, which further depresses the acceptance rate, and so on. Until the cycle gets vicious.

Because acceptance rates are so low at the most-sought schools, the majority of families are going to have to cope with some degree of disappointment in the course of the college application process. Parents may well find themselves having to manage their own disappointment that their child was not accepted at the first-choice school, while at the same time comforting a child who is heartbroken over a rejection letter. For some talented students, that disappointment may be the first after a long run of school successes.

Our main advice to parents as pressure and anticipation build is simply this: *Relax,* or as the emerging adults put it, *chill.* As parents ourselves, we know how difficult this is. The whole frenzy that has built up around the college application process in recent years makes it more difficult than ever to keep your cool. But remember this: In the end, having a college degree is more important than where it was obtained. There are hundreds of American and Canadian colleges and universities that provide the opportunity of an excellent education that will prepare students well for work and for life. An abundance of research shows that getting a four-year degree matters greatly to future economic success, but *which* college the degree is from does not. Getting into Harvard or Middlebury or Michigan won't ensure a happy and fruitful four years, much less a happy and fruitful life. Motivated students who really want to learn can find opportunities to learn at a wide range of schools. More important than getting into a "top school" is finding a college that's a good fit so students want to be there and will feel at home and motivated to do their best.

COLLEGE TALES

"I HAD to let go of that dream."

—Gail, a 49-year-old mother of an 18-year-old college freshman

I've been very involved from the beginning. I got him into good early childhood programs, and then into the gifted program in school, and then into a really good private school. But I wanted him to go to Harvard and he made his own choice not to go there and to go to [a small college] instead. He just felt the fit would be better—it was more like the private school he went to, lots of personal attention. But I'm like, "Wait a minute, he's not following the plan now!" I got a lot of pressure—all the people who knew him thought he was really smart, that he should go to the best college. The more I learned about this college, the more I could see he was right, it was the right fit for him. But it was hard for me; I had to let go of that dream.

He's majoring in teaching English and in Theater and Arts. He's done very well. He was on the honor roll his first year. He's really into theater and chorus, and he's gotten to do those there. I was hoping he was going to be my doctor, but that didn't happen.

We like to recall the observations of one college counselor at a competitive high school where whoops were heard and tears were shed when letters of acceptance and rejection arrived in the spring. She had seen dozens of students go off to college in September, some with a bounce in their step and others trying to make the best of a second- or third- or fifth-choice school. But by the time they came home for the winter holiday, she noticed, almost all of them felt things had worked out for the best. They were making friends, getting involved in their classes, spreading their wings in a new community. They were embracing what *is* rather than fretting over what might have been. Parents should do the same.

COLLEGE TALES

"SHE WAS devastated when she didn't get in."
—Ellen, a 64-year-old mother of a 24-year-old daughter, now applying to graduate school

I didn't really get involved much in her college applications. She's always made good choices, so it was never an issue. But she wanted to go to an Ivy League college, applied to a bunch of them, and she was devastated when she didn't get in. So she went to the state university and enjoyed it, actually.

After she graduated she wanted to go to medical school. Again she didn't make it, and again she was devastated when she didn't get in. Now she wants to study physical therapy instead. She got a master's degree in physiology this year and she's applying to Ph.D. programs in physical therapy. It's actually a good thing. She wanted more of a balance in her life than being a doctor allows. But it's still an adjustment. She always thought that being a doctor would be what defined her, so that change has been tough.

The College Transition, Parents' Version

Waving the kids off to college and offering emotional support through their inevitable ups and downs on campus is not just about them—it's also about you. About how you'll respond to the empty nest, what

Dos and Don'ts of the College Application Process

DO:

- Ask other parents who have been through it for their advice.

- Seek information online about the colleges your child might be interested in.

- Browse websites like collegeconfidential.com for objective evaluations and parents' perspectives.

- Visit the top schools on your child's list, if time and money allow.

- Find other good resources of information, such as the *Princeton Review,* which rates colleges based on over 100,000 students' feedback about their learning experiences.

- Encourage your student to build a good rapport with the college counselor at school.

- Remember that your student is likely to be more committed and engaged with the college experience if allowed to have the main influence in selecting a school.

DON'T:

- Believe everything parents tell you from their experiences, unless you can verify it elsewhere.

- Believe what colleges say, online or in person, about their own virtues without getting independent confirmation.

- Generalize too much from one or a few passionate parents' website ravings, good or bad.

- Make a decision based mainly on a good or blah college visit.

- Rely on resources that are popular but not credible, such as the *U.S. News and World Report* rankings, the unreliable, overhyped reference that relies on irrelevant metrics such as "percent of alumni who donate to the school."

- Rush to sign up for a private college counselor unless the school counselor is unhelpful or overbooked.

- Believe that the choice of college is going to determine the rest of your child's life, for better or worse.

you'll do to fill and refeather it, about your marriage, your work life, and the hobbies you might now actually have time for. It's about what you're going to do with the rest of your life. And that's a formidable question for most people, and not one that can be answered on the drive home from depositing your grown kids in their new dorms.

A couple of weeks after Elizabeth's younger son left for college, a friend dropped off an empty nest, a real one, at the door. Inside she tucked a flamingo-pink plastic egg and a note: "It's a love nest, of course, for your new life."

After twenty-plus years of trikes in the hallway, bulging backpacks in the kitchen, and soccer gear over the bathroom floor, Elizabeth and Bob finally had the place to themselves—and they felt unmoored. For those first few weeks after both boys were gone, their house felt less like a romantic hideaway and more like a hollow watermelon, as their older son used to call it before anyone got home. The phone was quiet, the rap music silenced, the zone from the front door to the kitchen hauntingly clutter-free.

> I worried about my dad all alone in our big, empty house. He did all right. He got a lot closer to my cat.
>
> DAUGHTER, 18

Adjusting to the empty nest is an emotional time, and your emotions may run from A to Z. First, you may cry—and for some parents the anticipatory grief can be almost more painful as you watch your high school seniors move through their season of lasts—last basketball game, last school dance, last parent conference, last SAT (okay, that one's not so sad). You cry if you loved being a parent of children underfoot more than anything and you cry for your regrets—that you yelled too often or worked too many long hours. And sometimes you cry because you're not sure who you are without your children. You cry for the empty self as well as for the empty nest.

But then . . . the fog begins to lift, you start to hear that your precious kids are settling into their new communities, and time begins to open up for you in delicious new ways. You can read a book at odd hours, stay late at the office, cobble a meal together from leftovers without complaints from the peanut gallery, or have a leisurely restaurant tête-à-tête with your spouse or a friend. Often the grief, self-scrutiny, and gift of time help catalyze an exciting new chapter in your life that you can't foresee until it's unfolding.

The College Experience

The American college is set up so that students have a wide range of options to explore as they develop a clearer sense of who they are and what they really want to do. They don't have to know what they want to be or what they want to study when they arrive. Students entering a four-year college typically have two years to sample the possibilities and take a wide variety of general education courses in the humanities and the sciences before deciding on a major, unlike universities in Canada and Europe. Two-year colleges also provide a lot of flexibility, allowing students to take a course here and a course there to explore options.

In the process of sampling a variety of courses, if students are lucky, something clicks—they have that *aha!* moment when an inspiring professor or something they read seizes their imagination and they feel the exhilaration of their future field becoming clear and an identity snapping neatly into place: "This is what I want to do. This is the thing for me." Even for those who are not so lucky, in the course of two years most find something to major in, at least for now.

What kind of experiences do emerging adults have at college? What kind of experiences do they seek? What kinds of goals and attitudes do they bring to their college experience? These questions have been the target of considerable research in the United States over the past fifty years. One useful way of characterizing students' experiences was developed in the early 1960s by the sociologists Burton Clark and Martin Trow, who described four student "subcultures": the collegiate, the vocational, the academic, and the rebel.

The *collegiate* subculture centers around fraternities, sororities, dating, drinking, big sports events, and campus fun. Professors, courses, and grades are a secondary priority. Students in this subculture do enough schoolwork to get by, but they reject or ignore any encouragement from professors to become seriously involved with ideas. Their main purpose during their college years is socializing and partying. This subculture thrives especially at big universities.

Students in the *vocational* subculture have a practical view of their college education. To them, the purpose of college is to gain skills and a degree that will enable them to get a better job than they would have otherwise. Like collegiates, students in the vocational subculture resist professors' demands for engagement in ideas, beyond the requirements of the course work. But vocationals have neither the time nor the money for the frivolous fun of the collegiate subculture. Typically, they work twenty to forty hours a week to support themselves and help pay their college tuition. Students who attend two-year colleges are mostly in this category.

The *academic* subculture is the one that identifies most strongly with the educational mission of college. Students in this subculture are drawn to the world of ideas and knowledge. They study hard, do their assignments, and get to know their professors. These are the students professors like best, because they are excited about and engaged with the materials their professors present.

Students in the *rebel* subculture are also deeply engaged with the ideas presented in their courses. However, unlike academics, rebels are aggressively nonconformist. Rather than liking and admiring their professors, they tend to be critically detached from them and skeptical of their expertise. Rebels enjoy learning when they feel the material is interesting and relevant to their lives, but they are selectively studious. If they like a course and respect the professor, they do the work required and often receive a top grade, but if they dislike a course and find it irrelevant to their personal interests they may slack off, and their grades will reflect their lack of effort.

But, you may say, Clark and Trow described these student subcultures more than five decades ago. Can the same subcultures still apply to today's students? Observers of higher education think so, and from Jeff's experience as a professor he would agree that their description is still true. All of these subcultures are likely to be familiar to anyone who teaches college students. But it is important to emphasize that these are types of subcultures, not types of students. Most students are blends of the four subcultural types, to different degrees, although most identify with one subculture more than the others.

To put it another way, the four subcultural types represent different kinds of goals that emerging adults have for their college experience. As collegiates they pursue fun, as vocationals they pursue a degree, as academics they pursue knowledge, and as rebels they pursue an identity. Most students hope to weave all these strands into their college experience. For example, in a national study of college freshmen conducted by the Higher Education Resource Institute, 77 percent responded that it was "very important" for them during college "to learn more about the things that interest me," an academic goal, and nearly as many, 75 percent, intended "to get training for a specific profession," a vocational goal, but 52 percent also intended "to find my purpose in life," a rebel goal.

Watching your children choose their college goals from among these options can be a satisfying moment—or a vexing one. Maybe you were looking forward to attending big-time football games with your child and reliving a bit of your own collegiate fun—only to find that he or she doesn't have the slightest interest in spending a beautiful autumn Saturday that way. Maybe you were savoring the prospect of talking all about the fascinating topics promised in the titles of your child's courses each semester—American Short Stories, Global Economics in the Twenty-first Century, and Atomic Physics—only to find that your child is just focused on the vocational goal of surviving them and getting a degree, and adamantly rejects any inquiries about the course content.

These kinds of disconnects may be hard for parents to accept, especially when they are paying the bills, but remember, seductive as it is to relive the glory days, now it's the students', not the parents', college experience. It's best for parents to honor college students' newly defined interests as a positive sign of their identities coming into focus. Then find common ground where possible—taking them and their roommates to dinner when you come to town, appreciating a good paper they've written, watching them play Ultimate Frisbee or have a role in a campus production. In most cases, you'll find ways to share at least some of their college experience while realizing that these are mainly their years to strive and, you hope, thrive.

College Challenges, for Them and You

Coll_ege life can be fun and exciting, but for most students there are challenges and stresses as well. Let's look at five major stumbling blocks and at what parents can do to help their emerging adults overcome them.

The First-Year Blues

That last summer before entering college is often a busy and emotional one for college-bound kids, especially for the ones moving away from home. Many spend a lot of time with high school friends in a last hurrah before they all scatter in different directions, promising to keep in touch online and get together again at breaks.

For families this is often a bittersweet time. Their grown-up kid is about to enter college, so of course there's excitement. Parents usually feel proud, and they should. True, most young Americans today get at least some college education, but not everybody does. Going to college, and graduating, sets the emerging adult on a path that is likely to lead to

---

Q: *I helped my daughter a lot during high school, often checking her math homework, typing her assignments, and giving her advice on projects. It paid off, she got into a good college—but now she comes home most weekends and still expects me to help with her schoolwork! I hate to tell her no, but I thought this would end once she was in college.*

A: You're right, your help on her homework should end once she enters college. However, her requests for your help could be part of the first-year transition that is difficult for many students, and it may be that after she gets used to college work she'll be able to do it on her own. Perhaps you could gradually reduce your role during the first year, encouraging her to do more of it herself. You could also encourage her to make use of the resources available at her college. Most colleges have a writing center to assist students on papers, and professors and teaching assistants are usually available to provide help outside of class.

---

a good life, certainly more likely than the noncollege path. It's an event to celebrate, so find a way to mark the occasion: a final vacation to a favorite family spot, dinner at a special restaurant, or a home-cooked meal featuring the guest of honor's most-loved childhood dishes.

For students who will not only be entering college but also leaving home, this separation can feel like a jarring loss for both sides. Of all the normal separations in our society, departure from home can be the most difficult. Young children enter preschool for the first time, five-year-olds have their first day of primary school, and adolescents take their first drive in the family car, but in each of these cases they come home again a short time later, and family life goes on as before. The fears that emerging adults (and their parents) have about the life-changing departure from home are natural and understandable. So much is unfamiliar and unknown for both generations.

For parents this transition means defining a whole new structure for their lives now that the child will no longer need to be picked up from soccer practice or helped with homework or have breakfast, lunch, and dinner provided. For college students, it means making a life from scratch and all at once: a new residence, new roommates, new friends, higher academic requirements, and, for many, the challenge of combining school and a job. The dropout rate is higher in the first year of college than in any year that follows as young people try to meet so many challenges at once and sometimes fall short.

So how should parents respond when their emerging adults leave for college? Follow your grown kid's lead. There is a great deal of individual variability in how much new freshmen need and want their parents to be involved. The greater the need for parental support, the more involved parents will have to be in order to help their children make it through.

On the one side are the many emerging adults for whom the transition to college is not hard at all. They seize it with enthusiasm from Day One. Maybe home life wasn't all that happy, because there was a lot of conflict between the parents, or there were divorce and stepparent complications, or there was a contentious relationship with a sibling. Maybe home life was happy as could be, but constricting, too, because of well-meaning parental advice and involvement, so the new college student is exhilarated by the prospect of having more freedom.

On the other side are the students who find the transition a rocky one. It could be that they don't like their roommate situation or that classes are harder than expected. Or they're distressed because home was a safe, secure, nurturing place, and the college world feels colder and crueler. They'll get used to this reality eventually, and they'll find friends and romantic partners who will provide new sources of support, but until they do, they may need more nurturing than they expected or parents realized they would need.

So parents may find that a lot of their time in this first year is devoted to supporting their emerging adults emotionally. This may mean visiting them or having them come home more often than planned for weekend visits. There may be many texts per day back and forth, especially in the early months, or frequent conversations on the phone. One mother reported that her daughter called home crying every day for the first three months of college. She was alarmed at first but always made time for her daughter to vent about the difficulties she faced and how lonely and homesick she was. After that initial three-month period her daughter adjusted and ultimately had "a great experience."

Another way parents (and grandparents) can support their emerging adults during the first year of college is to send an occasional care package that includes some of the student's favorite foods, maybe an article from the local newspaper or a drawing by a younger sibling, along with an encouraging note from Mom and Dad. Students love getting care packages. It makes them feel connected to the love and support of home even as they are striving to learn to be on their own. Even a real, mailed letter can be exciting in this age of email and texting.

But isn't this kind of parental involvement bad for emerging adults? Doesn't this mean becoming a dreaded "helicopter parent"? We say, nonsense. Don't pathologize a good and necessary thing, and don't let other people make you feel guilty about it. It's only helicopter parenting if parents are more involved than their college students want or need them to be. If kids are doing fine adjusting to college, happily making friends and learning new things, yet *parents* are calling *them* every day to moan about how much they're missed, then yes, that's obviously not a good idea. But most parents who are in frequent contact with their emerging adults during the first year are responding to their children's needs, not their own. Supporting college students when they need it will help them hang in there instead of dropping out. Support ultimately leads to autonomy, not dependence.

Sometimes the reluctance to stay in close contact comes from the students, not their parents. Even if they are suffering and feeling the need for parental support they may be reluctant to ask for it. They may feel that it is somehow wrong for them to need their parents so much after they have gone away to college. They may feel ashamed that they're homesick and having so much difficulty coping on their own. Parents who sense that their kids are struggling with this transition need to let them know the family's door is open and they shouldn't hesitate to ask for help if they need it.

Parents may also worry that involvement in their college students' lives delays yet again the day when they finally get to turn their attention back to their own lives. For eighteen years—or maybe twenty to twenty-five years, if they had more than one child—parents' first priority has been serving their children's needs. It's gratifying in many ways, of course, and the rewards of seeing them grow up, of loving them and being loved by them, are immense. But by the time children reach age 18, many parents are ready to move on with plans and projects of their own—change jobs, move to a smaller house, go back to school, travel, or do that special thing they've always wanted to do.

Then maybe it turns out that parenting isn't over after all, not nearly. Instead, the grown-up kid dropped off at college with hugs and smiles is calling every day, crying over one crisis or another, in need of time and emotional support, maybe even asking parents to intervene with a professor or a college administrator. Even the most dedicated parents can be forgiven for thinking to themselves, "Wait a minute, I thought I was done here! Wasn't I supposed to get a chance to live my own life again by now?"

It may help to remember that the first year is the shakiest for most students. After the first semester, even, most students have begun to feel confident enough on campus that they no longer need parental support

My son dropped out of college after one semester. He's *very* smart, there was no reason for him not to continue in school. He's roofing now, and he realizes what a backbreaking job that is. He comes home complaining, and we say, "Just think if you had stayed in school."

MOTHER OF A SON, 21

as much as they did getting started. By Thanksgiving, returning freshmen are sounding more secure, and for many, by the time they head back to campus after winter break, they're old-timers. Not that this means all their problems are over, but the issues are not likely to be as intense in later years as they are at the beginning.

Many students don't "go away to college" but stay home as they begin their college studies. Staying home is especially common among students from low-income families, who cannot afford the costs of living in a college dorm. It's also more common among students from ethnic minority groups; African Americans, Latinos, and Asian Americans all place a high cultural value on family obligations and mutual support, so parents in these cultures often encourage their emerging adults to live at home during the college years. Even when college students remain at home rather than going away, it is wise for parents to recognize their transition to a new developmental stage. Parental intervention that may have been appropriate during adolescence, such as supervising their choice of courses, enforcing a nightly homework period, and helping them out with assignments, is no longer appropriate now that they are emerging adults. Step back from this kind of involvement, even as you stay connected to provide encouragement and moral support.

What about having a gap year before entering college? Would that help ease the first-year blues and make success more likely? It probably would, but there is little research in the United States on this topic, perhaps because gap years are so rare—only 2 percent of Americans take a year off after high school and then enter college the following year. In Europe taking a gap year—or two, or three—is much more common, in part because young Europeans go to university to study in a specific field and don't have two years of general education requirements before they have to choose a major.

Based on his experience with students of many different ages at many different colleges and universities, as well as his own gap year experience as a musician way back when, Jeff would say that a gap year is an excellent way to gain maturity and prepare for the challenges of college life. Parents sometimes fear that if high school grads take a year off and start working or roaming the world they'll never go back to school. This may be true for some, but anyone whose interest in a college education is that easily snuffed out probably would not have made good use of the college experience in any case. And working for a year is probably more likely to have the opposite result. Once emerging adults find out how grim and low-paying the work prospects are for someone with only a high school degree, their motivation to complete college is usually intensified.

Roommate Issues

For most students today, the first time they ever share a room with another person is freshman year at college. Over the past fifty years, the typical American home has more than doubled in size, while the typical family has shrunk from three or four kids to two. Consequently, most American kids grow up with their own room, and sharing a room at college, with a stranger, can come as a rude awakening.

Fortunately, colleges do more today than in the past to make the roommate situation go smoothly. Rather than simply pairing students randomly, as in the old days, most colleges try to match up roommates who have similar interests and habits. Also, before students arrive on campus, colleges often provide future roommates with email addresses so that they can make contact and start to get to know each other.

Many students have high ideals for their roommate, imagining someone who will be a companion, a confidant, maybe even a best friend. However, when imagination meets reality, conflicts are likely and compromises are necessary. Maybe your daughter gets a roommate who also checked "early to bed" on the roommate selection questionnaire, but finds that her roommate borrows her stuff without asking, something the questionnaire didn't cover. Maybe your son selected "likes rock music" on a similar questionnaire, and his new roommate did, too, but he had not anticipated that the new roommate would like to play it at high volume on weekday evenings when he was trying to study. It could be that one roommate has a boyfriend or girlfriend who comes to visit from home on weekends, sending the other roommate into "sexile" to sleep on the sofa of someone down the hall.

So what can parents do, and what *should* parents do? Probably the first step is to resist the temptation to intervene immediately. This is certainly an understandable temptation. You've sent your emerging adult to college to learn and have fun, you're paying all this money, and now some selfish jerk is ruining it already?! Of course parents feel annoyed and want to do something to make things right. But at first it is probably best to have students try to handle the situation themselves, and frame it as an important step toward learning to take on their own responsibilities. Even if students are complaining bitterly on the phone, that may not mean they want parents to jump in right away to save the day. Maybe they just want you to *listen.* Start with that, and help the student generate options for how to handle the strains, but without dictating what to do. Sometimes confronting roommates calmly but directly can work wonders; they may not even have realized that what they were doing was annoying. Even calm and direct is not easy, because students want their roommate to like them and they don't want to seem like they're whining. But it's often the best first strategy.

If the problem persists, then it's time to raise the ante and get others to intervene—but it's still better if the student, not the parent, looks for extra help. College dormitories typically have resident assistants (RAs) living on each floor, as well as experienced administrators and staff who may be able to mediate a solution. If none of these strategies work, there is also the option of trying to switch roommates, a request most colleges will accommodate if possible.

Time and Money Management

One of the biggest challenges of college life is how best to manage time and juggle classes, assignments, exercise, a job, and socializing. Not as much time is spent sitting in class as in high school, but more work is required out of class. The average college student spends twelve to thirteen hours per week on homework, more than twice the amount for high school students. College students are also more likely than high school students to be employed, and those who have jobs work for more hours per week. And—crucially—parents are not present any longer to shake them awake in time to get ready for class, to encourage them to turn off the music and turn out the lights before midnight, or to forbid them from going out drinking with friends the night before a major exam.

One of the reasons the first year of college is so tough is that students now have to manage their time on their own. The freedom to run their own lives can be thrilling at first. They can sleep through their morning class, and nobody cares—nobody will even know! They can go out drinking on a Wednesday night, and no one will sniff their breath suspiciously when they come in the door. They can wait until the last minute to study for that econ exam and then stay up all night to finish the reading they had neglected—and it's all up to them.

Most learn pretty quickly that freedom isn't free, and if they don't learn to set their own limits, they'll suffer the consequences. During that morning class she slept through, there was a quiz she missed and now she has to swallow a zero or plead for a makeup. That Wednesday night he went out drinking, he found it difficult to clear his head the entire next day and couldn't study. That econ exam he pulled an all-nighter to study for—his grade was Exhibit D-minus for the effects of sleep deprivation on test performance.

> College involved a lot of ups and downs for my son. He has learning disabilities and attention deficit disorder, and that made it difficult. He struggled a lot, especially the first year. But in the end I think he really enjoyed college. He made lots of friends, enjoyed his social life, enjoyed having a girlfriend. He made it through and now he's an accountant.
>
> **FATHER OF A SON, 24**

Parents' roles in students' time management should be based on how much students want them—and allow them—to be involved. They may want advice, or they may want parents to listen and refrain from advising. They may want parents to call them at 7:30 a.m. the day of that 9 a.m. chemistry exam. Of course, parents have choices, too. It's not unreasonable for parents to say, "Look, just set an alarm. It's time you learned to get yourself up instead of relying on me." There are also students who will tell parents very little about when they get up, when they go to bed, and the consequences they are experiencing as they struggle to manage their time well.

Money management is just as new to most freshmen as time management, and can be just as daunting. For eighteen years, Mom and Dad have paid all or most of the bills. High school students often have part-time jobs, but most of them spend their wages on their own fun, not on groceries and utilities. Even in college, at least for the first year or two, dorm life is a kind of semi-dependence, where older adults are still in charge of providing food and paying the electric bill. Nevertheless, college students have to manage money for their other expenses, such as books, travel, and weekend leisure. Where should that money come from? How much should parents provide?

Each family has its own customs and values regarding money to guide the answers to these questions. Our advice is that it's best to have open discussions about money issues, before college starts and then on a regular basis through the college years. Sit down together the summer before college and work out a budget for the first semester. Figure out how much the expenses are going to be, and then decide who is going to pay how much. Have the student keep a record of how much was spent and on what, and at the end of every semester, calculate how everything worked out and adjust next semester's budget accordingly.

Of course, students who are paying their own way, as many are, also have the right and responsibility to manage their finances on their own. But in most cases, parents are contributing some, most, or all of the money required, so they should be involved in how it is spent. Even when that is the case, however, parents should keep in mind that their children's capacities are growing greater with every year of the emerging adulthood decade. The ultimate goal is for them to be able to handle life independently, including their financial lives, so allow them and encourage them to take on as much financial responsibility as they seem ready for each year.

Be prepared for some rocky patches along the road to becoming financially adept. Jeff confesses that when he opened a checking account for the first time, as a college sophomore, the $500 he initially deposited seemed like such a large sum, he didn't think he needed to bother to keep a record of his checks. A couple of months later, when he received a frantic call from a kind bank manager informing him that he had ten checks that were about to bounce sky high, he learned an important lesson. But it was a lesson that required an immediate bailout from the Bank of Mom and Dad (much to their irritation). Such debacles can be headed off by the kind of joint planning and regular communication we've described here. We'll have more to say about money issues in Chapter 10, "The Bank of Mom and Dad."

Changing Paths

For some, college is a smooth academic and personal journey. Students take the first two years to investigate a wide range of courses and the last two specializing in their chosen field. If all goes well, they stay on track and graduate in four years.

But often all does not go well, and the journey through college is not smooth and direct but wind-blown and delayed. Today it takes five to six years for the typical student to get a "four-year" degree. Students with health problems or learning disabilities are especially likely to need more time, but even students without those extra challenges often stretch their college experience an extra year or two. Along the way, students may switch majors, transfer schools, decide to double major, spend a semester or a year abroad, or take time off to work or reassess.

For concerned parents on the sidelines—often watching mounting tuition bills with dismay—it may help to realize that these changes are a normal part of the explorations of emerging adulthood. Most grown kids come to college with an unformed, open-ended identity. They don't know yet who they are and what they want out of life, including what to study and what kind of work they want to do. College is the place for answering these momentous questions, and some students can't box them into four years.

Yet even if parents understand the developmental issues involved—and the potential positive influence on later life choices—they may still find the changes of mind exasperating as well as expensive. When their children entered college, parents may have planned that they would be contributing to college expenses for four years and then they would be

---

COLLEGE TALES

"SHE FELT like she wasn't challenged."

—Sarah, a 54-year-old mother of a 25-year-old

She's been in college for six years. Now she's allegedly graduating in May, from [a big state university]. She spent her first year in Germany, at a college there, then moved back with me and has lived here since. She's not that open to answering some questions, like "Are you graduating this May?" She rolls her eyes, like, "You're meddling again!"

I thought I was being a good parent by telling my children they didn't have to be doctors and lawyers, just get a good education. Over the years we've had conversations about what they're interested in, what do you want to do, what do you want to study. My daughter has one side that is artsy, creative, musically talented. We said, "Why don't you go somewhere and do a fashion design program?" But she'd say, "I'm not good enough." She also has a very analytic side; she likes deep, intellectual stuff, so she leans toward philosophy. Now she's gravitated toward a middle ground, with a degree in philosophy and a minor in something artsy; I'm not sure what!

It's been disappointing, her experience. She doesn't want to go to graduation, for that reason. Her strategic error in high school was that she rebelled against the "overachiever" model of her private Catholic girls' high school, so she didn't apply to the more elite colleges. She was disappointed at college, because she felt like she wasn't challenged. She's felt very frustrated all along, by the lack of intellectual curiosity in the people around her. She's looking forward to going to grad school someday.

done with it. It's rarely a pleasant surprise to find that a fifth and perhaps a sixth year are being added on (to say nothing of graduate school). The money is important, but it's not only the money. They may also worry that their child is already falling behind in life.

Taking five or six years to finish a four-year degree does not mean your grown-up kid is falling behind; it means he's following the path typical for emerging adults today. Changing paths does not mean your grown kid is failing to grow up; it means she is sorting through the complex issues of identity and life purpose and doing her best to find a direction that will feel right and lead to gratifying and rewarding work. Of course, it's not unreasonable for parents to say, "We'll pay for four years, but after that you have to pay more (or all) of the rest." This approach depends on parents' views of what is appropriate as well as their finances.

Just keep in mind that getting that degree is ultimately the ticket to the good life in today's economy. And it's not easy to get, no matter what the school. Of the students who enter a four-year college or university, only 56 percent have graduated six years later. Attaining a bachelor's degree is a major accomplishment and a substantial boost toward adult success, even if it takes longer than expected. Do what you can, within reason, to help your grown-up kids get there.

Alcohol Use and Abuse

For most emerging adults, college is about a lot more than getting an education and a degree. It's also about making friends, finding romantic partners, going to parties, and getting drunk. The college years are the prime drinking years: Alcohol use peaks at ages 20 to 22, including *binge drinking,* which is defined by researchers as five drinks in a row for a man, four drinks in a row for a woman.

Binge drinking is higher among college students than among emerging adults who don't attend college, which should not be surprising. The college environment is well suited to social drinking in many ways. There are potential drinking partners and parties everywhere, and on many campuses the weekend starts on Thursday night. The desire to fit in and find a comfortable social place in college also contributes. Even if students might not feel like drinking, knowing there's that physics test in the morning, if a fellow student asks, "Hey, we're going out, wanna come?" it's not easy to say no; if they do, maybe next time they won't be asked.

Then there's the desire for romance—and sex. Potential partners are all around, and one of alcohol's attractions is that it is *disinhibiting*. A few beers may make students feel less fearful about getting their egos stomped if they muster the courage to talk to someone who looks good from afar.

So how much do college students actually drink? The Core Institute of Southern Illinois University-Carbondale surveys over 200,000 college students annually on their drinking attitudes and behavior. Here are the latest findings:

- 84 percent of students consumed alcohol in the past year.

- 71 percent of students consumed alcohol in the past thirty days.

- 46 percent of students reported binge drinking in the past two weeks.

- The national average per week for college students is 5.2 drinks.

Many parents may find these results worrisome. Almost half of students have been drunk—that's essentially what "binge drinking" means—within the past two weeks. On the other hand, the other half has not been drunk in the past two weeks, and almost 30 percent of students haven't had any alcohol at all in the past thirty days. Other studies have shown that drinking rates have gone down substantially since the parents of today's emerging adults were in college. Many students drink less, and more students than in the past choose not to drink at all. By now, there are enough nondrinkers on most college campuses that students who don't want to drink can easily find company on Saturday nights, rather than being left out of the social mainstream, as they might have been decades ago. However, schools vary a lot in this respect.

If your child is strictly a nondrinker, you may want to start with the *Princeton Review*'s list of "Stone Cold Sober" schools. At the very least you could avoid the colleges on their list of "Party Schools." Ask your grown kid, too, how important this issue is.

Is College Worth It?

Many parents today are shocked and dismayed at the high cost of sending their kids to college, and with good reason. With more families and young people than ever before buckling under huge college loans, there's a lot of understandable grumbling in the air about whether college is really necessary. Since 1970 the cost of college has risen *four times faster* than the cost of everything else. Many small colleges and elite Big U's cost about $50,000 a year for tuition, fees, room, and board—$200,000 over four years—and of course the grand total goes up if it takes five or six years. And what if parents have two or three kids? At that price they can kiss that summer house on the lake good-bye, and don't count on retiring early, either. Many expensive colleges offer financial aid that cuts the price for most families from 50K to maybe 30K or 40K a year, but that's still a lot of money.

Of course, a college education need not cost that much. The 50K-per-year figure that gets bandied about in the media is only for the most expensive schools. State universities are still a relatively good deal, usually costing about half as much. And community colleges are an unheralded treasure of American society, a place where students can get two years of education and training for very little money, often enabling them to obtain a credential in a field like computer science or nursing that is likely to lead to a well-paying job. Of the 70 percent of high school seniors who go on to college the next year, nearly half begin their college education at a community college.

Nevertheless, many parents and students face a formidable tab for four or more years of a college education. Even at a state university, college costs add up. If it costs $25,000 a year over five years, a pretty typical path for college students, that makes $125,000 for a bachelor's degree. And that doesn't count the potential income lost over five years of going to school full-time. If a person who did not go to college could make at least an additional $25,000 a year in full-time work, that's another $125,000 in lost income for the college student, making the total college investment $250,000.

So, is it worth it? $250,000 is quite a chunk o' change. Does it pay off in the long run?

The answer is an unambiguous YES. A college degree pays off big-time. Even with the rise in college participation in recent decades, only 30 percent of Americans ages 25 to 29 have a bachelor's degree (or more), so obtaining one instantly places young people in the upper echelon of the economy. In today's information-based economy, a college education is more important than ever to prepare for the best new jobs. The economic benefit of a bachelor's degree amounts to about *a million dollars* over the course of a career, according to most estimates. Furthermore,

COLLEGE TALES

"HE DOESN'T have an education, and that worries me."
Mary, a 53-year-old mother of a 21-year-old dropout

The school thing has always been a problem for him. He has a learning disability; he doesn't have much short-term memory. His comprehension was a problem from early on, reading and then understanding what he read. He passed everything in middle school and high school, though; he made it through. They told me he could be an A and B student, but I said, "You don't know my kid! He can't remember what he had for lunch!"

He went to [a nearby liberal arts] college for a year, lived there, but he did terribly. I didn't want him to go there, I wanted him to go to [the local community college], but my daughter said, "You're giving up on him!" But I wasn't. I just knew him.

At the college they had ways to help, but it wasn't enough. Anyway, he didn't really want help by then. He's not a school person. He passed, barely, the first semester, then had to withdraw the second semester. I think he regrets it. He liked being on his own.

He moved back home, and it was fine. We made him get a job, and he did, a month later. Then next semester he went to [the community college], just one course, but he flunked that.

Would I have liked him to stay in school? Yeah, but he's working, he's happy. But now he doesn't have an education, and that worries me, what kind of job he's going to end up in. Nowadays it's so much harder if you don't have an education.

the unemployment rate is consistently at least twice as high for 25- to 29-year-olds with only a high school degree than it is for those who have a bachelor's degree.

All of a sudden that $250,000 investment looks like a pretty good deal after all. And most college grads know it. A survey by the Pew Research Center found that 84 percent of college grads said that their degree had been a good investment; only 7 percent said it had not. Even if it takes your child a while to find a good job after graduating, be patient. A college education nearly always pays off over the course of a career.

And there is more to a college education than the economic payoff. A college degree provides a broad general education that enhances a person's life in multiple ways. Education researchers Ernest Pascarella and Patrick Terenzini have conducted research on this topic for decades. They report a variety of intellectual benefits from attending college, in areas such as general verbal and quantitative skills, oral and written communication skills, and critical thinking. In addition, Pascarella and Terenzini describe a long list of other benefits. In the course of the college years, students develop clearer values. They gain a more distinct identity and become more confident socially. They become less dogmatic, less authoritarian, and less ethnocentric in their political and social views. Their self-concepts and psychological well-being improve. All these advantages hold up even after taking into account characteristics such as age, gender, and family social class background.

Take a Deep Breath . . .

In closing this chapter, we'd like to underscore that there is no set-in-stone college plan that applies to every student. There is no Top 20, Top 50, or Top 100 list of schools that everyone should aspire to. Instead, parents and their emerging adults should make the decision about where to apply and where to go based on their own judgments of what schools are best for them. It is revealing that the *Princeton Review*'s Top 20 list of schools with the "Happiest Students" contains all kinds of schools—Big U's and small colleges, State U's and Elite U's, well-known schools and obscure schools.

Similarly, there is no one path through college that everyone should follow. For some emerging adults, traveling the straight-and-narrow path to a degree through four college years suits them well. For others, there will be detours to study abroad, U-turns to other schools, trails blazed to new majors or double majors, additional forays to graduate school, or a tough decision made that college is just not for them. Occasionally a young person dips a toe into college life and knows instinctively that he or she is not ready for it. This may be a warning sign to parents of academic, social, or emotional problems that may call for professional help. Or it might simply be a need for some extra time to mature, find a job, stay closer to home for a while longer, and pursue other, nonacademic interests.

For many ambitious young people and their parents, the expectations they have for college life may be so high and so expansive that no college will be able to fulfill all of them. On the other hand, most students, even those who don't end up at their top-pick school, will usually bond with the campus they're on and feel that it was the best choice after all. For those who decide their first college is not the right fit, there's always the possibility of transferring.

Perhaps the college transition so often becomes frenzied because it's so often about leaving home, about saying farewell. Emotions run high, not just because this is a momentous decision but because parents and children realize that once it has been made they have passed a fateful threshold, and family life will never be quite the same again. "How odd the college craziness is!" declares Andrew Ferguson in *Crazy U: One Dad's Crash Course on Getting His Kid Into College.* "All this expense of emotion and money and time, to make happen what I desperately didn't want to happen. But that's parenthood for you. You fulfill yourself by denying yourself, preparing people you can't live without to live without you."

6

The Boomerang Kid

*It is nice having our daughter around and
we do spend time together. I worry about her ability
to move on, though, and that maybe things are
a little too comfortable for her at home.*

MOTHER OF A DAUGHTER, 24

When you waved your grown-up kid off to college, cheered at graduation, congratulated her on her first job, or helped him move in with a girlfriend, you didn't expect that one day you'd be following up those milestones with "Welcome home!" But it's become one of the ironies of twenty-first-century life that just at the crossroads when emerging adults want to take a great leap forward toward independence, many are forced by circumstance to come home. And dropping out of college as well as graduating without plans, unemployment, poorly paid first jobs, and breakups or emotional upheavals can all send 20-somethings boomeranging back to Mom and Dad.

The results are not always pleasant. Anxiety, disappointment, even shame may show up in the mix. And we're not talking here about just what kids feel: Your heart may be sinking, too. But chin up: With foresight, planning, open discussion, and give-and-take on both sides, workable, even pleasurable arrangements can be made.

The Exploring Phase

What makes this move especially freighted is that life is so very up in the air for early to mid-20-somethings anyway, and now, for many, their struggles are happening under the family's roof. Age 22 to 26 is the *exploring phase* of emerging adulthood, and for many it's a bumpy ride. Most will need parents less than they did in the launching years—but more than they will by the end of their twenties. All's in flux as 20-somethings butterfly through relationships, struggle to find employment, then zigzag from one job to the next, and haul their stuff to three different cities—or back home—before declaring a permanent zip code. Even those with shiny new degrees and brash confidence can suddenly experience panic or helplessness as they're buffeted by an unsympathetic world. Without the strong scaffold of college that held their launching lives in place, they may find themselves feeling more alone and, at times, surprisingly lonely.

When parents were young, their postcollege transition occurred, most likely, in their own apartments or in a big old house with a self-styled family of roommates with whom to commiserate. But today those roommates are frequently Mom and Dad. It's Mom and Dad who become worried eyewitnesses to their grown kids dashing as fast as they can to keep all their plates spinning in the air, with frequent, to-be-expected crashes. It's not unusual for a young person to be settled in one or two of their major life decisions—work, love, and location—and adrift in the third. This imbalance leads to the good news/bad news syndrome of these exploring years. A son announces, "Good news—I met someone I really like; bad news—I lost my job. Can I move back home?" Or a daughter emails, "Good news—I landed a terrific starter job; bad news—I still can't afford the rent in this town. Can I live at home for a while?"

A parent's heart may be swelling with pride over the good news . . . only to be deflated by the follow-up news that's not so good. There's no choice but to ride the ups and downs of this roller-coaster exploring phase and encourage emerging adults to do the same. Trial and error are the brushstrokes of the early to midtwenties, and eventually, for nearly all, a self-portrait, a way forward—and a separate address—do emerge.

Welcome Home?!

Multigenerational living patterns have shifted sharply since today's boomer parents were launching their lives. During the second half of the twentieth century, one of the major milestones en route to adulthood was moving out of the parental home after high school. Among the midlife parents we interviewed, almost all reported leaving for college or a first job and not living in their childhood home ever again, except for visits and the rare return after a marital or financial crisis. Indeed, the phrase "I wouldn't have been caught dead living with my parents" was used more than once. But changing mores, closer parent/child relationships, smaller families, a later marriage age, financial pressures from high student debt, widespread unemployment in this age group, uncertain job prospects, and sky-high urban rents have created a perfect storm, bringing grown children home in droves to seek shelter.

A recent *New Yorker* cover captures the pathos perfectly: A 20-something son who's just finished graduate school is shown moved back into his childhood bedroom; his cap and gown from commencement are scattered around. He's hanging his newly minted and framed Ph.D. on the wall above his spelling trophy and golf award from yesteryear. Meanwhile, his none-too-happy parents watch him from the doorway with looks of strained befuddlement. There's no caption, but their faces make the message clear: "How have all the years of expensive education come to this?"

A 2012 Pew Research Center study of the Boomerang Generation confirms how extensive this phenomenon is. Using recent census data and Pew's own survey of more than two thousand adults nationwide, the study found that almost 40 percent of 18- to 34-year-olds are living at home with one parent or both. Looking at the younger, 18- to 24-year-old group, more than half have moved back home, at least for a time, in the past few years—or never moved out. The percentage is about the same for men and women.

Not having a job bumps the number even higher. For instance, among 18- to 34-year-olds who are not employed, nearly half have lived with their parents at some point or have moved back home temporarily (compared with 30 percent of those who do have jobs and only 17 percent of those who feel embarked on a "career").

Pew survey findings also suggest that, for most families, the pluses of this arrangement outweigh the minuses. As boomeranging becomes the new normal, there's less stigma and embarassment attached to returning to the nest. Almost 70 percent of young people 18 to 34 who are living at home with their parents say they are very satisfied with family life. Appropriately, the report is subtitled "Feeling OK about Living with Mom and Dad."

The reasons grown-up kids boomerang home (or never leave in the first place) are various, and parents may welcome some returnees or never-leavers with more open arms than others. If Jack parties late and sleeps until noon or if Jill turns down every job possibility as not quite perfect, you may understandably run out of patience. But if you see

---

Q: *Our son and our daughter have both moved back home after graduation, one after the other, and though we enjoy their company, what strikes us the most—and not in a good way—is their sense of entitlement about our apartment. They have taken "mi casa es su casa" to the extreme—playing loud music day and night, hosting frequent, last-minute, late-night parties for friends, and expecting that we'll still be cooking all their meals as if they were little kids. Help!*

A: Many parents imagine that once their kids have graduated from college, they'll instantly turn into responsible and generous adults, offering to cook, clean, and take the dog to the vet with no prompting. Alas, it doesn't happen quite that fast. It's probably time for a sit-down with your kids where you explain today's facts of life to them: You're now four more-or-less adults living together and everyone has to pitch in. What's more, you need to be aware of and respect one another's needs and timetables (e.g., no techno music or unannounced impromptu parties after 9 p.m.). In return, you'll play your Dylan records quietly and let them know when your book club is coming over for a potluck.

---

that your back-at-home children have a constructive Plan, a purposeful agenda that moves them toward a self-sufficient future, you'll be more supportive and more likely to forgive the occasional, um, regression. You may feel OK about the arrangement, too.

Some emerging adults in their late teens or early twenties are still too immature and unprepared to make it on their own. They are not ready to be launched at 18, or 19, or even 21 or 22. Parents usually have a sixth sense about which children will take longer to mature and depart. Perhaps children have been struggling for years with learning issues, mood swings, anger management, or social anxiety. They may well need a longer nesting period at home to address these challenges with continued parental support as well as therapy, medication, or other approaches. They may benefit from holding a job or taking just one course at a community college or even enrolling in online classes and continuing their education from the security of their own rooms.

Heartbreak can also send a previously launched child back to the nest. Most emerging adults cohabit before marriage, but most cohabiting relationships dissolve within a few months or years. Jane's daughter, Jenny, 23, had graduated from college, done a year of teacher training, and was engaged to her high school boyfriend. She'd been living with him in another city when she turned up on her parents' doorstep with a big suitcase for an indeterminate stay. The boyfriend and the shared digs had become history. "There have only been four or five times when Jenny has shared what's going on, so everything is undefined with no sense of permanence," explains her mother. But since Jane married early, then regretted it and divorced, she's hoping to spare her daughter that mistake. If that means providing temporary lodging while Jenny sorts things out, she feels it's a small price to pay for her daughter's future happiness.

Like Jane with Jenny, parents' own postcollege histories and choices often get tangled up with their sons' and daughters' dilemmas. Parents' experiences can become guideposts in helping their emerging adults work through an impasse—or occasionally turn into static interference. In this family, Jane's misguided early marriage made her extra sensitive to her daughter's predicament. Still, she wisely stepped aside to let her daughter resolve her romantic dilemma her own way.

"She was in transition, very much not an adult."

When grown kids land back at home instead of moving onward and upward on their own, the whole family is shaken up. With a 20-something tucked into a childhood bedroom and parents on call again, it's hard not to feel a sense of disappointment, even failure, on both sides. But it may be wiser to think of this stint as a transitional time, a time-out for your son or daughter to regroup, get a better financial footing and sense of direction . . . and then, like Kelly, move on.

After getting her B.A. at a women's college, Kelly, 22, an excellent, ambitious student, had her plan in place: She would go to graduate school in anthropology and live at home only for the bridge time before her advanced studies began. When she didn't get into the program she wanted, she was shocked and quietly devastated. It was, her mother Kate says, her first failure ever. At home, feeling rejected and purposeless, Kelly was floundering. It pained her parents to see their daughter so indecisive about what to do next (although it comforted them to notice that many of their friends' grown children were also returning home and similarly at loose ends).

Thinking that a job of some kind, even if not her dream job, would help get Kelly out of her funk, her father, Mark, gave her a Starbucks flyer. He encouraged her to pursue Plan B as a barista and take that all-important first step toward financial self-sufficiency. She landed the job at a neighborhood café, and it turned out to be a positive learning experience. "They trained her to smile—at 6 a.m., no less," says Kate. Her parents saw her gain confidence, social skills, and good work habits and turn into a friendlier person. Oh, and she could whip up a mean caramel macchiato.

They got a front-row seat to watch every quirk of her changing personality, because she ended up living at home for more than a year. "She was in transition, very much not an adult," says Kate. For a while, daily life fell into familiar, old patterns until things became almost too comfortable. Kate and Mark were happy having Kelly around but started to be afraid they were becoming codependent and standing in the way of her future progress.

Then, after a few months, tensions started to amp up. Kate and Mark realized that they were still treating their 22-year-old, gainfully employed daughter as a child. They understood that, even living under their roof, Kelly needed to get on with her own life. At midyear, they approached her about paying some rent. She hadn't been forced to think about a real budget, and even contributing a modest monthly amount to the family made her more aware of the need to plan ahead. And when another, better paying job in the tech sector came along nine months later, she moved into a small apartment with a friend and was able to make it work. She had already become used to budgeting part of her salary for rent, a routine that eased the shock of making monthly payments to her landlord. Her stint living with her parents had prepared her to handle the real world.

Different Cultures, Different Patterns

Maybe a small family of upscale, urban professionals like Kate, Mark, and Kelly will find themselves reeling when a daughter boomerangs home. But in many cultures both here and around the world, this pattern is normal, expected, and positive. Families in most cultures embrace multigenerational living both for emotional and economic reasons. The 2012 Pew Research analysis of census data shows that the share of Americans living in multigenerational households is the highest it has been since the 1950s and has jumped up significantly in the last five years. Among young people ages 25 to 34 this pattern has increased more than for any other age group.

The rise in multigenerational households in the United States is primarily the result of the corresponding rise in ethnic minority populations. Staying at home during emerging adulthood is more common among Latinos, African Americans, and Asian Americans than among whites, because there's more emphasis on family closeness and interdependence and less on independence in these groups. Protecting a daughter's virtue (and virginity) until marriage is also an essential value for families in certain ethnic groups; keeping a young woman at home is thought to shield her.

Two or three generations sharing family dinners together through the young people's twenties is traditional in many immigrant families. But as Ang Lee's 1994 film *Eat Drink Man Woman* shows, this pattern often frays with assimilation. The film's hero, a widowed father of three 20-something daughters, is a brilliant professional chef. He insists that his grown daughters sit down with him for the mouth-watering family meals he prepares. But though loving him—and his copious, classic Chinese dishes—they resist the pull to stay at home. One by one, they peel away, to marriage, an unexpected pregnancy, and a job in another city.

Low-income families have typically kept their living arrangements more fluid, adjusting them according to what is needed, and their willingness to double or triple up is a crucial buffer against homelessness in economically stressed communities. The rate among African Americans for multigenerational living is 23 percent, nearly twice as high as for whites; for Hispanics, it's 22 percent, and for Asians, 25 percent. Conflicting needs and demands among family members are accepted as a given, not an aberration.

In many countries around the world it's also expected that young people will live at home during their twenties, and often until they marry. Many European college students go to university in their hometowns. In any case, most of their universities don't have dorms or other on-campus housing, and apartments are scarce and expensive, so living at home is often the best solution.

Scandinavian young people tend to leave home earliest—usually at age 18 or 19—because the state provides free university education (including a living stipend), a housing allowance, and generous unemployment compensation; German and French emerging adults typically move out in their early twenties after they finish university. And Italian and Spanish youth stay at home the longest—and are happiest about it. In Italy, 94 percent of young people between 15 and 24 live with parents, the highest percentage in the European Union, yet only 8 percent view their living arrangements as a problem, the lowest EU percentage.

The Italians use the term *mammoni* or "mama's boys" for young men in their twenties who are still living at home under mama's care and don't move out until they find a wife to look out for them, usually by age 30. Teasing and affection are layered into this coinage. Belgians use another phrase, "hotel families," for the arrangement where parents provide room, meals, and laundry while emerging adults come and go as they please. With this much support along with the freedom to go out, socialize, and travel, it's no wonder that many European youths are in no hurry to check out of the Hotel Mom and Dad.

There's often a clash of cultural expectations about home-leaving for immigrant parents of emerging adults who have settled in the United States. Sandra, 59, for example, grew up in a small town in Spain and, like all her friends there, lived with her parents while she went to college in her community. "No one could afford an apartment," she recalls, adding, "generational tensions were taken as part of life." She stayed home until 27, when she came to the United States for graduate school, married, and became a teacher. She also had a son, Armando, and raised him here with annual trips to see her family in Spain.

Now Armando is taking the slow route through his higher education. For a while, he attended a local college and lived in the studio above his parents' garage. But tensions escalated when his father wanted him to have dinner with them every night, and Armando balked. "We butted heads," is how Armando puts it now. Before long, to keep the peace, Sandra was encouraging her son to move out. Using her teacher's salary, she helped set him up in his own apartment. Now he visits home—often with laundry in tow—a few times a week. The new arrangement is providing a good balance for their family of staying close while also stepping back and letting go. But still, Sandra points out, old traditions die hard. "Every time I visit Spain, my 90-year-old mother says, 'Why doesn't Armando live with you?'"

> Our daughter failed out of college in the first semester, .5 GPA. We took her out and she moved back in. It was rough at first, but she has found a job and a routine that works for all of us. She is trying to decide what she wants to do. I just want her working and gaining real world experience for now.
>
> FATHER OF A DAUGHTER, 19

Two Generations Under One Roof

When 20-somethings move home, the etiquette of once again sharing space, a dinner table, and trash disposal is reopened for discussion. The parents typically desire household order and predictability and some degree of control over how things are managed—from what time dinner is served to who empties the litter box. The emerging adult, by contrast, usually wants the freedom to come and go at will and be respected as an independent mover. He or she may not want to plan ahead or be pinned down to a particular timetable. The push-pull between parents' need for order and control and the grown kid's wish for autonomy without restrictions may stir up generational strains and cause quarrels.

Ten Questions to Ask Before the Boomeranging Begins

1) Do kids have a Plan while living at home—more education, networking and job applications, part-time or volunteer work?

2) Is there an end date (e.g., a few months or no more than a year) or is the arrangement open-ended?

3) Will they pay rent, contribute to household expenses, or provide other kinds of regular help (e.g., errands, grocery shopping, cleaning the bathroom)?

4) What are the expectations about chores?

5) Will they prepare or help with meals either regularly or once in a while?

6) Will they take care of their own laundry?

7) Will they be allowed to borrow the car?

8) Do they need to call or text if they'll be out for dinner or past a certain hour?

9) Can romantic partners sleep over?

10) Can they smoke cigarettes, or use alcohol or marijuana in the house?

The key to making a successful transition home is for parents to recognize the change in their grown children's maturity and treat them not as adolescents, but as adults. It's best if the move is regarded as a temporary necessity, not a backslide to old family roles. And home life will be more peaceful if parents hold back from over-vigilance, like waiting up at night for a grown child's return or pestering about his or her whereabouts. Now more than ever, parents and their grown-up kids need to observe mutual respect. Each side needs to give the other some breathing room so that times spent together will be freely chosen and mostly stress-free.

At the same time, life will be more pleasant if boomeranged kids meet parents halfway, taking responsibility for themselves and showing some progress in moving their lives forward—putting together and sending out résumés, going to networking events, making connections where they can, taking on part-time work to help defray expenses or volunteer jobs to build experience.

If grown children want to be treated like adults, it also makes sense that they do an adult's share of the chores involved in running a household. The willingness to pull their weight around the house is a major signpost on the road to adulthood.

We Can Work It Out

Before Junior's overstuffed duffels are unpacked into his or her old childhood room, it's a good idea to discuss living arrangements that feel fair and doable on both sides. Once you come up with a game plan, expect to revisit it after the first few weeks and then months to see if it's still workable.

But, no matter the planning, some hot topics are inevitable.

Money Matters

About half the boomerang kids who move home pay some sort of rent, and almost 90 percent help with household expenses, according to the 2012 Pew Report. But there are many ways to divvy up what it takes to run a household. Some parents ask for a monthly cash contribution, or if a grown child has a decent job, perhaps 10 percent of his or her monthly salary (that's still a lot less than the 30 percent of take-home pay that most adults put toward rent or mortgage payments). Other families collect rent but then funnel it into a "nest egg" fund, a kind of enforced savings plan for an emerging adult to use later on. Beyond rent, some families want a contribution toward utilities or car insurance, not just because Junior is using lights, heat, and the family car but also to help instill the habit of budgeting for these necessities when he's on his own. And, of course, emerging adults can contribute to the household in non-monetary ways as well—offering sweat equity when they don't have cash to chip in.

Some midlife parents are strapped financially themselves and don't have the wherewithal to continue supporting grown kids for an indeterminate stay. Most will do the best they can but may come to a point where they have to say, "Don't ask for money or rent-free shelter, because we don't have it to give." Skip the guilt because this is a hard truth for many of today's families.

For more about thorny financial issues, see Chapter 10, "The Bank of Mom and Dad."

Cleanliness and Chores

Cleanliness may or may not be next to godliness anymore, but messiness is the number one flash point when emerging adults move back home, especially if there's been a long break when order and serenity reigned in the empty nest. Definitions of "clean" tend to skew between the generations—dishes left in the sink (not in the bedroom or on the living room floor) may be considered tidy by an emerging adult and offensive to parents. Let grown-up kids know if you want them to wash their own dishes or at least put them in the dishwasher.

When a returning child's stuff spills from a bedroom to the bathroom to the kitchen, parents may rightfully squirm. Most parents at least try to contain the possessions to one room and leave the maintenance of that space to its owner. The milder offenders will usually respond to requests to keep some baseline of organization. And sometimes, the short-term surrender is worth the long-term relationship. Parents may decide that closing the door and forgetting about a grown child's chaos is the better path to peacekeeping.

Most of the time, negotiations about household duties can produce a solution that's livable for both sides. Many parents have high hopes that sharing chores will be easier the second time around, and boomerang kids will offer household help more readily than when they were teenagers. In the best-case scenario, emerging adults will demonstrate that they're taking care of business by pitching in around the house or doing spontaneous chores to work off their keep without being asked.

But optimism can fade to frustration when grown-up kids don't get the memo to help, especially when parents are straining under the financial and caretaking burdens not unusual for this sandwich generation. A warm welcome can turn chilly with unspoken resentment and tension.

Be upfront and specific about how much help you'd like or need: making dinner, grocery shopping, doing laundry, caring for a pet, or helping out with occasional big tasks like cleaning out the garage or taking stuff to the dump. Emerging adults may have outgrown the chore rotation list taped to the refrigerator, but spelling out the division of labor helps get the jobs done. And sometimes oblique reminders are more helpful than confrontations. One dad we interviewed sent occasional emails to his moved-back kids to jog their memories about putting towels in the laundry or dirty plates in the dishwasher.

Couple Relationships (Yours)

When the house fills up again, parents often react with mixed emotions. Yes, it's fun getting to know their grown kids as the adults they're becoming. Table talk at dinner grows livelier, and cherished childhood friends come around again. But what about the quiet, private, maybe more romantic, come-and-go-as-you-please couple time that many partners created when their kids went to college?

Since your kids' move home will (most likely) be short-lived and your couple connection will (you hope) be forever, take care to protect your time as a twosome. Emerging adults are totally capable of fending for themselves while parents have a quiet dinner out or go off for the weekend by themselves. Do what's needed to keep the romantic fires burning.

As at earlier stages of parenting, stresses build when couples are of different minds about shared living arrangements. Perhaps one parent is happy to extend the welcome mat for an unemployed 20-something into an unknown future while the other prefers a home-sweet-home for two. Divergent views are especially likely in stepfamilies, where both the emotional and financial pressures heat up if the biological parent wants to offer support to his or her grown kids and the stepparent objects. Talking through differences, compromising when possible, and setting some good boundaries (for example, a time-limited stay or contribution to expenses) will go a long way to preserving a happy home.

Couple Relationships (Theirs)

It's one thing to offer temporary shelter and three squares to an emerging adult son or daughter, but life can get complicated very quickly when one or more significant others enter the picture. Marie has a stepson, Peter, who moved back in with the rest of the family for three years after college despite having a good job. His active love life generated a lot of drama, as his stepmother recounts: "One day there was an emergency in the kitchen . . . the family cat had caught a rat, and I needed Peter's help dealing with it, so I knocked on his door. He opened it, startled, pulling his robe around him while a naked girl was clearly visible in his bed. 'What's the matter?' he said. I was horrified and ran off. Later, he said to me, all innocence, 'I don't know why you're so upset: I'm not even dating her!'"

Marie was not up to a major showdown, but shortly afterward, she wrote Peter a note saying that she needed his bedroom for other purposes. He got the picture and was out of there faster than the cat charging after the rat. But this tale has a happy ending: Years later, this mother adds, of her six grown children, Peter is the one to whom she's closest.

If an unmarried son or daughter wants to sleep with a partner—or a string of them—at a parent's house, it may become a shared decision that depends on the family's values and ease with the guest in question. Most parents know that their grown-up kids are sexually active, but not all feel comfortable hosting a sleepover at their home. Things to consider: whether or not this is a long-term relationship, whether there are much-younger children at home, and whether there's enough room to give everyone privacy. You need to feel comfortable in your own house, so, ultimately, it's your call. Keep in mind, too, that involuntary celibacy is a great incentive for finding a job and moving out.

Social Expectations

It may be lovely to think that grown kids living at home will show up for a nephew's birthday party or Uncle Espie's retirement bash, but it's best to lower expectations about how much entertainment will turn out to be shared. Emerging adults are used to leading their own social lives (much of which takes place after 11 p.m.) and may not want to join every event on the family calendar. Parents will do best requesting but not pressuring, being careful to prioritize the invitations, saving the full-court press for the most important occasions.

For those who are not used to seeing their grown-up kids plugged in 24/7, their inattention even while physically present may come as a bit of a shock. Some families are fine with parallel digital play—everyone sitting around the living room, transfixed by their own screens or checking cell phone messages at breakfast. For those who prefer some occasional face time, set some ground rules, like no checking email at meals.

"What's hard is wanting to please him and make him happy, which you can't."

Frances's relationship with her son, Justin, 26, had always been easygoing and harmonious. She describes him as a "classic firstborn son, very chivalrous," more even-tempered than his emotional younger sister. After college, Justin spent three years as a reporter in New York City, then volunteered in Nicaragua, and eventually was ready to be home. Frances, 55 and a research scientist, and her husband welcomed him back, especially knowing it would be short-term. He's been working at a restaurant while waiting to hear from graduate schools in journalism, and he's been living with his parents for almost a year.

After many agreeable months, things started to get difficult between him and his mom. The day of our interview is also the day after their first big fight since Justin moved back in. Frances, who has short gray hair and a ready smile, is raw and upset from the argument. The trouble started when Justin wanted to borrow her brand-new Prius to drive eight hours to visit his girlfriend, and Frances did the unthinkable: She said no. "He acted as if I'd stabbed him," she says, adding that his immediate reaction was, "'You don't love me.'" For Frances, the car is just a car—and one she needs for her own life. But for Justin, it has become symbolically loaded. In the twenty-four hours since their blowup, she has done her best to work it through with her son so that he doesn't take her refusal as a personal attack. "We don't know how to do this," she admits, but "we're learning."

Although she sees Justin as an adult in many ways—he's a hard worker, takes care of the house, and voluntarily gardens alongside her—she sighs as she realizes, "We're clearly still parent and child." Sharing the family nest once again, they're finding it hard to escape the old roles. Now she finds herself treading super carefully around Justin and being hyper-aware of his moods: "I have a hard time turning off the mother button if he's around me. Weekends when he's gone, I exhale. I can be myself. What's hard is wanting to please him and make him happy, which you can't."

The shadow of a difficult family history also colors their relationship: "My sister never really emerged," Frances says. "She married young and divorced. She worked only for five years, then took care of Mom. My mom was always trying to make my sister happy and she couldn't, and I don't want to repeat that."

During their long-term, living-together arrangement, Frances's mother and sister were never able to clear the air between them. But Frances hopes that her openness with Justin and their mutual willingness to work out disagreements will keep their relationship strong and close. Besides, Justin will head to grad school in the fall, so this boomerang phase will be short-lived. In many ways Frances is enjoying the found-time with her son that may not come again. He loves to cook, she says, so they often make dinner together, and afterward, the three of them play card games. "We are peers in some way," she says with her warm smile. "I like his friendship."

And therein lies the silver lining of the boomerang phase: the unexpected gift of time and companionship. It's also a second chance to round out Basic Life Skills 101 and finish off what parents may have failed to impart during the first eighteen years. Most parents relish the chance to get to know the adult who's emerging from the child they raised, and they take in stride the occasional flare-ups, the food left out on the counter, or the 3 a.m. return home. They say the benefits far outweigh the inconveniences.

But think twice before extending this living-together arrangement for too long, says family therapist Sheri Glucoft Wong. A longtime parent educator with a multigenerational practice, Wong cautions parents to question if and when the home situation becomes too symbiotic. "Our generation of parents was the first to be child-centric and now we've become twenties-centric," she says. She finds that parents sometimes define their own lives by the success—or struggles—of their grown children.

"Are 20-somethings moving back home because our generation is holding on longer to our children?" Wong asks. She wonders if some devoted kids feel they're giving their parents a mission by coming home. The balance between connection and separation is out of synch when parents are overly dependent on their emerging adults for companionship and a social life, when they're hurt if their grown-up kids won't sit down for family meals every night or come along on every social outing.

Lower Narnia

Ten years ago, when Nate was almost finished with high school and Will was just about to start it, Elizabeth and her husband, Bob, moved the family into a house that was roomier than the small one where the boys had grown up until then. A few acquaintances raised their eyebrows and wondered what sense this move made, when before too long, both boys would be leaving for college and the nest would be yawningly empty. Ha. As things turned out, the nest was more often full than vacant.

The new house had a small "in-law" unit in back that was walled off from the main living space to provide privacy and noise control. But Elizabeth and Bob decided to integrate these extra rooms into the rest of the house. Because they broke through an old closet to reach the new territory, they dubbed the salvaged space Narnia, after the magical world the children found behind an old wardrobe in C. S. Lewis's beloved series.

Upper Narnia became Elizabeth's office, and Lower Narnia, well, Lower Narnia turned out to provide shelter for a procession of 20-somethings in their extended family: both their sons returning home after college and a passel of nieces, nephews, and cousins who needed a homey way station on the road to their unfolding futures. One of them provided an

---

Q: *Our 23-year-old son has been living with us since he graduated from college almost a year ago, and things have gone from bad to worse. At first he sent out résumés and looked for work, but when months passed with no job offers in his field, he seemed to give up. Now it seems as if he's not even looking for work. He's stuck. He doesn't communicate with us much, but we wonder how to reach him and help him.*

A: Looking for work is stressful for everyone, and when your job-hunting son is still living at home, you share his stress. But it sounds as if in this case, the daily job-hunting grind has downturned into depression, and your son is hurting. You need to step up and put out the offer of therapy or perhaps a job counseling program that will address both career planning and emotional issues. The twenties can be an ideal time to get some support and counseling for the uncertainties that are the focus of this decade: not just a difficult job search, but also questions about identity, self-awareness, relationship-defining, and decision-making in many spheres. By the early thirties there's often more light at the end of what for some has been a dark tunnel.

Whatever the severity and length of these emotional struggles, they are painful for both emerging adults and their parents. But knowing that such struggles may come helps reduce an unnecessary layer of stigma or shame. Often despair will lighten as life choices are made—finding a job that also provides the camaraderie of colleagues, more financial stability, absorbing outside interests, a stronger friendship network, and, eventually, a special significant other. We'll have more on the problems of emerging adulthood in Chapter 12, "When Things Go Wrong."

---

illustrative tableau when he moved in between gigs elsewhere, carrying an open box of books. Sticking out of the top was a beloved old copy of *Where's Waldo?* and a fifth of vodka: the symbolic straddling of the line between childhood and adulthood.

During the past decade, Lower Narnia has borne silent witness to the exploring years of the twenties. There were many unpaid or underpaid internships that landed these houseguests in free lodging in the first place. One worked at the local modern art museum, another at an environmental action agency, still a third at a political magazine. These assignments usually began in bursts of enthusiasm (so much to learn! such great people! terrific for the résumé!). Then, about six weeks in, the work started getting tedious and the lack of pay became oppressive. Out of such discouragement plans for graduate school were often hatched, as well as job searches, both fruitless and fulfilled.

> I enjoy the company of both of my kids who are living at home, although I will admit to looking forward to it just being the two of us, once again. We were married for ten years before we had kids, and it would be cool to experience that level of independent togetherness again.
>
> MOTHER OF A DAUGHTER, 21, AND A SON, 19

There were late nights and parties and hangovers, dating and heartbreak and dry spells watching Netflix videos solo before falling for someone new. There were apartment hunts and group interviews and Googling to research new neighborhoods (one houseguest even created a giant spreadsheet listing all his options). And inevitably, plans for coming and going shifted frequently, reflecting the instability and sense of possibility that marks emerging adulthood. One young relative, for instance, stayed for three months, then dreamed of taking a road trip around the West with friends, which segued into helping a family friend in New Mexico, which morphed into driving to southern California to see his brother, until finally every plan was jettisoned in favor of flying back to his parents' house on the other coast.

Elizabeth's oldest niece, now 34, married and a mother herself, looks back on her midtwenties' stint in Lower Narnia with bemusement: "At one point I was living in my aunt's and uncle's house, driving their car, tutoring at a job they'd recommended me to, and dating the son of one of their friends!" Elizabeth and Bob's family enjoyed every minute of her stay, especially those five blissful words they'd rarely heard from their sons: "Can I make a salad?"

Moving On

When grown-up kids move out for good (or what looks like for good), it's an exciting turning point in emerging adulthood. No matter how much parents have savored this bonus family time together, a part of them is likely to sigh with relief when Junior moves out those boxes of college textbooks and old baseball cards to set up independent living. To visit a son's or daughter's first apartment is a thrill right up there with first steps and words. It's a move toward autonomy and maturity and another glimpse into the people they're becoming.

Elizabeth's son Nate had been living in Lower Narnia for a while but recently moved out and into a big, old, San Francisco Victorian with four other guys: his brother, Will, two old friends, and one newcomer found on Craigslist, along with other household treasures: a set of kitchen knives, trash cans, a bed, and a dining room table with six chairs. Nate and Will also took with them two hand-me-down orange armchairs to complete their living room seating. Once they were so small the two of them squeezed into one of these chairs together to watch TV. Now they have jobs, girlfriends, and this new place of their own.

They still come over often for brunch or dinner. When the meal is done and conversation winds down, one of them will say, "Time to go home." There's a moment of startle, then acceptance, and pleasure: the next stage.

7

You Can't Hurry Love

Around our campus, people are either single or in serious relationships. There's not so much casual dating, but we hang out in groups a lot. Then sometimes we hook up.

COLLEGE SENIOR, WOMAN, 22

Boomers thought they had invented sexual freedom when they were young, and their grown kids certainly owe a debt to the expanded options their parents fought for. But the millennials have pushed the envelope farther, startling even the Free Love Generation. And their slow-track to adulthood—and marriage, if it happens—means that they spend more time dating than any previous generation. In what might be a decade or longer journey to find a life partner, there's more trying this and that, more boyfriends and girlfriends, more hookups, breakups and makeups, and more living together that may or may not lead to the altar. All these choices and all this relationship drama can add up to a lot of confusion for young people and also bewilder their parents.

Consider these contemporary "love stories" from our interviews:

• Peter and Peg, both age 20, have been dating for six months. But Peter always introduces Peg as "my friend," never "my girlfriend."

- Sally, age 21, has dated both guys and gals at her Ivy League college. When she says she's bringing someone home for a visit, her parents don't know which gender to expect.

- Tom, age 22, is too shy and socially awkward to meet people in bars or at parties. But he's made many friends—and even met a couple of romantic partners—by playing social games on Facebook.

- Amanda, age 23, uses online dating sites when she's in the mood for a quick hookup. She recently arranged to meet up with a guy on a street corner at 11 p.m., made out for an hour, and went home by herself, feeling more lonely and lost than she had before.

- Rebecca, age 28, had a law degree and a good life but no one to share it with. She posted a photo on JDate but didn't get many takers until a friend helped her tweak her profile and replace the old photo with something more appealing. This time, replies flooded in. Among them, she met the man she would marry a year later.

- Clay, age 29, has a busy professional life and travels the world for his job. He would like to marry and have kids, preferably beginning soon, but he wonders if the demands of work would make it impossible for him to be a good husband and father. He thinks about cutting back his hours or finding a less taxing job, but he knows it would be painful to trim his ambitions, just when his career is taking off.

As with the lengthening of emerging adulthood itself, there is both good news and bad news about today's extended mating season. On the plus side, the more leisurely timetable means that this generation of 20-somethings has more of a chance to explore their talents, dreams, and needs before they become coupled. Move across the country, change jobs, train to be a medic, teach English abroad, crisscross the globe—as long as young people stay unattached, with no one else's agenda to consider, these decisions remain in their hands.

In Erik Erikson's theory of development across the life span, once an independent identity is established, the main challenge or "crisis" of the twenties is resolving the push-pull between *intimacy* and *isolation*.

To Erikson, this meant finding (or failing to find) a lifelong, intimate partner, usually in marriage. By taking more time for this quest, young people today have a better chance of knowing what they want both in a mate and in life. From the point of view of their parents, history's most-divorced generation, this could be a very good thing. For their grown kids, divorce rates have declined, in part because a longer mating season produces unions with a better chance of lasting.

But there's also a downside. Today's wider stage for experimentation, which is expanded exponentially by social media, online dating sites, and digital porn, can lead to frustration, disappointment, and the very loneliness all these tools are trying to assuage. Isolation feels more acute in the midst of constant connectivity, and sometimes, intimacy seems harder to achieve. The old rules of courtship have disappeared and been replaced by uncertainty and ambiguity.

Talking About Love, Sex, and Dating

When talking about dating mores, parents and their grown-up kids have some common ground but are not always speaking the same language. Parents remember "making out" and one-night stands; 20-somethings have hookups both with people they've just met and people they know well. Today it's "friends with benefits"; yesterday, parents had platonic relationships that sometimes drifted into bed and sheepishly out of it the next morning. Then again, some of today's young people may be doing things in private for which, thirty years ago, the words hadn't even been coined. "NIFOX," anyone? (That would be "Naked in front of the computer.") Or "sexting"—sending around naked pictures by text?

Yet another difference shaping this younger generation's perspective is the Pandora's box of easily available, online pornography whose use is higher among emerging adults than in any other group. In a 2008 study called "Generation XXX" of eight hundred college students from age 18 to 26, 86 percent of the men reported "interacting" with porn at least once a month, compared with 31 percent of women. And while for some the use of porn, like the habit of violent video gaming, is a way to walk on the wild side without real-life repercusssions, porn use can also generate some unrealistic expectations. Frequent exposure to porn can create an alternate universe where all things sexual seem possible, where the popularity of less common sexual activity is overestimated, and where sexual exclusivity is deemed unlikely and uncommon. Overexposure to porn can turn a romantic cynical and make ordinary sexual relationships seem a lot more ordinary . . . and not in a good way.

In an extensive study of the sex lives of young people ages 18 to 23 for their book, *Premarital Sex in America,* University of Texas Professor Mark Regnerus and Jeremy Uecker found other striking generational differences as well. Young Americans are, on average, losing their virginity earlier than their parents did (and certainly earlier than their grandparents did). Their study estimates that two-thirds of 18-year-olds are sexually active, and only 16 percent are still virgins by 23. As they put it, "A good life in the minds of many Americans now involves delayed marriage and childbearing but accelerated sex."

Yet despite media ballyhoo about the hookup culture on campus, revolving-door "friends with benefits" relationships, and ubiquitous casual sex throughout the twenties, Regnerus and Uecker's conclusion is more reassuring: Although most dating includes sex, most sex, indeed, the vast majority, is still experienced in romantic relationships and in a pattern of one partner at a time. In the early twenties, especially, these relationships may be fragile and short-lived, but as the decade goes on, most young people are looking for a lasting romantic partner or soul mate.

The dream of a soul mate is not just about finding someone to love passionately; it's also someone who feels just right, who sees the world the same way you do and likes to do all the same things; in short, someone who is a perfect identity fit. In one study by the National Marriage Project, 94 percent of emerging adults said they want their marriage partner to be their soul mate, above all other criteria. This dream of an ideally matched soul mate has also been inherited from boomer parents—never mind all the times when it didn't work out as planned.

"On the one hand, among young people today, it's more OK than ever to have casual relationships," says University of California, Berkeley, professor of psychology Philip Cowan. "On the other hand, there's a romantic template that's still highly idealistic and that makes it harder to commit to a relationship if it's not perfect." The dream persists for children of both divorced and nondivorced families, he adds. "Children of divorce still want that long-lasting relationship even if they haven't seen it with their own parents."

When it comes to talking with emerging adults about their dating lives, proceed with caution. One son may be relaxed and forthcoming, bringing a girlfriend home from college as if she were already part of the family—even if she might be outdated a year later. Another grown kid plays her romantic cards closer to her chest than a CIA agent with classified information. Still a third is figuring out his sexual identity and not ready to disclose anything.

> I'm very opinionated and hard to please. One of my son's girlfriends I really liked: He took her to the prom. Now she's training to be a nurse. But he's not ready to be serious. He says, "I don't want to be a father, so it's best to be by myself."
>
> MOTHER OF A SON, 21

Here, more than anywhere else, parents and their emerging adults do best seeking out the comfortable middle ground between privacy and openness, independence and communication. Each family measures out its own comfort zone based on history and traditions, personalities, and values. Parents should enter this zone with care and tact.

Just as most parents wouldn't share excessive details about their private lives with their kids, it makes sense to return the favor: Let grown children draw the curtain of discretion around their intimate lives as well. In our survey, almost half of the parents responded that they knew "a little" about their sons' or daughters' love lives; about a third knew "quite a lot"; and fewer than 10 percent knew either "nothing" or "a great deal." One mother of a 23-year-old daughter expressed well how she found the right balance between being available and hearing too much: "I guess I'd say that I know 'enough,'" she said. "Enough—with appropriate boundaries—to know my daughter is happy."

When to say something, what to say, or whether to say anything at all is not black-and-white, but more nuanced, says Philip Cowan. Adds his wife, Carolyn Cowan, also a family therapist and coauthor of *When*

Partners Become Parents: The Big Life Change for Couples, "It's one of the biggest challenges for parents—how much can you say about your children's choices, about their relationships?"

The Cowans made their reputation studying the transition from couple to family, when baby makes three and the family system is recalibrated forever. But as parents of three married children, they've lived through that equally complex—but hardly as studied—passage when emerging adult children begin finding their own partners.

The Cowans' children are all partnered and parents now, and over the years, as they've settled into their own marriages, they've become more open, more curious to talk with their parents about what makes a relationship last. But when the kids were first tumbling in and out of love, their parents did a lot of waiting and keeping a low profile on the sidelines.

"We'd always had good relationships with our children when they were little kids, middle school kids, and then in their teens and twenties," says Philip Cowan. "But still, we always asked ourselves, 'Do we voice our feelings or just wait?'" For the most part, they leaned toward holding back.

Some of their friends, they noticed, couldn't contain themselves and barged into their children's romantic lives with strong, dramatic judgments. But that kind of intensity can quickly spell "end of discussion." Says Carolyn Cowan, "You have to be careful, because sometimes your kids can feel misunderstood or as if you're treating them as if they're not adults. Then again, we also have friends who've backed off too much and then regretted it."

The Cowans preferred to take cues from their children and waited for them to come forward with any concerns. Sometimes an appeal for feedback would be vague, couched, or indirect, and parental antennae would have to be especially fine-tuned to pick up a conversation's subtext. Still, even if something felt serious, they would wait before jumping in. "We didn't want to jeopardize anything, and we'd check that we weren't coming across too strong or critically," says Carolyn Cowan.

When a potential partner started to look serious, they asked themselves one question, and, if given an opening, passed it along to their kids: "Is this a relationship in which you can be the best you can be?"

Q: *Our 25-year-old son has had a number of lovely girlfriends stretching back to high school. We were especially close to one of them. Is it okay to see this ex even if our son doesn't?*

A: When your child's girlfriend or boyfriend spends a lot of time with the family, it's only natural to become close and feel the loss if the pair splits up. But except in rare circumstances (and of course if there are grandchildren involved), it may be too hurtful to grown children to keep contact with their exes after a breakup. As one mother of a 24-year-old made clear, "We liked our daughter's college boyfriend a lot. It was hard to go cold turkey when they broke up, but to honor her, we couldn't see him." The parents' relationship with their own child is the forever one. Best to leave the ones that got away in the annals of history.

"Talk to us but try your life on for yourself."

Both in looking for love and talking about it with Mom and Dad, young people travel the road between confession and discretion as they pass from launching to exploring to landing. A pivotal task of the twenties is establishing an independent identity, and although the need for closeness between generations continues, it's age appropriate as the twenties-decade proceeds for young people to become more private and not to share every romantic hit or miss. "Parents don't need to know every gory detail about their kids' relationships," points out Susan Waisbren, a clinical psychologist and the mother of four daughters, now 22 to 31. "If kids tell parents everything, it's too hard to make the break," she explains.

When one of her daughters left home for college at 18, she was still rather tied to her parents' opinions: Should I date the shy guy in Romantic Lit? Now that we're going out, should we break up before the summer? After the first few months of their daughter's wobbly launching year, Waisbren and her husband suggested that she limit her calls home to once a week. "Talk to us but try your life on for yourself," Waisbren

counseled. As her daughter made her way through college, then graduated and began settling into her own life, she came to know her own
mind better and got more confident about her choices, both romantic
and otherwise. Then mother and daughter found more and more relaxed
chances to communicate.

Knowing when or when not to speak up is an art in itself. If a parent
gives a blunt two cents about the guy or gal who dropped by the night
before or the one who has suddenly stopped calling, the grown child
might well accuse the parent of meddling. And yet there's also the chance
when parents hold back and don't ask about someone or something that
a grown-up kid might think they don't care. And if a parent sees a red-
flag situation brewing, it may be a lifesaver to speak up.

"I hate it when you bring up things that are the most stressful, but
those are the things that I probably need to talk about," is how one of
Waisbren's daughters recently framed the dilemma to her. One of a parent's roles going back to the childhood years can be holding up a mirror to their children's behaviors—anything from tone of voice to table
manners—even when the reflection is not flattering. But this kind of

---

Q: *Every time we see our 24-year-old daughter she seems to be dating
someone new. The guys she's brought around to meet us don't look like great
future son-in-law material (what really scares us: thinking about the ones we
haven't met). We dearly love our beautiful, talented daughter and want her
to be happy. What should we do if we're afraid she's heading down the wrong
road again and again and doesn't see the pattern?*

A: When the exploring years involve a young person taking a lot of scary
risks—like a daughter churning through a wild carnival of dates or a son
involved with someone with a serious alcohol problem—that's when it's
time for parents to step up and be frank about what they're observing.
Parents can say, "You're endangering yourself and you're scaring us." You
can also consider the offer of therapy as a way to better understand herself and her choices.

mirroring becomes more delicate as kids grow up, and it's particularly touchy around amorous choices.

By the later twenties, dating often takes a more serious turn and veers toward marriage, as Waisbren has observed with her daughters. "'Is he the right person?' they've all asked me, and my answer is always, 'When you find him, you'll know.' You may have to try out a lot of apples and oranges, but when you find the right one, you'll look back on your earlier encounters and say, 'How could I have?'"

"You're never the worse for having loved," has been her best counsel during her daughters' love-torn twenties. "What was it that you loved in the one you lost? That quality is what you can look for in the next one. You need lots of practice in relationships, and it's hard if you marry the first person you fall for. And painful as it is, you'll break up with all the people you don't end up marrying—or they'll break up with you."

Dating as Data Gathering

On the way to making a good partner choice, grown kids may end up making a bunch of bad ones. Watching their mistakes is difficult, and parents may wish they could swoop down like Superman to save the day and spare their kids the heartbreak. But mistakes are part and parcel of emerging adulthood's data gathering and identity explorations; they put a young person on the learning curve toward better choices later on. In any case, parents have less sway over their 20-somethings' dating and mating lives than they might wish. Sighs a father of three sons in their twenties, "Their partner is the biggest decision they make, but we have no control over it!"

Although it may be agony for parents to see their easygoing son with a high-maintenance girlfriend or their diligent daughter with a guy who's perpetually unemployed, intervening can also backfire. Sometimes a thumbs-down from Mom and Dad can cement a young couple's love faster than you can say Romeo and Juliet. Unless a parent feels a child is in harm's way, wait-and-see is usually the best policy. Many ill-matched partners will seal their own doom, like a wacky political candidate who makes one crazy comment too many until all support is lost. Better to low-key your opinions and keep the door to future conversations open.

Remember, too: It's a rare parent whose own romantic choices were above reproach. One mother of a 25-year-old son was starting to find fault with his live-in girlfriend—she was too needy and wishy-washy, couldn't settle on a career, and didn't contribute enough to household expenses. Eventually, she caught herself. "I brought home a lot of loony tunes boys," she realized, "so why do I expect my son to be perfect?" Most parents made their fair share of relationship mistakes and need to give the same growing room to their kids. Seeing a grown-up kid fall for the same kind of Mr. or Ms. Wrong that a parent did can be especially frustrating, but every heart has to learn from its own on-the-job training.

"I don't volunteer anything about my children's relationships unless asked," is how family therapist Leah Fisher phrases her policy toward her late-twenties' son and daughter. "I act as if anything I say will go back to their partners." And since sooner or later one of those partners will become an in-law, she wants to make sure to keep their future connection amicable.

Q: *Our question is one of the oldest in the book: What does our daughter see in her boyfriend? He's lazy, sloppy, and not very nice to her.*

A: It's certainly upsetting to see your precious daughter or son dating someone you feel is not worthy of them. If you're puzzled or concerned about your grown-up kid's choice of partner, try looking at the relationship from the emerging adult's point of view and asking, "What's this relationship providing that I'm not seeing?" Just considering the question reframes a parent's perspective from criticism to greater empathy.

When you do see something truly worrisome, it works best to comment on the behavior observed, not on the person in question. Instead of "I don't think that person is right for you," consider, "When I see the two of you together, I notice that . . ." For instance, "He puts you down" or "She interrupts you." Sticking with observations rather than sweeping judgments gives grown kids room to explain or reassess things for themselves—or tell you to back off.

But, like any good outfielder, she'll go after any ball hit her way. "If a kid gives you an opening, you can ask questions," she says. "Your girlfriend likes you home for dinner every night at six; how will she feel about your international travel for work? How will your boyfriend's family from a different culture want you to raise your children?" Fisher doesn't always get answers to her probing questions, but by putting them out there, she feels she's urged her children to think more deeply about their decisions, their futures, and how their lives will be intertwined with their partners'.

Not Their Parents' Dating World

In many ways, today's emerging adults are looking for love in the afterglow of their parents' Sexual Revolution. Condoms at the drugstore and widely available birth control, sex before marriage, cohabitation, no-fault divorce, gay rights—many sexual practices and relationship trends that today's young people take for granted were pioneered by their parents.

But in the long shadow cast by AIDS and its aftermath, some of these freedoms have turned out to have a dark, if not dire, side. Young people may have all the leeway to experiment that their parents had—and then some—but today that same sexual liberation comes with the frightening prospect of contracting a dreadful disease with no cure. This double-edged sword hangs over the sexual lives of most emerging adults, affecting their attitudes and how they approach potential partners. Fortunately condom use has increased sharply since the late 1980s among both high school and college students, and the greater practice of "safer sex" has led to declines in the consequences of unprotected sex. Throughout the 1990s and into the new century, there were steady declines in unintended pregnancies, abortions, and sexually transmitted infections (STIs) among young people.

Most emerging adults are quite responsible about contraceptive use. Only about 10 percent of 18- to 29-year-olds who are sexually active report never using contraception, but an additional 35 percent describe inconsistent or ineffective contraceptive use. Consistent condom use is more likely among college students, and for this reason their rates of STIs are lower than among emerging adults who don't attend college.

And college grads have the highest rates of contraceptive use, almost 90 percent.

HIV/AIDS is not the only STI young people have to watch out for. Emerging adulthood is also the peak period for chlamydia, gonorrhea, human papillomavirus (HPV), and herpes simplex virus 2 (HSV-2). One

---

Talking the Relationship Talk

For families who want to keep the conversation going from the launching to the landing years, here's what works well, according to respected family therapists and couples experts we interviewed, all of whom are parents who've guided their own kids and many others from age 18 to 29:

Start talking together early.

In the best-case scenario, parents have kept channels open with kids from an early age long before any hot topics surface. Kindergarten confidences about a playground bully have eased naturally into a trusting rapport about ups and downs of first friendships, first crushes, and first dates. Ideally, said the late psychologist and divorce expert Judith Wallerstein, author of *The Unexpected Legacy of Divorce,* parents have asked 10-year-olds, "How do you choose a friend?" and 15-year-olds, "What do you look for in a girlfriend or boyfriend?" These relatively stress-free discussions set the tone for honest dialogue and pave the way for future heart-to-hearts. But even if there's not a long family history of confiding in one another, it's never too late to start.

Hold back on Big Opinions.

Parents may still have strong feelings about what's best for their children, even when those children are emerging adults, but at this point, Big Opinions are best left on the cutting-room floor. The secret to being a good listener is patience—if your son or daughter is confiding in you, don't jump in, finish their sentences, or push the conversation where you want it to go. You might ask for a clarification—"What makes you say that?"—or just keep the conversation moving along with a few choice phrases, such as, "Tell me more" or "I never thought of it that way." If a relationship is

half of STIs in the United States occur in young people between ages 15 and 24. Even if sex takes place between people in a committed relationship, most youthful romances do not endure for long, and partners eventually break up and move on. The gain: Having the chance to see what it's like to be involved with different people. The pain: Having sex with

brand-new, take a wait-on-the-sidelines approach. Avoid extreme responses, both gleeful and glowering—from "She's a keeper!" to "He's not worthy of you!" They often have the opposite effect of what you intended.

If a relationship hits a snag and your child confides in you about it, again, do your best to stay neutral. Although you may be tempted to offer a quick fix to a difficulty, instead listen with empathy and support your grown-up kids' own problem-solving resources and decisions about where a relationship is headed. And before you pile on criticism of a recent ex, remember that many exes end up back in the picture. You don't want to be on the record as an enemy of a reinstated ex.

One size doesn't fit all.
As any parent of more than one child knows, what works with one may fall flat with another. Couples therapist David Treadway makes his living giving relationship advice but proceeds cautiously with his own sons. "I have a handout in my office for every human problem, and my sons have gotten every one of them," he jokes. His 30-year-old son treats Dad's advice with some interest and respect. But the 24-year-old is oblivious. "He probably folds my handouts into paper airplanes!" says Treadway.

So Treadway tailored different approaches to his sons' two personalities. "With my older son, we can problem solve, and he might even use the advice I offer." Maybe his son wants to deepen the commitment to a relationship—or end one without causing too much pain. Treadway keeps him company while he thinks out loud, asking probing questions, occasionally sharing pieces of his own experience. But with his younger son, he mostly listens. "I ask if he wants any feedback. If he says no, I don't give it."

a variety of people, even within a series of relationships, carries with it a substantial risk for STIs.

STIs such as chlamydia and HPV increase the risk of infertility for women, but fortunately these STIs can be treated effectively with antibiotics. Also, a vaccine for HPV is now available, and public health advocates are vigorously promoting the vaccination of adolescents before they become sexually active.

To support your sexually active grown children's health, parents are well advised to make sure that both their daughters and sons get the HPV vaccine. Encourage daughters to build a relationship with a trusted gynecologist to get contraception, annual Pap smears, and sexual health check-ups, and urge grown sons as well to have a stable relationship with a caring doctor who will help them protect their health, sexual and otherwise.

And before your kids head out the door to live on their own, it's perfectly appropriate to have one more Talk. Remind them about safe sex practices and share your own values about sex and relationships. Be frank about the steps required to avoid STIs and unintended pregnancy. If they do contract an STI and unintentionally infect a partner, emphasize the importance of integrity about informing that person, however embarrassing it might be.

Do As I Say, Not As I Did

What about the dreaded moment of truth when kids ask parents who came of age in the sixties and seventies about their own checkered histories—the nude encounter groups, stoned couplings, or the parade of flagrant Mr. or Ms. Wrongs? Parents would sooner forget some of these youthful dalliances, and most certainly don't wish them repeated by their own kids. Judicious editing of your wilder escapades—from losing your virginity too young to rowdy partying—may be the better part of wisdom; that or provide an honest reflection on past mistakes made: "I didn't realize the consequences and I regret what I did." If you were in and out of multiple relationships and had your heart broken too many times, share some of those stories, as discreetly as you can. There's no need to go into detail about the love and sex of your single days, but you can reference them in broad terms—"I remember what it's like"—to empathize with your kids' painful breakups . . . and also to hold out hope that eventually they'll find their special, lasting someone (and yes, you can still offer hope even if your special someone didn't stay special).

Some young people hear about or view their parents' runaway love lives and want to zip in the opposite direction. So confesses Molly Jong-Fast, the daughter of four-time married, feminist novelist Erica Jong, whose *Fear of Flying,* published in 1973, became a sexual bible of liberated women around the world. Perhaps to her mother's chagrin, Jong-Fast, now 33, married at 24 and already has three children. She reflects on being the traditional one in a nontraditional family in her essay "Being a Prude in a Family of Libertines":

> *My mother fought for free love and the right to sexual expression. I fight the traffic as I squire my kids up and down Madison Avenue. Both sets of my grandparents had open marriages. I have a closed marriage (that's where you only sleep with the person you are married to). If it is every generation's job to swing the pendulum back, then I have done mine.*

Every generation hopes to improve on the happiness quotient of the one before, and to some emerging adults, this means forging a couple relationship that is very different from the one their parents had. But overall, today's emerging adults have inherited their parents' Sexual Revolution without thinking of it as revolutionary. With some exceptions, they expect sex to be part of their romantic relationships, no big deal.

"We can drop people as quickly as we can type."

Rachel is a 22-year-old senior at a small liberal arts college, and like other 20-somethings who've been surfing the Web since they could hunt and peck, the Internet and all its tools are the main stage of her social life. The instant gratification of email and social media—Twitter, Facebook, and the like—has become the cadence of how she dates and couples. "We can drop people as quickly as we can type," she says. Most of the time, she loves being connected to friends and potential lovers any time of the night or day. But the dark side of easy-come, easy-go, she admits, is complacency and boredom. "If you can get anything quickly, you don't value it as much."

Rachel can reinvent herself daily on Facebook, a socially acceptable place to flirt, screen people, and hit on someone almost anxiety-free (or at least less so than phoning or texting). Rachel keeps up her profile like a publicist spinning a client's public image. "You're creating a personality or persona," she says. She makes sure she puts up just what she wants people to know, the side that's "hip or snarky."

However, what seems like an ideal fit in cyberspace may not withstand the cold light of day. A few years back Rachel met a boy on Facebook who went to the same college she did, admired the same bands and—this clinched it—"liked the quotes on my page." Their virtual chemistry was instant and before long, it was "LMIRL"—"Let's Meet In Real Life." But when they did meet in person, she was blindsided: They had nothing to talk about beyond, "I took Philosophy/You took Anthropology."

"Facebook doesn't translate into real life as easily as it would seem," she says. "In reality we might find each other annoying. We'd divulged things that we'd never say in person, because we didn't have to look at each other. Then we saw each other, and it was"—she grimaces—"embarrassing. This person knows more about me than I want him to know," she realized. And yikes: "He was a flesh-and-blood person." The transition from screen to flesh can be trickier than it seems.

Peter Pearson, a California couples therapist and author with his wife, Ellyn Bader, of *Tell Me No Lies,* agrees. Meeting up through social media keeps things more detached, he observes. "It's easier to open up—like on an airplane with someone you'll never see again—and it's easier to break up. If you have to break up face-to-face with someone, that's anguish." But a virtual kiss-off can be painless and fast. And among today's young people, including his own three daughters, fast is the dating pace du jour, he says, and it's enabled by texting and other digital tools.

"It's the new social phenomenon: Things happen spontaneously at the last minute. It could be 9 or 10 p.m., and kids come together like swallows who know when to fly together." His youngest daughter is a college senior, and when she's home, he notices that the word to meet up goes out like a mating call (by whatever mode of communication is handy)

YOU CAN'T HURRY LOVE • 143

Q: *We are baby boomers who were not part of the Free Love generation. We have brought up our four children with conservative values. Now our 18-year-old daughter is heading to a coed college, and we are worried. We hear from friends about the wild parties on campus, the drinking and hookups, and behaviors we couldn't even imagine. We don't want our daughter to be hurt emotionally or physically. What can we do?*

A: True, sex on campus gets a lot of hype (although research shows that noncollege emerging adults are actually the most sexually active). While there's unquestionably a party scene on many campuses with the hookups and possible regrets that come with it, many researchers conclude that casual sex is not as common as parents might fear. Most students wait for the right person and the right time and want to feel love first. College students often overestimate the amount of sex all their friends are having. Many may be more sexually conservative than they let on but don't want to seem prudish to their peers.

Share your values with your daughter. If you believe that sex is better saved for marriage, let her know your feelings before she leaves for college. Then trust her to make her own decisions once she's there.

---

and her friends "swarm with each other," often hanging out in big groups.

"Do they feel uncomfortable with just two of them?" he wonders about these aptly named "group hangs," or unpaired collective outings. Going out in a crowd provides a cover for someone too shy to initiate a private date.

Traditional, paired dating is definitely on the downswing. To some, it's a quaint, culturally conservative custom that requires blocks of time that many college students don't have. So sometimes the old dating model has gone topsy-turvy. Parents remember going out with someone a few times and then deciding to have sex. That's still a common pattern, but today there's also the option of having sex a few times and *then* deciding to call it dating.

All that said, parents, take heart: Even given today's explosion of social media, online dating sites, and digital connections, the overall

My older son has had three serious girlfriends. He's dated a lot outside of that. He made business cards, and he'd hand them out to girls. Once I was in the grocery store checkout line, and he was in the car, and I got a text, "Give the bagger a card."

MOTHER OF TWO SONS, 22 AND 19

romantic trend through the twenties is not that different from thirty years ago: falling in and out of some number of relationships until the right one comes along. The recent Toledo Adolescent Relationship Study, which followed 1,300 young people from adolescence into adulthood, found that relationships show increasing levels of intimacy and commitment over the course of the twenties. And the vast majority of those who reported recent casual sex experiences slept with friends or ex-partners, not random Internet matches.

Is This What Feminism Looks Like?

Not long ago, while waiting to get her computer fixed, Rachel ran into someone who felt like a keeper. The day they met, they listened to jazz and went to bed together. But then, on their first real date, he explained his theory of exclusive relationships, which was: He didn't believe in them. Just for good measure he tossed in that rejecting monogamy "wasn't a chauvinistic throwback but quite the opposite: the ultimate nod to feminism."

Rachel's mother, Serena, is a sixties-bred feminist, divorced since Rachel was a baby. Serena raised Rachel to be an independent-minded, liberated woman, and to follow her own dreams. So was this the liberation that Serena and other feminists had marched for back in the day? Rachel had to wonder. Had her mother's cohort struggled for their daughters' easy access to quick partner-changing and non-monogamy? "I don't think that's what Gloria Steinem had in mind," is how Rachel responds to her own question, and Serena surely agrees.

Feminism's forward strides have been a boon and a curse, says David Treadway, Massachusetts couples therapist, author of *Intimacy, Change, and Other Therapeutic Mysteries*, and the father of two sons, 30 and 24. "Changes in women's roles over the past several decades have caused young women's sexuality to become freer and released them from the standard of saint versus slut," he says.

On the one hand, the new landscape of sexual freedom has distinct advantages for today's young women, some, like Hannah Rosin, author of *The End of Men*, argue. Her take is that female college students have more important things than long-term relationships on their minds, "such as good grades and internships and job interviews and a financial future of their own." It's great that they can have sexual adventures without commitment or undue shame while pursuing their other, long-term goals.

But to other observers, the new casualness and social fluidity on campus and postgraduation looks like a step backward. *Premarital Sex in America* authors Regnerus and Uecker see the more disturbing side of today's dating scene for young women. They offer the paradoxical theory that the remarkable educational gains made by women have tipped the sex ratio in favor of men. In the past fifty or so years, who attends college has changed dramatically: In 1947, 71 percent of college students were men; now it's only 42 percent.

Women now outnumber men both in college and postgraduation, when, in some big cities where highly educated young professionals flock to find work, young women exceed men by significant margins. Regnerus and Uecker argue that this gender imbalance can leave women at a disadvantage in "the sexual marketplace," as they call it. When men are more numerous than women, women have the upper hand in the dating pool, but where there are more women than men, men call the shots. As Regnerus and Uecker frame it, some men in their twenties take advantage of their status by staying free agents, rather than signing a long-term contract. And women end up competing for the increasingly rare, desirable men who are willing to commit.

Other research shows that young men are more content than young women to have casual sex. In Jeff's national Clark University poll of 18- to 29-year-olds, 52 percent of young men agreed that "It's OK for two people to have sex even if they are not involved with each other," compared to just 33 percent of young women. And according to the 2002

National Longitudinal Study of Adolescent Health, for young women between 18 and 23, having a lot of partners is not beneficial for emotional health. The more partners these young women had, the higher their likelihood of depression and emotional struggles. For young men, there was no similar correlation between having many partners and emotional problems.

While it may still be true that young men are more likely than young women to be happy with casual sex that stays casual, it's also true that most young men, like most young women, want to end up with a soul mate and are happiest when they find a long-term monogamous relationship.

Meanwhile, as the dating years stretch out longer, friends of both sexes become more important than ever before. That means both those ubiquitous Facebook friends and the good old-fashioned kind who can be counted on for company and moral support when the twenties get lonely or bumpy. Not all the benefits that go with friends need to be of the sexual kind.

Q: *Our 21-year-old daughter is soon to graduate from college. She's quite shy and rather geeky and seems out of step with the wild-and-crazy social life of her peers. She's bright and attractive but prefers to keep to herself, often spending hours in her room on her computer. We're proud of her and want to support her lifestyle, but we're also concerned that she'll never find a partner. Thoughts?*

A: Each of us dates to our own drummer, and your daughter may need more time to feel comfortable with herself before looking for companionship. That said, the Internet can be a godsend for the socially self-conscious, and it's possible that she's making connections online that could lead to real-life friendships later on. If she has other strong interests—and gives you an opening—you might gently suggest that she look for groups that support those interests, either on campus or in your community, so that she has a chance to meet people while doing something she enjoys.

LGBTQ

Only a generation ago, same-sex couples were stigmatized to the point of invisibility; today, same-sex relationships have taken a huge leap out of the closet. Same-sex marriage is legal in a growing number of states and countries, including Canada, Belgium, and Spain, and is likely to become more widespread.

Words for sexuality and the attitudes and practices that go with them have changed radically in the past thirty years, especially in matters of sexual preferences. LGBTQ is the current acronym that reflects this younger generation's rainbow of choices—lesbian, gay, bisexual, transgender, and questioning. That *Q* is key, especially during emerging adulthood when so many lifestyle choices go under the microscope, and curiosity and flexibility are everything. Bi-curious has also become popular as a term for someone who doesn't identify as bisexual or homosexual but has some interest in having same-sex relationships.

Although the research remains controversial, the past few decades have seen increasing evidence that human sexuality is more flexible than it is fixed, not polarized but unfolding along a spectrum. Especially among teenage girls and young women in their twenties, there's more of an openness to relationships with both genders that may be a temporary experiment—or become a way of life. LUGs (lesbian until graduation) or BUGs (bisexual until graduation) are new coinages for the transitional nature of relationships during this period of perpetual questioning.

The 2002 National Study of Family Growth, for instance, showed that in the sexual experiences of 18- to 23-year-olds, same-sex behavior is more common than self-identifying as homosexual, and more so among women than among men. More than double the number of women as men report same-sex attractions (18 percent versus 7 percent) and have engaged in same-sex behavior (14 percent compared to 5 percent). Only about half as many women as men call themselves homosexual (1 percent versus 2 percent) but twice as many women as men identify as bisexual (5 percent versus 2 percent).

Although these overall numbers represent a small portion of emerging adults, gay youth culture has come out strong in many high schools and on college campuses. And being young and gay today is not what parents remember homosexuality to have been in their youth. Contemporary LGBTQ young people have opportunities today that were unimaginable even a decade ago. With Gay-Straight Alliances a dynamic force in more than four thousand high schools and queer communities active on many college campuses, today's young people are more at ease with homosexuality than their parents' generation was—and have a more flexible view of human sexuality overall. There's been a huge cultural paradigm shift, according to Ritch Savin-Williams, a professor of clinical and developmental psychology at Cornell. His twenty-five years of research about gay and lesbian young people and books like *The New Gay Teenager* have helped redefine attitudes about gays and lesbians and bring them into the twenty-first century.

The old paradigm was a deficit model, he says, with an equation between gay youth and troubled youth: isolated, confused, suicidal, and in need of clinical services. This negative image has been ingrained for so long in the culture that some have taken it to extremes. Savin-Williams reports a gay teen he interviewed who told him, "I don't think I'm gay because I haven't tried to kill myself."

Contemporary LGBTQ young people, Savin-Williams argues, are diverse, resilient, positive, fluid, and less given to labels than their parents. Today's under-30 generation is more tolerant of sexual diversity across the board than older people are: of same-sex marriages, adoptions by same-sex couples, and gay people serving openly in the military. With greater tolerance and less social stigma, today's young people are first identifying as gay at a younger age: 16 for girls and 15 and a half for boys, about five years earlier than occurred in the sixties or seventies. Even the optimistic Savin-Williams observes that young people who come out early may have a harder time in school, at home, and with friends than those who wait till later. Nevertheless, by the time many LGBTQ youth reach their twenties, they've had more experience and may be more comfortable with their sexuality than past generations who didn't acknowledge their sexual preferences until later.

Mainstream society has become increasingly, if slowly, accepting of differences, but there's a long way to go. Despite Savin-Williams's upbeat picture, homophobia persists in American society, as it does in most of the world. Young gays and lesbians still suffer teasing and bullying in high school and have high rates of depression and substance use and abuse, with bisexual youth the most susceptible to relationship violence and substance abuse.

Multiple studies have also shown that gay kids are at higher risk for suicide than their straight friends. Several devastating cases of campus intimidation have received major media attention, including that of a Rutgers student whose 2010 webcam spying on his roommate's tryst with another man may have contributed to the 18-year-old roommate's suicide. A tragic spate of gay teen suicides after bullying episodes in 2010 prompted the creation of the It Gets Better Project, a series of YouTube videos promising struggling LGBTQ youth that harassment eases and happiness increases in adulthood. President Obama and Hillary Clinton, Ellen DeGeneres and *American Idol*'s Adam Lambert are among the more than fifty thousand people who have created videos amassing over fifty million total views, offering hope and changing minds, one by one.

What do these social changes and increased openness about sexual orientation among emerging adults mean for parents? First, understand that for young people—young women, especially—a period of experimenting with both same-sex and opposite-sex relationships is not unusual. It may be seriously disconcerting to see a daughter dating both women and men, but for some undecideds, this pattern comes with the explorations of the twenties. Some may continue to be bisexual; others will choose one sex or the other. As with any of your children's partners, gay or straight, it makes more sense to be accepting than dismissive if you want to keep a strong relationship with your grown-up kid.

If and when your gay or lesbian sons or daughters tell you about their same-sex orientation, it's best to accept them at face value and not dismiss their feelings as "just a phase." Most LGBTQ youth disclose first to friends at about age 16, and somewhat later to parents, typically around age 19. Many parents know intuitively that their kids are gay from a young age, but let them go at their own pace to reveal their sexual identity and choose the moment when they're comfortable enough to open up. Parents can create an atmosphere of acceptance with the message "We love you regardless of your sexuality."

Some parents prefer to be private about their children's same-sex orientation; others benefit from reaching out to other parents or joining organizations like PFLAG (Parents and Families of Lesbians and Gays), a 200,000-member organization with five hundred chapters nationwide. At PFLAG meetings parents can get information, share feelings, and get support going through the process of understanding and acceptance. It may help to remind a gay son or lesbian daughter that while they may have had a long time to get used to their sexuality, their path is new to you. Ask them to give you time to be comfortable with their newly revealed sexual orientation or gender identity.

Even the most loving and liberal parents may receive the news that a child is gay with confusion or mixed emotions. They may be disappointed that their child will be following a nontraditional path and may not marry or have children (although same-sex marriages are becoming increasingly possible, and 20 percent of gay men and 30 percent of lesbians do have children). They may be concerned about the social pressures their child may face and be fearful of HIV and AIDS. They may wonder how (or if) they're going to share the news with more conservative relatives. And sometimes, they may self-blame, as in "What did we do wrong?" or "We should never have divorced" (or sent her to that camp or him to that school or whatever).

But parents may also feel relieved that their gay or lesbian kid trusts them enough to disclose and share such an important part of their lives. Parents may feel pleased that openness has replaced secrecy, and be admiring that their grown kids want to live with honesty and integrity. Now they can enjoy getting to know their kids' same-sex partners. And they may be optimistic about their emerging adult's chance for finding a loving mate, someone to cherish them over a lifetime.

Keep in mind that sexual identity is not under conscious control and is present from a young age. No parent created a child's sexual orientation and no parent is going to be able to change it. Even for those parents who believe homosexuality is wrong, or have mixed or disapproving feelings, consider what's in your best interest and the best interest of your child. It's surely not going to serve family harmony to reject or disown a child. To preserve a close relationship with grown-up kids, whether gay or straight, embrace them and the people they love.

Q: *We recently learned about mobile dating apps where users can instantly connect with each other for casual dating and sex. For our 25-year-old gay son, we're especially concerned about a popular geosocial networking app geared toward gay, bisexual, and bi-curious men that uses GPS to show users where interested men are nearby. Forgive the pun, but this scares the pants off us.*

A: Perhaps your parents winced thirty years ago when they heard about people posting personals in *The New York Review of Books*. But just because the possibility was out there didn't mean that you were going to use it to find your true love, and the same may hold for your son. That said, online dating sites and mobile dating apps absolutely open up a new universe of ways for grown kids to get into trouble. These technologies can lead to dangerous behavior and scary situations, so your concerns are understandable. Sometimes it's easier to open a sociological discussion than a personal one on a touchy topic. You might say to your son, "I've been reading about mobile dating apps, and I'm wondering what you know about them and how common their use is among your generation." You can follow up by sharing your fears about where this technology might lead. At the very least, it's one more opportunity to underline the importance of safe sex practices and responsible condom use.

"My parents, my boyfriend, and I went out on a double date."

During sophomore spring in his Northern California high school Tad appeared in the first amateur production of *The Laramie Project*, a groundbreaking play about the small-town beating and murder of a young gay man. He and his dad were out on a neighborhood jog the day after the performance, critiquing it together. "I don't understand homophobia," his dad ventured. "Men have been involved with men since ancient Greek times."

Perhaps Dad had been waiting for this opening for years, and like many parents was aware of his son's homosexuality long before the news was shared. But he let his comment hang in the air, and Tad stepped up. "Dad, I'm gay," he said.

Dad kept up his pace and didn't miss a beat. "You are," he answered, agreeing, acknowledging, accepting. Then, between huffs and puffs, he added, "You should tell Mom, because we have no secrets, and she should hear it from you."

"I knew I was gay very young," Tad said, reflecting on the evolution that brought him to that confidence shared. "I broke up with my seventh grade girlfriend because I was gay." He closed the straight chapter of his dating life with an enigmatic, "Eventually you'll understand."

Still he bided his time: "I wanted to come out when I was comfortable with it myself, and I wanted to tell my parents first, because I value our close relationship and didn't want to have secrets."

Tad, now 27, remembers, "It was a little more complicated with Mom than with Dad. It took her a while to adjust to it." He walked her through the paces. "I understand it's new for you," he said. "I've been living with it for years, and it's not a phase."

It took yet a few years longer for his parents to be comfortable enough to meet one of his boyfriends. But on a visit to campus in his sophomore year in college they asked if he would like to introduce them to the guy he was dating. "My parents, my boyfriend, and I went out on a double date," he recalls about that historic night. "We all shared a giant martini, got a little drunk, and had a lot of fun. Any lingering weirdness was gone." He pauses. "It was the beginning of a new framework for my relationship with my parents. I could stop viewing them as parents and now think of them as friends." Most important, they were friends who accepted his boyfriends just as they accepted him.

Tad's brother is only 16 months older, and he married his longtime girlfriend at 23. Their mother threw herself into every detail of planning the storybook vineyard wedding so that the groom and his new wife were literally walking into the sunset as the ceremony ended. Tipsy and content, all the guests agreed it was the most fun they'd ever had. On the way home, relishing every detail from rehearsal dinner to garter toss,

Dad said wistfully to Mom, "It's a shame we can't do the same for Tad."

"Of course we can," she replied.

In 2008, it seemed as if California had cooperated by legalizing gay marriage, but shortly after, the decision was overturned. Although there's still legal controversy entangling the final outcome, a future wedding for Tad does seem increasingly possible. But he also admits it's unlikely he's going to settle down anytime soon. "I'm always with someone"—he laughs—"but does it last long? No!" He adds: "I've had lots of wildly romantic one-month relationships, where I'm truly, madly, deeply into infatuation with men who don't live anywhere close."

Although Tad would like to be a dad someday, that day still feels far in the future. Every year at Christmas, his mother inquires, "Will you be bringing someone home for the holidays?" It hasn't happened yet, but someday, he promises his mom, it will.

8

Saying "I Do" or "I Don't"

My parents, now divorced, were never a super
affectionate couple. They fought a lot.
So now I say, I expect more than that from a
relationship, I have much higher expectations.

DAUGHTER, 26

Since Adam got together with Eve, Elizabeth Taylor wed Richard Burton (twice), and Ellen DeGeneres found bliss with Portia de Rossi, the decision to marry has been a major developmental milestone. But as the marriage age rises, the state of matrimony itself is losing ground as the organizing institution in American society—and even more so in Europe. According to U.S. census data, barely half of adults ages 18 and older are married—51 percent in 2010, compared with 72 percent in 1960. This decline is especially notable for emerging adults: Only 20 percent of 18- to 29-year-olds were married in 2010, compared with 59 percent in 1960. Indeed, today's marriage delay is one stand-out reason why emerging adulthood has become a distinct stage of life for this generation of 20-somethings.

Thumbs Up or Down on Marriage

Your grown kids' lack of marital enthusiasm may be unsettling. If you're happily married yourself, it makes sense for you to believe that marriage is a vital ingredient of lifetime contentment, a commitment that infuses everything else in life. No matter how much you celebrate all the exciting options for today's young women and men, if your own marriage sustains you, you can't help but want the same for your loved ones. As one mother of twin 18-year-old daughters put it, "All the happiness I have as a mother, as a lawyer, everything, begins with having a great marriage. And I want my daughters to find that, too. I want them to know that marriage affects their happiness on every level."

If you're in that camp, there is hope: Although 39 percent of Americans say they agree that marriage is becoming obsolete, according to a 2011 Pew Report, most people who have never married say they would like to marry someday (including many who agree that marriage is becoming obsolete). More evidence that 20-somethings are not giving up on marriage: In Jeff's 2012 Clark University Poll of Emerging Adults, 86 percent said they expected to have a marriage that lasts a lifetime. But they're also realistic about reaching happily-ever-after: 61 percent said they expected to give up some of their career goals to have their dreamed-of family life.

Fine. But what about your 20-something daughter who's dedicated to her job in law or social work or managing a store and seems content dating quite casually? Or your son of the same age putting in 12-hour work-days in finance or technology or for a nonprofit while darting from flower to flower with no firm prospects in sight? Beneath your pride and admiration, you may secretly fear that these young people are wasting precious time. Why aren't they getting on with their personal lives: settling down with someone special, planning weddings, and decking out nurseries? "When I was your age," a well-meaning parent might be tempted to say to a son, who's 25 and blithely single, "I was already married with my second baby on the way." Or an anxious grandparent might harrumph to a career-minded, unmarried 29-year-old granddaughter: "At your age, I was ten years married with four children under eight."

With emerging adulthood's expanded time line, the personal decisions about marriage and family that young people used to make in their late teens or early twenties are often pushed to their late twenties or thirties. As noted earlier, the average marriage age has risen sharply since

1960: from 20 to 27 for women and from 22 to 29 for men. Young people with college degrees marry even later—an average of 30 for women and 31 to 32 for men—and with that extra maturity also comes a better chance of staying married.

Most emerging adults expect to marry eventually. By age 40, 85 percent will be wedded, and another 5 percent living together—a statistic that neatly matches the 90 percent of their parents' generation who married. So, not to worry: Young Americans today are actually as likely to find partners as their parents or grandparents were. It may just happen on a different schedule.

If you're impatient to become a mother of the groom or father of the bride, also take note: Early marriage comes trailing plenty of extra baggage—for starters, a higher divorce rate. According to the 1973–2002 National Opinion Research Center's General Social Surveys, 50 percent of women who were first married before turning 19 ultimately divorced, compared with just 24 percent who married when they were 26 or older (for men, the corresponding figures are 54 percent and 21 percent).

Arguments over money are a perennial source of marital strife, and getting hitched young usually means a wobblier financial footing, which, in turn, means more money woes. So delaying the age for entering marriage may well be a good strategy for being more financially stable as a married couple as well as avoiding divorce later on. According to the 2011 Pew Report on Marriage, for every year a woman delays marriage into her early thirties, she reduces her risk of divorce. This statistical nugget should help parents with unmarried 30-ish daughters or sons to relax a bit. Life as a single person may sometimes be lonely, but it sure beats an unhappy marriage or a bitter divorce.

While we're talking trends, the range of ages when young people marry has also spread out for this millennial generation. As a glance at *The New York Times* wedding pages will confirm, some couples still marry in their early twenties, and most of the rest are spread out among the midtwenties, late twenties, and early- to mid-thirties. There's no longer a clear-cut definition of what's "normal," so young people can make their choices according to their own development, education, career decisions, financial security, and when they happen to meet their soul mate.

The freedom from the social pressure to marry young can be a relief, but the choice-overload can also prompt confusion and anxiety among today's grown kids as they consider when or whether to say "I do." Now it's up to the individuals themselves to decide when the time is right to take this momentous step. And it's the rare parent who likes to hear: How about never?

At the same time that the decision to marry is on hold longer, the state of matrimony itself is also changing. As Andrew Cherlin points out in *The Marriage-Go-Round*, over the past century marriage has become more fair, more fulfilling, and more effective in fostering the well-being of both adults and children. But on the downside, it's also more optional and more fragile, less likely to last. Since the 1960s, divorce rates have been rising until now nearly half of marriages break up. But a college degree seems to have a protective effect on staying married. The divorce rate for college graduates who married between 1990 and 1994 is about 25 percent. That's compared with a more than 50 percent divorce rate for those without a bachelor's degree.

> I always thought I'd marry when I was 26. Then I had an aunt who married young and divorced, and she said don't get married before 30. I used to be obsessed with having kids, but I know they take a big toll on a marriage, and I care more about having a good marriage. If I marry a guy and he wants kids, he'd better be really open to being involved. I could also adopt or foster; I don't have a need to have my own kid.
>
> — DAUGHTER, AGE 26

Yet despite our widespread pattern of divorce, Americans continue to idealize marriage. It's only in the United States, Cherlin says, that gay people are fighting for the right to marry. Most gay men and lesbians in Europe, he argues, view marriage as another oppressive heterosexual

Talking the Marriage Talk

Don't wait till the rehearsal dinner to start sharing your thoughts about what nurtures a good marriage. Even when kids are still teenagers and certainly as emerging adults, parents can trust them to understand the shifting seasons of even the most well-suited couples. Here are several talking points from marriage and family therapists:

Practice, don't preach.
Being a loving role model and a kind partner are more important than anything a parent might preach about holy matrimony. Creating a good, lasting marriage doesn't mean having all the answers; it means being open to working out the inevitable. Couples therapists Peter Pearson and Ellyn Bader, authors of *Tell Me No Lies*, did their best to model to their three 20-something daughters "openness, candidness, asking questions even if the responses make you uncomfortable, and appreciating the vulnerabilities of the other person when your partner is being open." Most valuable of all, they've tried to demonstrate how even with conflict, their marriage is still strong. "What a gift to give children—to show them you can disagree and work it out," Pearson says. "Too often children either see no conflict or constant fighting. Let them see how differences can be solved."

Marriage doesn't have to be perfect.
Kids often demonize or idealize their parents' marriage, and it's helpful for them to know that marriages are complicated propositions with inevitable ups and downs. "Some couples talk about good and bad days," says David Treadway, Massachusetts couples therapist and author of *Intimacy, Change and Other Therapeutic Mysteries*. "We talk about good and bad decades."

institution. Pointedly, his last chapter is entitled "Slow Down." Think before you rush into new relationships, he advises. It's just this slow-down that emerging adults are practicing these days.

Parents, a word of caution here: No matter how much you may wish for your grown-up kid's marriage to someone who loves him or her as much as you do, don't let your goals for your children's personal lives

And our first decade was a bad one." But the Treadways are going strong four decades later, and Dad is proud that they've been honest about themselves with their sons. "They see our limits and our flaws as people and as a couple," he says, adding the message he wants his kids to take away: "You don't have to be perfect people to have a good relationship."

Offer hope even if your marriage didn't last.

If parents are divorced or single, they can still be optimistic about their grown kids' marriage plans and potential. Parents might be open about what derailed their marriage, and what their children should avoid, from spending too much time at work to being unwilling to compromise. It's possible to show the next generation that with awareness, kindness, and patience they can make better choices than their parents did.

Get ready for give-and-take.

As teenagers morph into emerging adults, conversations shape-shift as well, from "What time will you be home from the movie?" to what matters in a life partner and how to weather the storms to make a marriage endure. Now parents need to be ready to answer some tough questions as well as dish them out. "How open do you want your kids to be as they get older?" asks Treadway. What that question also means is, "How open do *you* want to be about your life?" Your kids might well ask you, "You've stayed married, how?" or "You got divorced, why?"

"There's room for quite meaningful collaborative communication," Treadway says—and room to negotiate what's too private for discussion, on both sides, but still keep the lines open.

intrude on their plans. No one likes to be rushed or challenged or spied on in matters of the heart. Okay, if you feel strongly that time's a-wasting, go ahead and share an occasional phone number or email address of your colleague's cute son or daughter who's just the right age for your son or daughter. But most of the time, step back and give your grown kids room to roam romantic playing fields on their own timetable.

One more thing about timing: Biology remains a factor. Even with today's more relaxed timetable and less peer pressure to get hitched, biological clocks keep ticking. Despite medical advances, like in vitro fertilization and gestational surrogacy, a woman's alarm bell tends to go off when she nears thirty, and starts clamoring by thirty-five. Young men usually feel they have the luxury of extra time and the liberty to choose younger partners when they're ready to settle down. But even for them, the pleasures of singlehood tend to wane in the course of the twenties. Both young women and young men tend to feel an "Age 30 Deadline" by which they would prefer to be married—provided their soul mate comes along by then.

Being single may offer occasional excitement and a sense that anything (and anyone) is still possible, but it also makes for lots of lonely Saturday nights. And new research suggests that age may also be a factor, though a much smaller one, for would-be fathers. The sperm of older men is associated with various neurocognitive problems in children, including autism, schizophrenia, and dyslexia (still only a risk of 2 percent overall for fathers 40 and above).

Q: *Our 26-year-old daughter and her boyfriend of several years just broke up. For a while it seemed as if this guy was The One, and now she seems kind of down about her future. What encouragement can we give her?*

A: The Supremes had it right: You can't hurry love. Finding the right person and building a good relationship take time. It's rare to find your soul mate the first time you try. First you need to know yourself and what you truly want. Painful as it is to split up now, when your daughter looks back later at the one who got away, she may well be relieved. Research shows that people who wait longer to get married and those who have had a handful of relationships before marrying have more stable marriages in the long run. Your daughter is learning things from these early relationships that will benefit her later on.

Is Marriage Just for White People?

Among African Americans, there's less marriage and more divorce; in fact, African Americans have become the most unmarried group in the United States. In the 1950s, nine out of ten African American women married at some point; today only two out of three expect to marry, and these marriages are often unstable: The divorce rate among African Americans is 70 percent, compared with 47 percent among whites. Since two African American women graduate college for every African American man, there's also a real concern among well-educated African American women that they won't find an equally matched partner when they're ready to marry.

As Stanford Law professor Ralph Richard Banks explores in *Is Marriage for White People?,* the black middle class is disproportionately female and the black poor are disproportionately male, with the gap widening. High rates of incarceration for black men and the long-term consequences of a prison record on future employment make this situation worse. Banks cites studies showing that in evaluating potential mates, African Americans give more weight to economic stability than do other groups. Yet many never find someone who can offer that security, and therefore never marry. And African American women are less inclined to marry out of their ethnic group than African American men are.

The Shadow of Divorce

There are all sorts of reasons why young people are delaying marriage these days. They want to finish their education and pursue their career goals. They don't think they can afford the big wedding they envision, or they're not yet ready to have children. They want to travel, stay unfettered, be their own person. Besides all that, a major influence on emerging adults' caution about the *M* Word . . . is the *D* Word. By age 18, only half of today's young people are living in a household with two biological parents. Or to put it another way, half of today's young people are children of divorce or dissolved relationships. For them, their parents' divorce was a life-defining moment. Their parents' problematic histories may cast a long shadow on their search for long-term love.

Anxiety not to repeat their parents' mistakes often leads to anxiety about commitment.

Even young people whose parents stayed married may feel the fallout of widespread divorce among their contemporaries. Jake, a 22-year-old, once asked his freshman seminar classmates how many of their parents had stayed together. When he surveyed the room, he saw "like three raised their hands." Awareness of that low success rate has contributed to his wariness of marriage, despite his parents' contented and enduring partnership.

Q: *We have always told our son: Date or marry anyone you like, but please, don't bring home a Republican. Well, now, you've guessed it: Our liberal son has fallen madly in love with a conservative girl, and they're planning to marry next year. How do we handle our extreme political differences, both with our future daughter-in-law and her parents?*

A: If you're surprised—or taken aback—by your grown child's love interest of a different stripe (whether red, blue, or any other color) do not rush to express your feelings. Few things will cause your child's hackles to rise like perceiving your stereotyping or, worse, your rejection of a beloved. Give yourself a chance to get to know the young person in question and see her through your child's eyes. It's very possible that when this new family member is making you a special meal, driving you to the hospital for an emergency, or putting that first grandchild in your arms, you will forget the differences that used to bother you and appreciate everything she brings to the party instead. And if you want to preserve your relationship with your son, his future wife, and the children they might have together someday, it makes sense to accept her even if you don't agree with her every political opinion. As for her parents, you may not end up being best friends, but give them the benefit of the doubt as well and keep it cordial for the sake of your kids. Until you know each other better, leave politics at the door, and concentrate on what you have in common: your pleasure in this young pair.

Without a Marital GPS

In marriages that are working well, just the presence of caring, compatible parents may be enough to set the next generation on its way without elaborate advice and instructions. But grown children of divorce have had a front-row seat on all the ways that couples come apart: their anger and accusations, infidelities, and failed attempts to reconcile. And whether or not their parents' divorce has been handled well or poorly, no grown kids want to repeat this pattern, nor do they want to inflict the pain they may remember experiencing as children on their future kids.

Still, divorce seems to spawn divorce. In the combined 1973–2002 General Social Surveys, among individuals 35 and older, those whose parents were divorced by the time they were 16 were nearly two-thirds more likely to have been divorced themselves than those from non-divorced families. The marriage stories of today's emerging adult children of divorce are still being written. But how best can parents, divorced themselves, instill confidence that a relationship can be fulfilling and for keeps?

In an interview before her death in 2012, psychologist and international authority on divorce Judith Wallerstein, author of *Second Chances: Men, Women, and Children a Decade After Divorce,* was blunt: In families of divorce, parents need to talk straight to their kids. In other matters of the heart discretion may be a wise policy, but here, straightforward is the best course. Undoing an old layer of sugarcoating may be the right place to begin. "In the past, parents were told to offer pablum to their kids about their breakup and merely to say, 'We're different people,'" she said. She scoffed at this. "That's foolish, because it doesn't address the children's anxiety. The chief reasons for divorce are serious—addiction, unemployment, lack of trust, infidelity, loneliness. It's not just that parents are different people—we're all different people."

Divorce is the ghost at the table, she added, when grown children from marriages that didn't last start looking for love themselves. They worry that their own relationships will also fail. They don't commit readily or trust easily. *"When my boyfriend is half an hour late, I wonder who he's with"* was typical of the anxious comments she heard in her research. Or a perpetual state of apprehension takes hold: *"I'm married to a great man and we have two wonderful kids, but I'm fearful that the second shoe will drop. If I get something beautiful, I'm afraid that I'll lose it."*

Despite parents' histories, their job is to create a sense of hope and possibility for their kids. "You can say, 'I want you to feel that you're not me. You will be able to trust someone.'" Then, admit your mistakes: "'Your dad and I were young, we didn't understand what marriage involved.' Or 'Your dad's drinking was out of control.' Or 'I broke out of the marriage with another relationship and didn't realize the consequences.'"

There are ways to say things without blame, she suggested, and help empower grown kids to create partnerships that last. You might say, "I think I made a mistake, and I don't want you to make the same one." If a parent has created a successful new marriage, he or she can explain what was learned from the first and why this time it's working better. Meanwhile, however wronged or fuming divorced parents may feel, it is crucial for exes to refrain from bad-mouthing the other in front of their kids, both young and grown, and spare them the agony of having to take sides. If there's been lingering conflict after a split, consider burying the hatchet when grown children form their own couples. What could be a better wedding gift than parents who are ex-partners acting civilly, even cordially, at the ceremony?

"I'm not itching to get married just because I know I can get divorced."

Kevin, 24, whose parents divorced when he was seven, shows how cool realism can be mixed with buoyant optimism and romanticism in a grown-up kid whose parents' marriage did not last. Kevin was raised primarily by his mother; his father remarried, and Kevin had less contact with him over the years growing up. Kevin is now fairly clear-eyed about his parents' ill-fated marriage: "From my parents' divorce, I learned that marriage is not a fairy tale, and relationships don't always last forever. If two people are going to be happier apart, then they should be apart. Staying respectful and responsible is what's important."

But the sting of what went wrong between his parents is still there and provides a cautionary tale, a tough reminder of what he hopes to avoid: "What upsets me is that they no longer speak, and that they could have been married for that long and arrive at this point. I think of my mom and dad's relationship as true love gone wrong, and my dad and stepmom's relationship as a more practical arrangement where it's relatively clear what the give-and-take is on each side."

Knowing how widespread divorce is among the parents of his friends does not make him any more comfortable with this option for himself: "The prevailing wisdom is often 'getting a divorce is no big deal.' That said, I'm still somewhat of a traditionalist and I'm not itching to get married just because I know I can get divorced. It feels depressing to think of the mainstream nature of divorce as a contingency plan because it sort of deflates the mystique of the institution."

Despite his parents' marital history, Kevin still dreams of a forever mate: "I have a feeling 'the One' will be someone I'm willing to sacrifice and change my plans for," he says. There is someone special in his life now and he's just beginning to contemplate a long-term commitment to her. "The last year of my life has been the first time when marriage has ever been on my radar, and since it's still distant enough not to cause panic attacks, it's a nice feeling. I'm beginning to understand that marriage is more of a rational decision than I ever expected. I just want to make sure I'm with someone whose reasons for marriage agree with mine. And maybe that's not as unromantic a thought as it sounds."

Romantic or rational, a meeting of souls or an arrangment of convenience? On their way to the altar, emerging adult children of divorced parents may be dogged by ambivalence even more than their peers.

One Foot In: Cohabitation

For more and more young people, living together without marriage presents itself as a way to test the waters of long-term commitment without taking a permanent plunge. Boomer parents mated in the heat of the Sexual Revolution, but cohabitation remained relatively rare back then: Even in the late 1960s, only 8 percent of couples did it. By the 1980s and 1990s, unmarried-but-living-together had begun to look like the norm, and today, two-thirds of young people live with a romantic partner before marriage. It's a test-drive for a long-term relationship, a chance to check their compatibility, practice as householders, make life more convenient and sex more available, and save on paying double rents. Without the public commitment or legal ties, it's also a lot easier for either party to say adios. Many young people have gravitated to cohabitation as a touchstone, a way to guarantee that they're well suited enough to marry and a hedge against the pervasive divorce in their parents' generation.

The jury is still out on whether the strategy works. In fact, there's an active debate among marriage researchers over whether living together before the wedding does or doesn't point toward a more stable marriage later on. For many years, research suggested that couples who lived together before marriage were actually *more* likely to divorce than couples who didn't.

But more recent studies suggest that this old caution may no longer be true, as living together has become so prevalent and popular. Among women who married since the mid-1990s, cohabitation is not tied to a heightened risk of later divorce, concluded Bowling Green State University researchers Wendy Manning and Jessica Cohen, using data from the National Survey of Family Growth. But living together before marriage does not lower divorce risk, either, although many people believe it does.

Among parents in our survey, many more support their emerging adults living together than are against it—39 percent strongly favor the arrangement and 30 percent slightly favor it, compared with only 15 percent who are strongly or slightly opposed. Of the accepting parents, some see the decision as the couples' own choice to make. Others believe, either from firsthand experience or because the custom is now so widespread, that a trial period does provide a benefit to the long-term success of a marriage. Living together before marriage, observes one mother of an 18-year-old daughter, is a "good way to get to know each other intimately before choosing a mate for life and a good way to learn about yourself and how to compromise and work together." Another mother who's in favor points out the importance of seeing how the other person reacts to the day-to-day things "like what happens when the grocery bag breaks." All these daily exchanges accrue over time and add up to knowing what it would be like to be married to a person.

But some parents are vehemently opposed to cohabitation, whether for religious, moral, or personal reasons. They feel very protective, especially of daughters, like this mother of a 24-year-old woman: "I think, and my daughter agrees, that cohabitating, at least for women, is the worst of both worlds: You get all the crap of being a wife with none of the benefits and all the crap of being a girlfriend with none of the benefits."

Not all living-together arrangements look the same. On the most casual end is a kind of default cohabitation where a girlfriend or boyfriend has no other place to go, so moves in on a short-term basis. There's also semicohabitation, where two people are still in the dating stage but spend several nights a week together, so that, as Taylor Swift puts it in her song "Mine," "There's a drawer of my things at your place." Among the more committed forms of cohabitation, some are more well-defined than others, up to premarital cohabitation, where couples have made a long-term pledge to each other, and have maybe even set a wedding date.

Of the several varieties of cohabitation, some are more likely to lead to permanence than others. It's helpful (and saves later heartbreak) if both partners discuss their motivations and intentions before they start sharing rent, although it's not a sure thing that their level of commitment will be the same. If given an opening, you can encourage your grown child to discuss and be clear about hopes for the impending arrangement with a live-in partner, but don't expect the negotiations to be shared with you. This is just the kind of topic—like anything involving love and sex— that emerging adults tend to keep to themselves.

As a parent watching on the sidelines, you might also wonder what your grown-up kid's living-together status means. Will wedding bells be ringing soon, or is this just an experiment that will eventually fail? Depending on your openness, patience, and values, you may feel more accepting of a live-in relationship that seems to be heading toward marriage than a shared, just-for-convenience arrangement. But expect to remain in a period of uncertainty for a while. Your questions about the relationship's future may well be rebuffed, as often the unmarried pair is trying to figure out those very same questions.

Grandbabies, Ready or Not

In a chapter on marriage, we have so far talked about everything but. We've covered delay and hesitation, divorce, and living together, and now we may seem to be putting the cart before the horse once again by talking about grandbabies before we've even gotten our young couples to the altar. That's because, first, we want to point out that later marriage usually means later parenthood (and later grandparenthood for you), and second, because there's been a huge boom in babies born to unmarried mothers in the 18-to-29 age group.

The average age for having kids today is 26 for women and 28 for men, up from 22 and 24 fifty years ago. For parenthood as for marriage, among the college-educated, baby-makes-three happens later: 30 for women, 31 to 32 for men.

When friends start whipping out their cell phones to show off their grandchildren, grandbaby lust may set in. The majority of boomer parents we interviewed admitted wishing their daughters would start a family by age 30. It's well known that health risks for mother and baby rise steadily from a mother's twenties to her thirties. Post-30 and especially post-35, the risks of infertility can be considerable. Boomer parents of grown kids who themselves had children in their thirties or early forties may know about fertility issues firsthand. Now they want to make sure their grown kids won't wait too long and be disappointed. And they want to be spry enough to toss a ball or play hide-and-seek with grandchildren.

When grown children delay marriage and postpone parenthood, a youthful grandparenthood starts looking less likely, and parents of dallying emerging adults may feel this delay as a real disappointment and loss. If your prospects for knitting those baby booties seem dim, consider reframing your attitude: Do your best to enjoy your 20-somethings' increased freedom to explore, travel, continue their education, learn about themselves, and accomplish things in this decade. Meanwhile get on with your own life and your own projects and dreams.

Ah, but be careful what you wish for. On the other side of the cradle sit the boomer parents whose daughters become single moms at a young age. The rate of single motherhood in the United States has skyrocketed in recent decades, from low single digits in the sixties and seventies to 40 percent of all births by 2010. Among 20- to 24-year-olds, unmarried motherhood is as high as 60 percent of births (up from 20 percent in 1980). These days, it's not just poor girls who have babies outside of marriage, it's young women from across the economic and ethnic spectrum.

> I think 29 was a good age to get married, for me. With women there's always that sense of, if you want to have kids, you have to get started by your thirties.
>
> MOTHER OF 18-YEAR-OLD
> TWIN DAUGHTERS

And it's not just girls who are too young to grasp fully how babies are made. Despite all the concern over "teenage pregnancy," most single moms today are in their twenties, not their teens. Rates of teen births have plummeted since 1990, and today, the highest rates of abortions and births to unmarried mothers take place during the emerging adult years.

African Americans have had high rates of single motherhood since the 1970s, and their rates are close to 70 percent today, but the steepest rise in recent decades has been among young white women, whose rate of nonmarital births is now about 30 percent. Annie, 24, is one such mom. When she was 20, she and her college boyfriend had a sexual relationship and used condoms, except when they didn't because none was available at the moment. She became pregnant, signaling the end of college, and the end of the boyfriend, too. After much internal struggle and tearful conversations with her parents, Annie decided to have the baby rather than have an abortion. (Among unmarried women in their twenties who become pregnant, about half obtain an abortion and half carry the pregnancy to term.)

Now Annie works part-time as a waitress, and she and her daughter, Madison, age 3, live with her parents. She appreciates their support and could hardly survive without it, but moving back in with them after living on her own at college has felt like a step backward in her own development. "I feel like a kid with a kid," she says. "My parents boss me around, they boss her around, and then they tell me what to do with her, so it's like I'm her sister rather than her mother." Nevertheless she realizes that it is only her parents' willingness to take over some of the child care that allows her an occasional break from it. "Living with my parents gives me a lot of freedom because whenever Maddie goes to bed and if they're home, I can go do what I want. Eight o'clock comes and I'm at the mall!"

For young single moms like Annie, even with substantial support from parents, having a child essentially means the end of the self-focused freedom of emerging adulthood. The demands of parenting a young child make it difficult to pursue educational and career goals as other age-mates can. Many, like Annie, drop out of college or take fewer classes, and so take longer to graduate or never graduate at all. Single moms have lower educational attainment than other emerging adults. They also have much lower incomes, because without college credentials they have a more difficult time finding a job that pays a decent wage. Of all groups in American society, single moms and their children are most likely to be living in poverty.

The parents of these young single mothers often have long packed away the baby clothes from their own children's infancies and are look-ing forward to some years of freedom ahead. They may greet the news of an unmarried, 20-something daughter's pregnancy with surprise and dismay. Melinda, 52, found herself in this unexpected situation when both her daughters became pregnant young and unmarried, the elder at age 21, the younger at age 19. Both decided to have and raise their children rather than choose adoption or abortion. In both cases, the babies' fathers contributed little more than twenty-three chromosomes. Although both daughters managed to live in their own households with their new babies, Melinda and her husband have been called on to be sur-rogate parents for the past ten years, providing almost daily child care in the early years and financial support even now.

Melinda sounds as if she still has trouble believing this is how things turned out for her girls, and for her. "We're upper middle class!" she protests. "This kind of thing isn't supposed to happen to people like us." She doesn't understand why her girls chose this future for themselves: "It was no accident. They knew what they were doing. This is what they wanted." As for her, and for her husband, this is not what they wanted, but this is what they've got. "I didn't expect to spend my fifties this way," she says, looking wistful. "I thought I'd have more time for my career [as a public relations executive], and we'd have the time and money to travel." Nevertheless, she loves that she is still in close daily contact with her daughters and her grandchildren, a boy and a girl. "We adore those kids!" she says about the grandchildren, who have won her heart even though she wasn't quite ready for them.

Their Marriage and Yours

On the trail between stepping back and staying connected, a child's marriage can be an emotional turn in the road. Adding a new permanent partner into the family mix changes all its relationships—not just among parents, their grown-up kids, and a new son- or daughter-in-law, but also between adult siblings and brothers- and sisters-in-law as well. Once a married child has made the commitment to a beloved mate, it follows naturally for him or her to put that person first. When it comes to big decisions, plans, or handling hardships, even the most dutiful grown children, the ones who have been closely intertwined with their family of origin, will form their primary attachment to their mate. If they don't, watch out: Marital trouble may follow.

Parents are in the business of putting themselves out of a job when the time comes and knowing when to gracefully exit stage right. "Every mother must acknowledge that she'll no longer be the most important person in her son's or daughter's life after they marry," says California family therapist Leah Fisher, adding pensively, "All parents have to go through this, so they better have some dreams of their own."

At every life passage, grown children's choices also make parents revisit their own. The emotional buzz can be especially intense around the next generation's choice of a life partner, as young people's individuation and their mate selection stir up parents' own memories and feelings, for better or worse.

In the best-case scenario, happily married parents will be thrilled by the news of their grown kids' approaching marriage and wedding plans. If they feel close to their child's new mate, they will be joyful about expanding their family circle—and eager to increase it further if grandchildren come along. Pride, joy, relief, tenderness, excitement, validation, and hope mingle with the wedding toasts when parents are celebrating what they feel is a good match, and perhaps one that's been long awaited.

A choice that is mistaken, at least in parents' eyes, can be very upsetting. All sorts of marital prospects can push parents' buttons—a marriage that's too rushed or a relationship that's been on-again, off-again for years, a match with someone much older or younger or already divorced once, perhaps with kids, or someone who's not earning a living, or is having emotional problems, or from a different faith or background. Yes, you can share your feelings ahead of time, and once in a blue moon, you might change a grown child's mind. But more likely, the wedding will go on even without your blessings. So this is a time to weigh your comments carefully and do your best to build a bridge to your grown-up kid's new partner. Refrain from an *I told you so* if the union doesn't last, and let yourself be warmly surprised if the mate turns out to defy your low expectations and be a keeper.

For parents no longer living together a grown child's marriage can be a sensitive time. Ghosts of past hopes and broken promises mingle with

---

Q: *Our son is getting married in six months, and we've been wondering if it's appropriate for my wife and me to talk about marriage with him.*

A: It's not only appropriate—you should feel obligated to share your thoughts about marriage when your grown children head to the altar. If you've lived the experience and have wisdom to offer, it's important to share it. Your kids will make their own choices, and it's their decision to accept what you offer or not.

Consider talking points like these: "Your father and I always had a joint bank account (discuss pluses and minuses); what do you guys plan to do?" "I remember that there was a little tension between us before our wedding, but we worked it out this way and that. Are you two managing to do that?" "One of our secrets to a happy, lasting marriage is that we've learned to disagree and then move on; we don't hold grudges and we don't speak harshly to each other. How are the two of you at handling conflict?"

---

best wishes for a child's future—along with occasional personal regrets, especially if a parent remains unattached and lonely. Plus there's the tangle of relationships from first and later marriages to be accommodated at the wedding without creating pyrotechnics. Will semi-estranged Dad walk the bride down the aisle or will that honor fall to her stepfather, who's been a steadier presence? Where will Mom sit, and where Stepmom? And who will foot the bills? The goal should be to keep in mind that it's the young couple's day, not yours. It's a time to honor dreams for their loving and harmonious future; do your best to keep it free of the emotional baggage of the past.

Your Midlife Marriage Checkup

Although divorce rates are generally low once couples have been married for more than ten years, the launching-kids time of life can be a perilous crossroads in a long marriage as couples question their relationship, ask if they're truly happy, and review twenty years of issues they may have swept under the rug in the hurly-burly of child raising.

Freed from the daily demands of parenting, you begin to reflect on your own well-being and take the temperature of your marriage. You may be more haunted than ever before by your mortality, wondering, "Is this all there is?" and "Have I achieved all I want?" Sometimes one partner blames another for holding him or her back from fulfilling dreams, or longtime marrieds are tempted by another relationship to prove they're still desirable. In a long marriage, it's not uncommon for one or both people to get frustrated with decades-old habits and dream of more vibrant ways of being. Sometimes partners have drifted apart after too many years of inattention, too much time spent focusing on everything but each other: work, parenting, aging parents, financial pressures, home maintenance. In a lengthy marriage with many moving parts, there's always something that needs fixing.

"Do we renovate the old house or do we sell it and start again?" asks Clark University associate professor of clinical psychology James Cordova, author of *The Marriage Checkup*. Okay, a marriage isn't exactly like a house, he says, but nevertheless, be careful not to burn it down in the upheaval of this transition. It gets harder to start again later in life—the divorce rate for remarriage is 60 percent, not the least because of how tough it is to blend two separate families together.

One constructive way of coping: putting extra time and energy into your own marriage and sharing dreams for the next stage of your lives together. Although some marriages may flounder after kids depart, this relatively child-free time of life can also be a real period of renewal in a long marriage. Now marriages can become partner-focused instead of child-focused. "As our children [now 26 and 18] became more independent, we discovered we still get a kick out of each other," observed one mother among the 45 percent in our survey who called their empty-nested marriages "excellent." As people are living longer, they realize that the without-kids years may be more numerous than the with-kids years, and they want to tend their flame so that it's glowing till the end.

Because it's so easy to lose track of time together while absorbed in full-on parenting, Cordova suggests anticipating the transition before the kids leave home. Consider an annual marriage checkup for two or three years before kids depart for college, to bring attention to what's working well and what could be changed for the better. This can be as simple as a conversation over dinner out or while celebrating an anniversary. Are there habits you've fallen into that may not serve well after the kids are gone? Do both of you feel listened to and supported, or is there an imbalance or unspoken gripes between you? How can each of you nurture the other's growth as well as revitalize your time together?

Sometimes one partner may grow in a new direction that threatens the other person. One may want to train for a marathon (that Over-50 age category looks tempting), while the other is happy to stay home, nose in a good book. Or one wants to travel the world and the other hates the hassles of flying. Challenges may occur because each member of the couple will continue to grow and change, but comfortable compromises are possible. He works out, she reads, then they take a leisurely walk together. Or she travels with her BFFs, he fishes with his buddies, and they both plan a weekend getaway within driving distance. "The fabric of a long relationship is constructed of interdependence and independence," observes Cordova. Each partner needs to allow the other to grow as a person while taking the time to keep the bond between them strong.

Marie's 18-year-old daughter, for example, was head over heels about her first boyfriend and soon to leave home for college. Meanwhile, Marie woke up to notice that her own marriage was suffering from neglect. While she'd been lovingly tending her only child, her husband had grown more distant and discouraged. He'd gotten to the point where he didn't care anymore: "You want to do your thing," he'd say, "I'm going to do my thing." The chasm was growing so big between them that Marie started to fear divorce might follow.

But they pulled back from the brink, admitting their vulnerabilities to each other and focusing on their marriage again, talking and spending more time together: "Now he wants to be with me all the time! He even sold his dirt bike! We're communicating more now, and he realized, 'Wow, I really have been hard to talk to.' It's like a roller coaster, but we're working on it. I've told him, 'Listen, I'm going to give it one hundred percent, and if it doesn't work, at least I'll know I tried.'"

The result's been positive through the whole family: not a big surprise, but a pleasant one. At first, this couple didn't share their issues with their daughter, but after she sensed trouble brewing, they were honest with her, admitting they were having problems but were committed to working on them. Now things have improved all around: They're happier and their daughter is happier with them and with herself. With her parents taking care of their relationship, she's freer to live her own life without worrying about them.

The Wedding-Go-Round

Young people today may ponder the marriage question and delay answering it years longer than their parents did. But that expanded time of living in "the question" just builds up anticipation for the big day itself. When a wedding finally happens, it has turned into a bigger deal today than ever before. If movies are any reflection of what's on our minds as a society, consider the confetti storm of popular American films about weddings just since the new century began: *Wedding Crashers, The Wedding Planner, Margot at the Wedding, Rachel Getting Married, 27 Dresses, Bridesmaids, Bachelorette* . . . and more. This generation may be marrying less but they're buying tickets to watch other couples do it more.

What's up with that? For many couples who have waited till their late twenties or thirties, marriage equals achievement, and a wedding is an announcement to each other and the world that a long-postponed milestone has been reached. A large, fancy wedding has become a symbol of "having made it"—like having a flashy car or buying a first house—so no surprise that these ceremonies have become bigger, more lavish, and more expensive than ever.

Estimates for the average cost of an early twenty-first-century American wedding range from $18,000 to $40,000, depending on size, city, and season. *The Wall Street Journal* reporter Brett Arends crunched some extra numbers and concluded that the real cost of an $18,000 wedding was more like $90,000 to $200,000. That's how much a couple would end up keeping if they invested the same amount of money at 4 percent interest over four decades of marriage. Or they could use the same cash to buy a car, make a down payment on a house—or pay off their student loans. (Ironically, the average cost of a wedding and the average amount of student debt in 2012 are just about the same big number: $27,000).

Q: *My ex-husband and I haven't seen each other in years, and now we're both hosting and attending our daughter's wedding. Any advice to avoid fireworks?*

A: In divorced families, serve extra helpings of discretion with the wedding supper. Stay flexible about who walks the bride down the aisle— perhaps it will be her father, or her stepfather, or both mother and father with the bride as a buffer in between—or the wedding couple may choose to glide down the aisle together. At the reception, instead of having both parents seated awkwardly at the newlyweds' table, consider a separate, special table for each of you with your new partners, if any, and an array of appropriate guests. But keep this in mind: A grown child's wedding is probably not the best place for exes to introduce a brand-new significant other to the extended family. Keep the glowing spotlight on the blissful new pair.

"If [people] did the math, they'd probably get married in flip-flops," Arends wrote.

When many boomer parents married, it was not unheard of to get hitched barefoot on a beach with the vows ending, "As long as we both shall dig it." But barefoot or flip-flops these days? Not too likely.

Today weddings are a big business involving a retinue of expensive helpers: wedding planners and stylists, makeup artists and videographers. Some "destination weddings" last for days and cost guests a small fortune on travel and hotels (and families a larger fortune to keep these guests wined and dined once they arrive). Proposals are intricate, choreographed affairs—from hiring a mariachi band to serenade the intended to returning to the site of a first date, this time with major engagement bling in hand. In the months leading up to the big event, multiple showers and elaborately staged bachelor and bachelorette parties take place with guests often crisscrossing the country to attend just these warm-up parties. Las Vegas is a popular destination for brides-to-be and their entourage, with a male stripper revue a must for more bachelorette parties than you might believe.

The average number of attendants these days is ten—five bridesmaids and five groomsmen, according to the most recent annual survey by *Brides* magazine. But it's not unheard of for a bride to have more than ten women friends dancing attendance on her, accompanying her to "mani-pedis," having their hair coiffed and makeup done together before the wedding itself—and shelling out big bucks for the wear-once dresses and sky-high heels. Elizabeth's niece Sara estimates she had been to about twenty weddings and was a bridesmaid in six of them before becoming a bride herself at 33. Her closet, she notes wryly, is lined with jewel-toned silk dresses and matching shoes she'll never wear again. Her 30-year-old sister has been to about fifty weddings and was a bridesmaid in eight, and *her* closet is stuffed with dresses in unflattering shades of brown, the inexplicably hot color those years.

Something Paid for, Borrowed, or Blue

Devoted parents want a memorable wedding day for their beloved daughters and sons, and it's hard to go up against the Wedding-Industrial Complex that screams that grander and more expensive is better. But if your own family style has always been "less is more," encourage the new couple to do some soul-searching about what will make for the most meaningful day. One bride sent her guests home from her wedding with homemade chocolate chip cookies, a nod to the sweets she baked for her husband on their second date. Those sentimental treats were more eloquent than elaborate wedding favors.

Communicate early and tactfully with your grown kids about what you're willing and able to spend on the nuptials and discuss how costs may be shared. Some families still follow the old rules where the bride's family takes care of the main wedding costs, but there are a variety of alternatives these days as well. The bride's and groom's families may split the costs between them, or the new couple and the two families might divide the costs three ways. Or either set of parents might offer to cover particular expenses (flowers, photographer, a live band) or to contribute a set amount (from $2,000 to $10,000, for example). As young people are marrying later, more and more couples who have lived together and shared household expenses for years choose to plan and pay for their own weddings and receptions, with minimal family help. More power to them!

When parents are footing some or all of the wedding bill, it's natural to want some say in the planning, the guest list, and where and when the event will take place. But mothers of the brides, especially, remind yourselves that this time, the choices are not all yours, and gracefully acquiesce to the new couple's desires. Take on the tasks you're given or offer to do what you're most comfortable with—from booking hotel rooms for out-of-town guests to tracking down names of caterers, wedding cake bakers, or shoes that complement the bridesmaids' gowns.

With same-sex marriage now legal in a growing number of states, planning a wedding with two brides or two grooms is starting to be more commonplace. The set-in-stone etiquette for tying the same-sex knot has yet to be written (and maybe it never will be), but for now it seems as if most same-sex celebrations merge some of the old traditions with creative new ones. From gift registries to Pachelbel's Canon in D to personally written vows to cake toppers, many same-sex partners want to retain the familiar customs (while perhaps tweaking them a bit as well). Dress for the couple, for instance, may be more inventive than when

Mom and Dad walked down the aisle . . . both brides in gowns, or one in a gown and the other tuxedo-clad.

In many same-sex weddings, lifelong friends may fill the roles traditionally assigned to family (and a trusted friend may officiate as well, thus sidestepping the need to find a willing clergyperson). These new traditions recognize the important relationships LGBTQ folks form as they come out and establish their gay identities, as *Complete Gay and Lesbian Manners* author Steven Petrow points out. Since same-sex couples typically marry later than their heterosexual counterparts, they're also more likely to be financially established and able to take care of the wedding costs themselves. That means, parents, you'll be welcomed guests and may be invited to stand with the couple for the ceremony, but don't expect to orchestrate the event. If you're given a say about the guest list, make sure it favors your friends who love and support the newlyweds. If Great-aunt Mildred might harangue against same-sex marriage at the wedding party, respectfully leave her name off the list.

All those turn-of-the-millennium movies about weddings with all their raucous humor, mix-ups, and pratfalls give us permission to acknowledge something basic about getting married: Few things stir up anxiety like weddings. It's true for the wedding couple, for their families, and for the friends watching from outside. During the instructive time Elizabeth's niece Sara put in as a bridesmaid before becoming a bride, she once participated in a friend's wedding in the grand garden of the parents' summer home. As she read her assigned verses, her high heels sank deeper and deeper into the wet ground, and she struggled to keep her game face on. "Carrying on while sinking was kind of a metaphor for the whole experience," she says. Sometimes amid the joyful tears for her just-wedded friends trickled a few sad ones that her own prince had not yet come. But her wedding, when it happened, was all the sweeter for the waiting. And the ceremony was lovely, warm, and just a little understated, as if she'd learned from her years of bridesmaiding and wedding-guesting that public hoopla doesn't make a couple any more married or provide a better guarantee that they'll live happily ever after.

9

For Hire

I give advice about jobs if I'm asked, but
I haven't been asked in three or more years.

MOTHER OF SON, 23

When Jeremy graduated from a midwestern liberal arts college in 2008 with a degree in English and a minor in theater, he was full of optimism about his prospects, bursting with creativity and confidence. He was a solid student, a good writer, resourceful, and well spoken. During his first six months after graduation, he sent out hundreds of résumés. He was met with the same response that's greeting too many emerging adults of his generation: silence.

But he was not one to take no, even hundreds of them, for an answer. He'd been brought up to believe he could be or do anything he put his mind to, and he refused to give up. He decided to take advantage of Craigslist, the online networking site that had helped dozens of his friends set up their lives—find apartments, roommates, odd jobs, and used couches. Desperate times call for desperate measures, or at least some bold thinking outside the box, so he posted this notice: "Won't someone give me a goddamn job?" it read.

Someone in cyberspace admired his moxie, needed his skill set, and hired him. Today he's employed at an interactive Web development company—not his dream job, nor one he'll stick with too long, but it's something. It pays the bills and gives him a toehold on the digital frontier, where so much innovation takes place these days. Meanwhile, he wants to develop his voice as a writer and sees journalism as a longer-range career goal. So on the side, he's starting to publish in a local newspaper and racking up the first of those ten thousand hours that Florida State University psychology professor K. Anders Ericsson says are the training ground for achievement. Ericsson's twenty-five years of research found that steady practice—twenty hours a week for ten years or forty hours for five years or some variation—is, even more than talent, the route to success in many fields.

A word to the wise for parents to pass along to their grown-up kids: If they want to roar out of the starting gate and make their mark overnight, remind them that steady, tortoiselike perseverance rather than a hare's fast dash often gets the better, more lasting results. Persistence, practice, and an in-it-for-the-long-haul attitude might mean writing for a bunch of local publications, as Jeremy is doing, even if the work is low-paying or unpaid at the start. But it gives him a chance to hone his voice, skills, and contacts to lead him to his next break. Other emerging adults could be building up the ten thousand hours in a graduate program in a chosen field. Or volunteering after-work hours for a political campaign and learning from the grassroots up. Or apprenticing to a master electrician to study the trade. During these many training experiences, young people get to learn from both their successes and mistakes, receive important feedback, and perhaps find the mentorship that will help them build a lifelong career.

"He's always plotting," says Jeremy's father, about Jeremy's strategic employment tactics. He's proud that his son is purposeful and on a path. This skill of "planful competence," as psychologist John Clausen calls it, is one of the golden tickets to succeeding in the workplace for today's emerging adults.

For Hire . . . But When, Where, and How?

As Jeremy's story illustrates, the nature of work is fast-tracking in new directions for this generation of 20-somethings, and so is the way they're finding jobs. As we have noted earlier, the economy and the kinds of jobs that are available have shifted dramatically in the past fifty or sixty years. In the manufacturing-based economy of the 1950s and '60s, there were abundant, well-paying jobs in industries like automobiles and steel, available even to those with only a high school degree (or less). But the more complicated, globally connected twenty-first-century economy, which is information-, technology-, and service-based, demands more sophisticated skills and thinking. Most high-paying jobs now require a bachelor's degree or more, and many of today's jobs pay less than the manufacturing jobs of previous years.

From the early 1970s to the late 1990s, inflation-adjusted incomes rose slightly for college graduates or those with even higher degrees, but fell in all groups with less education. Overall, from 1973 to 1997, the average earnings for a full-time male worker under age 25 declined by almost one-third, adjusted for inflation.

Today's emerging adults take most of their twenties to find a long-term job, but their prospects here, too, depend a lot on how much education they have. According to U.S. Census data, it takes college grads four years to find a job they will keep for five years or more; for high school grads, finding that five-years-or-more job takes six years, and for high school dropouts it takes *seventeen* years.

Some young people, like Jeremy, may proceed with a well-considered plan. Others meander or drift into McJobs that provide no satisfaction beyond a paycheck. Still others seem to lack any plan at all and are clueless about how to get started. They may not know how to create a résumé or make contacts that might lead to jobs. They may feel overwhelmed (or apathetic) about taking the initiative to begin job hunting at all. Particularly when grown kids are living at home and you're still paying their bills, it can get old quickly to arrive home from a long day at your own job and see your 20-somethings doing . . . not much.

While we always advise balancing offers of help with making room for your job hunters to find their own way, some young people do need a firmer helping hand than others, particularly when they're looking for their first "real" jobs. You may need to make it a prerequisite to moving home that your child devote herself to job hunting as if it were a job. Show her what you know about résumé writing. Offer her a few contacts to call for job openings or informational conversations. And teach her some essential job interviewing skills, like being on time, researching the company before the interview to show what she can contribute, and following up with a thank-you note (or at least a polite, well-written email) reaffirming her interest in the position.

Once grown-up kids land their first jobs, the reality of the daily nine-to-five (or much later in some fields) may be a rude awakening: needing to show up on time, getting out of bed and going in when they've been out late the night before or have a sore throat, cooperating with difficult colleagues, having only two weeks' vacation per year (if they're lucky). And in some high-pressure starter jobs in finance, consulting, law, medicine, or politics, the digital connection may become a cyber ball and chain as bosses email young hires at any hour (including weekends) to get a job done. "Doesn't anyone believe in taking a break and recharging around here?" moaned one just-hired worker in a nose-to-the-grindstone office. Overnight, it seemed, the gentler pace of college life—classes two hours a day and gobs of free time—was over.

> I don't like to admit this, but my son thinks online poker is all the job he needs until he wins enough to start his own business.
>
> **SINGLE MOTHER OF SON, 28**

Besides the embattled feeling of some young worker bees, there are others who have a sense of entitlement that may read to employers and coworkers as "too big for their britches." These are the 20-somethings whose parents told them they were special since they brought home their first preschool finger painting. Now they're filled with such high expectations that they wonder why they're not directing the company at 23. "Entry-level" is not part of their vocabulary. Sometimes a little reality-testing from parents may be necessary here, as in, "Even if you're asked to do tasks that you feel are beneath you, do them well and without complaint; they may enable you to move up the ladder later on."

What's even more typical among new hires, though, is a mix of confidence and insecurity. One day, a self-assured young staff member will be "overtalking the boss," as one employer remarked about a brash, new 22-year-old employee; the next day the same guy will be hurt because one of his ideas was shot down. It's okay: Experience brings perspective and a more grounded self-assurance.

With the slower track to marriage and parenthood, young people have more years to try out various possibilities in school and work and a greater chance of zeroing in on an occupational direction that will fit their interests and abilities. Just as they hope to find their soul mate, they also hope to find their dream job, and their quest may involve both exploration and instability. The average young person holds seven different jobs during the decade of the twenties; one out of four has more than ten.

Be prepared for some unexpected U-turns here: The daughter who completes a teacher training program at 23 and is in the classroom for a few years may wake up to find it's not a good fit after all; at 26, she may decide to retrain for a different career altogether. Yes, these about-faces can be frustrating and disappointing for all concerned, particularly if large amounts of time and money were spent getting established. But "career overboard" is not an unusual scenario during the twenties. Sometimes it takes the experience of a poor fit to know when the right match comes along. Without a family to support, grown-up kids are in a better position to take a chance on something new than they will be later on.

What's come to be called the "quarterlife crisis" is mainly provoked by this instability and uncertainty about work; it's actually an identity crisis. Asking, "What kind of work do I really want to do?" is another way of asking, "Who am I?" And these days, answering that question can take most of the twenties-decade.

In the United States, where there's little support for making the school-to-work transition and few programs that offer information and guidance (besides colleges' mostly underwhelming career counseling), this crisis seems to be especially common. Unlike European students, who start to specialize at a younger age, well-educated American graduates seem to have almost unlimited options for their futures. (In theory, that is, unless they're job hunting in a challenging economy.) Some scholars, like Swarthmore professor of psychology Barry Schwartz, feel that the American system results in too many choices, a "tyranny of freedom" that leaves emerging adults confused and insecure about what comes next. A range of alternatives for their futures is welcome, but too many can become overwhelming. As Kafka once wrote, "There are many possibilities before me, but under what rock do they live?" For today's emerging adults, these words are still apt.

A 2004 study by Schwartz, Sheena Iyengar, and Rachel Elwork found that as the number of job possibilities available to college graduates goes up, applicants' satisfaction with the job search process goes down. This is particularly true for job seekers who want to get the "best possible" job. While young people in this group receive more and better job offers

---

Q: *Our 22-year-old son graduated from college with no job in sight. Then he took the summer off to decompress, and now summer's become fall, and he's still partying late most nights, sleeping through half the day, and hardly getting up off the couch. My wife and I are tearing out our hair! What can we do to motivate him toward gainful employment?*

A: It's surely time for some straight talk with your son. Let him know your expectations of him—and your belief that he has what it takes to be self-supporting. Job hunting can be scary, so put the emphasis on the process, not the final offer, suggests New York City career counselor Marianne Ruggiero. Tell your son, "As long as you're being accountable for your time, not just watching TV and playing video games, it's fine with us." Help him set reasonable goals: Make five calls a week, do informational interviews with two people, and become a miniexpert in his field of interest. "Kids learn critical thinking and research skills at college," says Ruggiero. "They shouldn't leave them on campus, but use them to find out about industries, companies, and job functions."

Encourage your son to build skills even if he's not on a payroll: say, two days volunteering for your state senator combined with three days waiting tables. Sometimes short-term jobs through a temp agency can lead to something permanent or at least help a confused young person explore a possible career.

than those who are aiming for "good enough" jobs, they also tend to be less satisfied with their career decisions than their less demanding counterparts. They are also more anxious, pessimistic, disappointed, frustrated, and depressed. What's the antidote? Suggests Schwartz: Learn to be satisfied with "good enough" instead of always seeking the best, and practice being grateful for what's good in choices made rather than regretful about what's disappointing.

Patience, Patience

Expensive college tuitions may create a parental expectation of a return on an investment—good-salaried first jobs for their graduates that will help repay college loans, fund graduate school, or contribute to the lease on a first apartment. But the work lives today of many young people are a very different reality. For years they may be cobbling together a series of part-time, short-lived, or temp jobs that barely pay the rent, don't offer benefits, and may not be in their chosen field nor leading down any promising career path at all. Even in a strong economy, emerging adults generally experience twice the unemployment rate of older workers, and in a down economy, that's a double-digit number.

Parents may be understandably concerned as they eagerly, anxiously await their sons' and daughters' emergence into life-work that will also be life-supporting. This mother of a 24-year-old college grad expresses the widely held ambivalence of many parents of the underemployed. She reflects on her daughter's work life in the worthy but underpaid non-profit sector:

> She patches together an "almost full-time" job status with part-time jobs. No benefits, which is one of my concerns—and also one of the realities of today's workplace. She is finding creative ways to adjust her lifestyle to her part-time jobs' income. Part of me is impressed, part of me is uneasy with the "fluid" nature of things, because it isn't quite what the adult threshold was like for us thirty-some years ago.

Patience is the invaluable currency of this life-stage, for grown kids as well as their parents, especially when hiring is constricted, say many college career counselors we interviewed. "Parents need to calm down their expectations," advises Don Kjelleren, the Director of Career Services at Middlebury College in Vermont. "Seniors may not have a dream job either by the time they graduate or on any predictable time-line. But taking time to figure out what they want to do gives them more of a chance to explore their options, discover unforeseen possibilities, and have less regret for rash decisons later on." That's the silver lining, however difficult to accept, of a more drawn-out job search.

Q: *My son graduated from a good college with a degree in economics and has spent six months looking for a job in his field to no avail. His dad and I are getting increasingly anxious about his prospects. Is there anything you can say to get us to relax a little?*

A: First, keep in mind that the path to a solid first job is littered with false starts and turnarounds, interviews that bomb, and ones that seem just great . . . until the phone turns silent afterward. If you can afford to help support him, encourage your son to volunteer or take an internship in his field, something that might lead to a paid position later on. Also let him know if and when you can't continue to support him so he can look for a job to get by on until something comes along that's more appropriate to his academic preparation. Meanwhile, manage your anxiety by talking privately with your spouse or friends with grown-up kids who are probably feeling just as stressed as you are. But stay positive for your son and don't add your uncertainties to his.

Your Midlife Career, Take Two

While your 20-something is dedicated to searching for a first job, you may be coping with your own work/life concerns and questions. At an age when many people imagined they'd be firmly settled in a career, or on the downslope toward retirement, some parents at 40, 50, even 60 may be riding out their own period of instability that intersects with their grown kids'. It's not uncommon for a parent and an emerging adult to be job hunting at the same time, the young person for a starter job, the parent for another position in a long career, after being downsized. As one 60-something, single mother remarked after being unemployed for more than a year, "I need a job so I have something to retire *from*."

To recoup the losses of the economic recession and to fund their longer lives, both employed and unemployed parents are learning to see their work lives extending into an unknowable future. In 2000, only 13 percent of American workers were 55 and older, but that number is expected to rise to 25 percent by 2020, according to a 2012 analysis by the Bureau of Labor Statistics. The size of the boomer cohort itself contributes to creating this bubble, but other trends also have their influence: longer, healthier life spans; the elimination of mandatory retirement and the enactment of age discrimination laws; increases in health care costs and a decrease in the availability of health benefits; and changes in the Social Security laws. All told, it's no longer your parents' gold-watch retirement at 65.

But working longer is preferable to not having a good job at all. "I am transitioning between careers," says one mom in our sample, and another remarks that she would like regular employment again, "rather than consulting/freelancing for the past two years." Unemployment, underemployment, working part-time instead of finding a full-time position with good benefits, or being stuck in a job that's no longer the right fit—these pressures on midcareer workers parallel the ones plaguing their job-hunting kids. Yes, it may be a bonding moment to share these career ups and downs, and it might help parents be more sympathetic to their grown children's first forays into the work world. But it may also make parents more impatient with their kids' inflated expectations or reluctance to stick with a less-than-ideal job. And the older generation's job insecurities can also compound a family's financial anxieties. When Mom or Dad doesn't have a stable paycheck coming in, it's tough to subsidize an out-of-work kid.

Midlife can also be a time for reflection on work choices made earlier and a reevaluation that leads to making a change. You may make a lateral move within a long-standing field, or reinvent yourself with an "encore career." Often retirement becomes rewirement as working lives extend; there's more time than ever before for reinvention. When that Hallelujah moment arrives and your emerging adults are finally self-supporting, and their mountainous college tuition bills have been paid (or the loans assumed by them), you may feel liberated to pursue a long-deferred dream of your own. The architect who opens a cupcake company, the stockbroker who becomes a classroom teacher, the teacher who takes over a bed-and-breakfast—many parents we interviewed were embarking on their second acts just as their grown-up kids were raising the curtain on their first acts.

There are some notable differences between younger and older workers in the job market. The rate of unemployment is lower among workers 55 and up than for their 20-somethings, the U.S. Bureau of Labor Statistics reports, but when older people do become unemployed, they spend more time searching for work than younger workers do. However, older workers have a lot more job stability than people in their twenties and don't switch jobs nearly so often. For example, the median years on their current job of workers ages 55 to 64 is ten years, compared to three years for workers ages 25 to 34.

But don't fear that your decision to work longer will stand in the way of your grown kids' getting hired or moving up. Economists, like University of Colorado professor Jeffrey Zaks, dispel this widely held belief. "Work comes from the ability to do something useful, and there is no fixed limit on how many useful things can be done," explains Zaks. "History shows we are always thinking of new things to do that are useful." A 2012 Pew Research study from the Economic Mobility Project concludes that a rising economic tide raises all boats, boosting the hiring of older workers as well as young. And just because an older worker might vacate a desk in a big company doesn't mean the position will be filled by a young worker. Young and old have different skill sets and experience, so that young people can't just step into a vacated job that had been held by someone who's been plying the trade for decades.

A flexible, adaptive approach to your own work life can send a message to your grown kids that a career is long and varied, full of both rewards and disappointments. If a first job or first choice of vocation turns out to be a dead end, it's not irreparable. Reinvention and redirection are also possible. That's a message of hope your emerging adult may need to hear.

Despite midlife job losses, stumbles, and retrenchments, overall job satisfaction is higher in middle adulthood than in any other life stage.

Like a couple who model a good marriage (complete with rocky patches), parents who are satisfied with their jobs (despite setbacks) are good role models for their grown children trying to get established. Parents who are unhappy in their work and feel like they're stuck with it have a message to send that can be just as valuable to their emerging adults, about how to avoid that fate and how to survive in a less-than-ideal job. Parents can be open about getting along with difficult bosses or coworkers or rebounding from criticism. If your grown kids are receptive, share your strategies for coping with common workplace strains or moving forward in a competitive environment without creating enemies.

Occasionally, a young person just starting out who sees parents at the peak of their game may suffer by comparison. Are those shoes too big to fill? One mother, a successful intellectual property lawyer, describes how her 25-year-old son has floundered, going from job to job without finding the perfect match. Now he's pointing the finger of blame at his parents: "Our son says it's our fault that he doesn't like his work and has too high expectations for it. He's romanticized work, as he thinks we've found the perfect jobs. My dad liked what he did—accountant. But his attitude was, 'That's why it's called work. Pick something and do it!'"

In just three years her son has picked up—and discarded—two jobs and is settling into a third. The verdict on that choice is not yet in, but his mother takes the long view. She's not sure this choice will be the sticky one either, but though she has moments of impatience, she has also come to accept the necessary zigzagging of her son's career search.

The Dream of Meaningful Work

Meaningful work? The boomers invented the concept, and now their children have grown up to expect it as their birthright. However, this dream was always optimistic, and a decade of economic stagnation has made it an even more elusive goal to achieve. Especially in a tight economy, and entering it at the bottom of the ladder, today's first-time job seekers find fewer jobs of any kind are available. When faced with a long stretch of unemployment, a young person may be tempted to take anything that will cover the rent and expenses. Still, this generation, particularly the college-educated portion of it, holds on to dreams for work that makes a difference to them and to society. Many want to find a job that's an expression of their identity, even as this identity may be constantly shape-shifting. They hope for a decent paycheck—and a fat one would be fine—but most also want work that's creative, uses their talents, and helps others. In the 2012 Clark University poll, for example, 86 percent of Americans ages 18 to 29 said it was important to them to have a career that does some good in the world. A full 80 percent said enjoying their job was more important that making a lot of money. But reality bites: 61 percent said they had not been able to find the kind of job they really want.

Researchers at Harvard's Project Zero, Howard Gardner, Mihaly Csikszentmihalyi, and William Damon, have been discussing work goals

---

Q: *Our daughter is our only child, and we've always hoped she would go into a worthy, well-paying (and, OK, prestigious) career like law or medicine. Instead, she's determined to spend her twenties seeing if she can make it as an actress. To us, this seems like a recipe for disaster. Is there anything we can say to change her plans?*

A: All parents have dreams for their children, but now's the time to give your daughter the freedom to follow her own. As one mother phrased it about her 20-something's job searches, "She has to find what lights her fires, not what lights mine." Even if your daughter's dream of becoming an actress seems grandiose or improbable, it's best to stand aside while she tests it out and sees where it leads her. Encourage her to take small steps to fulfill a big dream. If you're still paying her bills while she's waiting for her big break, it's legit for you to set a limit on how long your support will last. Then it's up to her to decide if she wants her name in lights badly enough to take on a day job to support herself while going to auditions and taking unpaid roles to get exposure. Do your best to be supportive and keep your second-guesses to yourself. You want to be the parent thanked at the Academy Awards for having had faith in her, not the one who stood in the way of her trying out her dreams.

---

with young people for the past fifteen years in an effort to understand what they think constitutes an optimal job. In their book, *Good Work,* they define these worthy jobs as "excellent in quality, socially responsible, and enjoyable," rather than solely focused on the bottom line. Even if landing any job at all is a challenge for young people today, emerging adults will still benefit from asking themselves questions about the quality and contribution of the jobs they take on—for instance: What kind of work would make the best use of my talents and interests? How much would I be willing to give up, in standard of living, in order to do something I really want to do? What are the societal consequences of the work I want to do? Will I be able to balance this job with having children and taking care of a family?

This 26-year-old artist is representative of many of her generation as she puzzles out the equation between her economic needs and staying true to her dreams:

> *A large percentage of my college-educated generation is not willing to settle for a career that sits them at a desk all week, despite the lure of comforts like health insurance and a 401(k). I sleep in a lightless box so that I can afford to experiment with my sources of income. At this time in my life I would rather struggle financially in order to carve out an ideal, authentic profession than fill an eight-hour workday to earn the money to afford a one-bedroom apartment.*

The Lure of Community Service at Home and Abroad

In their search for good work, more young people than ever are looking for first jobs in community service programs like Teach for America, AmeriCorps, and the Peace Corps. Graduates are signing up for these programs in record numbers, finding satisfaction in service while also gaining invaluable experience and fringe benefits. Peace Corps volunteers become fluent in the language of their host country and gain helpful cross-cultural skills. Over 90 percent of them say afterward that they would make the same decision to serve if they had it to do over again. Research shows that AmeriCorps volunteers experience a wide range of benefits, from better analytical problem solving to enhanced information technology skills. Teach for America volunteers not only get two years of fast-track training to become teachers but often use the organization's excellent reputation and network of contacts as an entry ticket to a wide variety of careers afterward.

It doesn't hurt that these programs pay a livable wage, do good for society, and in the case of Teach for America, cover the costs of a master's in education. All three programs also offer postponement of qualified student loans, and the Peace Corps offers partial cancellation of certain Federal loans after a year or more of service.

Increasingly, emerging adults are drawn to service opportunities outside the borders of the United States. Pollster John Zogby calls the millennial generation the "First Globals," international citizens whose "planet is their playing field." His polling research shows that today's emerging adults see their lives as public, interconnected, and continent-spanning in ways that were unimagined before the Internet, cheap travel, and surging study abroad programs. Coming of age in an increasingly multicultural world, they're drawn to global music, sports, fashion, and social service. Almost a quarter of the 18- to 29-year-olds Zogby polled expect to work abroad. For many of them, one part of their consciousness as citizens of the world is the desire to devote time to an international service organization. This experience serves the dual purpose of allowing them to express their ideals of helping others in need while also preparing them well for the international occupation they seek to have someday. And, of course, there's also the adventure of it.

Is there a role for parents in guiding these international explorations? It's useful to make a distinction between different kinds of service and destinations. There are many countries where young people will be safer, statistically, than they would be in most of the United States. This is true for every country in Europe, as well as for Australia and New Zealand. It's also true for some developing countries. In China, for example, a popular destination for postcollege grads to teach English for a year, crime rates are extremely low.

In other developing countries, risks are a much greater concern. Most countries in Central and South America have crime rates that are relatively high, especially in urban areas. Young Americans who are accustomed to going where they like, by themselves, any time of day or night, may be vulnerable if they don't adjust their behavior to take into account their new surroundings. Young women are especially at risk. In many developing countries an unaccompanied young woman is rare among the locals, so she stands out, especially if her hair and clothes are in a style that is obviously "not from around here." In countries where the custom is that a woman is always accompanied by a man in public, a lone woman may be viewed as fair game for sexual harassment.

In other countries, especially in Africa, disease is a greater threat than crime or harassment. Many sub-Saharan African countries have high rates of diseases such as malaria and tuberculosis that are rarely or never seen anymore in developed countries. Fortunately, vaccinations for most of these diseases are readily available in Western countries, and medications can be taken to protect against malaria.

Parents can play a crucial role in preparing young people for a year or two abroad by encouraging them to learn all they can about the risks most relevant in their destination country. Young people may shrug off the risks, because they are so used to living a comfortable and protected life that they assume nothing bad will happen to them. The twenties are the healthiest decade of life, in terms of susceptibility to illness and disease, and they may well feel so healthy and vigorous that they deem themselves invulnerable to anything that may come their way, wherever they may go.

If emerging adults seem casual about investigating and preparing for risks, parents can, and should, do the research themselves and share it with their children: The crime rate in the capital city is X times the crime rate in your hometown; the most common diseases in the country you are going to are as follows . . . Make sure that they see a physician knowledgeable about international travel and get the necessary inoculations (and do it well ahead of the departure date, as sometimes a series of shots is needed). You may be met with resistance, but at least you'll know you've done what you could to help enhance awareness of the risks and increase protection and safety.

Even if you have researched the destination carefully, seeing your child leave for a year in a foreign country may inspire anxiety, because so much remains unknown and potentially perilous. But the twenties are the prime time for having an adventure and making a contribution to the world, so be proud of the choice your grown-up kid is making.

Although young people today are often scorned for their reputed self-ishness, their zeal to serve others around the world is unprecedented and casts them in quite a different light. Call them the Generous Generation, a group more likely than their parents or grandparents to see the problems of people in far-flung parts of the world as their problems, too, and endeavor to do something about them.

Getting a Foot in the Door: Internships

Internships have become a common stepping-stone in the job-hunting quest of emerging adults, and, some might say, a necessary evil. Internships may be unpaid or low-paid (usually a small stipend or minimum wage), but they're a way to gain real-world work experience during (or instead of) college, the summers, or after graduation. They've become more important than ever in a competitive job market, where having experience in a field of choice gives a first-time job applicant an extra edge. Indeed, in a difficult economy, there's competition even for unpaid internships because they're seen as a gateway to future paid work.

Toni Littlestone, a career counselor in California, has helped numerous young people find their bliss. Like many others in her profession, she believes that an unpaid internship in a field of interest is a better choice than a paying but dead-end job. "When young people have a variety of experiences, it's like money in the bank," she points out. "If they have the wherewithal [to support themselves in other ways], those early internships will get them a job for the next ten years." As a case in point, she cites a young client who was weighing a minimum-wage, burger-flipping job offer from McDonald's against an unpaid internship at an environmental agency. He took the internship, and six months later, he got a job at the Trust for the Public Land and was well launched doing good work as an environmentalist in a career he loved.

On the plus side, internships provide a foot in the door, an opportunity to observe a field and try it on for size. When it's a good match, an internship offers a route to gain experience, build a résumé, make

contacts, and ideally parlay the newly gained skills and a glowing recommendation into a full-fledged career. Internships can rule out a profession as well, as a summer intern at a law firm finds out she doesn't
like the minutiae (or confrontations) involved in legal cases or a restaurant intern realizes that he can't stand the heat and the relentless pace.
During a short-term internship, these lessons can be learned without
too much time or money expended, and with the chance to find a better
match next time out.

On the minus side, interns are the lowest figures on an office's totem
pole and are often assigned the tasks no one else wants. These duties can
be repetitive, boring grunt work that really should be compensated, at
least at minimum wage. It has become almost too easy for companies or
nonprofits to take advantage of young interns eager to make an impres-
sion and snag a much-needed recommendation. Critics call internships,
at their worst, indentured servitude and another distinction between the
job-seeking haves and have-nots. The haves can take these poorly paid
or unpaid apprenticeships and still rely on parents' support to sustain or
supplement them; the have-nots, without that crucial parental financial
backing, are forced to take starter jobs that pay, but not very well, and
that may not lead into a field of real, sustaining potential. That said, if
parents are able to offer any financial support to supplement an internship, their initial backing can be a wise investment in an emerging adult's
future career success: A good internship leads to contacts, and some even
lead to real employment.

For young people who can't afford to take an unpaid internship, if
they're in college they might consider getting a work-study job or taking a course that gives credit for doing an outside internship. Either one
could lead to a future job in a promising career. Another possibility is
volunteering a few hours or evenings a week for an organization that
needs help and might offer contacts or leads later on, whether a political
campaign, a health clinic, or an arts program. There are also programs,
like Year Up, especially targeted to give employment opportunities to
young people who don't have family resources and connections and may
not attend college at all. For more on this topic, read our portrait of Otis
later in this chapter (page 204).

Flying Solo

What seems to be history for today's emerging adults is the single, lifelong career track with one steady job and decades of dependable benefits that winds up with a shiny gold watch and a comfy pension. The security (but monotony) of one lifetime employer has been replaced by a more freestyle pattern for today's young job seekers: frequent job changes coupled with stints of unemployment and a medley of careers rather than a singular, uninterrupted occupational path. For many in this generation, it's a "gig economy," in the phrase of Daily Beast founder Tina Brown. In 2012, according to Gallup, more than a third of young people between 18 and 29 were either unemployed or underemployed, and instead of full-time jobs with decent benefits, many of them were living "gig to gig"—that is, making do with part-time work, juggling several short-term assignments at once, freelancing, or starting their own business. What's attractive about such project-based work is its independence, creativity, and mobility; what's risky is the lack of security and benefits. And it's not just in America where gigs have replaced jobs. According to Elance, a site that helps freelancers find their next assignment, gig-to-gig work has increased more than 100 percent in countries with high youth unemployment like Greece, Spain, and Egypt.

This ambitious, 27-year-old young man we interviewed describes a patchwork of starter jobs as he struggles to make it (and make ends meet) in New York City:

> I have three careers: performer, writer, and fitness trainer. I go to auditions and moonlight as an actor when I get a part. I daylight as a fitness trainer with sixteen clients in a lovely "bougie" club with skylights and glass tiles. And I'm trying to sell my book of essays about my generation of "You can be anything you put your mind to" Americans. If we don't make it to president, we'll feel like we've failed. So let's own that we'll be failures and have fun!

His juggling act illustrates the gig economy at work: Perhaps one of his three part-time jobs will eventually expand to support him full-time. But more likely, he'll be doing his balancing act for a while.

The entrepreneurial urge is particularly strong in this generation of emerging adults. A common dream is owning a small business, and the Internet has made it easier than ever to establish a dot-com with little more than a business card, a list of contacts, and a vision. Cafés from Berkeley to Brooklyn are filled with entrepreneurs who can't afford an office but set up shop with their laptops and their ambition. Some might be forced entrepreneurs who've come up empty-handed in the full-time job search and decide to hang out their own shingle as a tutor or freelance editor, a web designer, caterer, or consultant for organizing homes and offices. They can easily shift if something more lucrative and steady comes along.

Others are entrepreneurs by choice, unfurling their own dream before even looking for a "real" job and building an infrastructure they hope is sustainable. Among the most fortunate are the 20-somethings who graduated into a shaky economy and still managed to leverage their initiative, talents, good ideas, contacts, and networking skills into start-ups that have weathered their initial three-year incubation period. In our interviews, parents mentioned an impressive range of entrepreneurial projects that this generation is capable of: a New York City taco shop (Dos Toros Tacqueria); an artistic, online invitation service (Paperless Post); an online clothing company for made-to-measure clothes (Bonobos); an online video production studio (Portal A); a company that offers off-the-beaten-path travel adventures (Vayable); and several tutoring businesses (A-List and others).

But a heads-up to parents: If your grown-up kid decides to start his own business, keep your expectations reasonable. It's the rare emerging adult who launches Facebook from his dorm room. Most young entrepreneurs or self-employed creative types will struggle to keep above water. The reality of owning a small business or launching a start-up is often harsh, because many small businesses fail in the first few years, and the ones that succeed often require long hours and relentless attention from the owners. Nevertheless, for some emerging adults, entrepreneurship is an attractive dream that seems to hold the promise of independence and self-sufficiency, of being their own boss and being in control of their fate. It also holds an identity allure, because they can choose as their business area something that reflects their sense of themselves—like a bright student starting a tutoring firm or an artsy social butterfly creating a company that provides decorative invitations online.

Some young entrepreneurs will be able to call on Mom's and Dad's support and contacts at some point in the start-up phase. Sharing an email list of friends or introducing young people to acquaintances who've run a successful small business are no-cost ways that parents can help. Beyond that, willing and financially able parents can contribute some initial funding to a promising project, either as a gift or a loan, or they can help young people make connections to other possible funders.

For those who can't tap the Bank of Mom and Dad, online crowd-funding networks are another contemporary way for young people to approach the wider community for financial support. Kickstarter, the largest of these as of this writing, has funded tens of thousands of projects since its inception in 2009, anything from a cool, new tech product to a winebar to an art, music, film, or design project. The way it works: Entrepreneurs describe their project on the website as well as what amount of funding they seek. Anyone—parents, friends, or strangers—can contribute at any rate; their reward is the product when it's launched, free tickets to an event, a T-shirt—or just knowing they've helped hatch a young person's dream. If the designated amount is reached or surpassed, it's the young mogul's to keep—minus a small percentage to Kickstarter and their credit card service. By 2012, 2.8 million people had pledged $368 million to jumpstart hundreds of dream projects and gone a long way to leveling the playing field for start-up entrepreneurs.

How Parents Can Help (and When to Step Aside)

Parents can provide a variety of resources to their job-hunting kids, as long as their contacts or advice are welcome. Observing the balance between stepping back and staying connected is as important when emerging adults are launching their work lives as when they're exploring their love lives. Based on our interviews with career counselors who specialize in working with young people, here are suggestions for how best to support (but not overwhelm) and guide (but not micromanage) an emerging adult's quest for a job:

Remember: It's their job search, not yours. Just as some parents of high school seniors talk about the application process as *"We're* applying to college," it may be tempting to think about a son's or daughter's first job hunt as *"We're* looking for a job." But an emerging adult who's ready for a job is also ready to search for one. Many recognize that their inexperience in job seeking is a disadvantage and will appreciate some assistance, but parents need to be careful that their well-intentioned help doesn't send the message that grown kids can't take care of business themselves. Beware the temptation to be what Middlebury's Kjelleren calls "snowplow" parents, who storm into the college career center clearing the road ahead for their kids. This practice is not empowering.

Be supportive even if children's career decisions don't jibe with your own. One emerging adult might accept a first job at a struggling start-up that a parent would never consider, or another kid might pass up a position with benefits and a pension that sounds fabulously secure to Mom and Dad. But young people need to make their own choices launching their work lives as well as learn from their own on-the-job mistakes.

In Jeff's original study of how emerging adults make career choices, parents emerged as figures of work inspiration less often than you might expect. In response to the question, "Did your parents' occupations influence your own choice of occupation?" emerging adults were about twice as likely to answer "no" as "yes." Some of the "no" responses were so insistent—"The last thing in the world I'd want to do"—that their vehemence suggested they saw their parents' work making them miserable and

> When my kids ask me about balancing work and family, I say, you don't necessarily need to follow my pattern. I left work as a psychology professor when they were in elementary school to be with them. But I'll be a feminist grandmother and help to the degree they want. Our society still doesn't support caring and working.
>
> MOTHER OF DAUGHTERS, 22 AND 18

leaving them unfulfilled. For many grown children, observing their parents' work struggles provided an extra incentive to find work of their own that is meaningful and enjoyable.

Offer a menu of possible choices of help—and let young people pick what works best. Some young job hunters value parental expertise—after all, parents are often the same generation as future employers and know how they think (e.g., no to flip-flops for interviews, yes to a firm handshake). These young people welcome their parents' two cents and feel well supported by their guidance. But other children may interpret any advice as criticism and want to look for a job on their own terms.

To navigate between those who appreciate advice and those who dismiss it, parents might present a smorgasbord of possible assistance and ask their emerging adult if any of their offers sounds promising—"I could

---

Q: *My husband and I are both lawyers with many contacts in the legal world. We have two sons who are interested in going into our field: One is hoping to work as a paralegal before going to law school, and the other has just gotten his first job offer at a big firm. Would it be appropriate to work our contacts for our younger son and help negotiate our older son's pay package?*

A: Of course it's tempting to smooth the way for your two aspiring attorneys into a profession you know so well. It would be fine to give your younger son some possible people to contact himself or let your older son know the range of starting salaries in comparable firms. But beyond that wisdom shared, let your sons handle things themselves.

In a 2012 study, the Collegiate Employment Research Institute sponsored by Michigan State University surveyed 725 employers regarding parental involvement with job applicants and employees. The study found that 31 percent of parents submitted a résumé on behalf of their child, 12 percent made interview arrangements for their child, and 9 percent were involved in negotiating their child's salary or benefits. Fair warning: Most employers saw these kinds of parental involvement as negative.

help you brainstorm different people to call, I could review your résumé, I could ask you how it's going, or role-play an interview with you. Do you want me to do any of these, or something else, or just back off?"

Assist in creating a jobs advisory network. Sixty to seventy percent of job possibilities come through networking rather than listed openings, says Kjelleren, so it makes sense to help young job-seekers build a network of contacts and advisors for their search. Parents can be key players, but they should not be the only ones. A teacher, coach, college faculty member or career counselor, neighbor, mentor, or older, gainfully employed friend may broaden their job search in pivotal ways and keep young people in the driver's seat.

Parents, resist the temptation to call or network yourselves. Hearing from parents that their grown child wants a job can be a turnoff to a prospective employer. Those who hire prefer red-hot candidates with the confidence and initiative to phone, email, and do follow-up by themselves.

Be sympathetic and supportive—and stand aside. Looking for a job can be more stressful than working nine to five, so give young job hunters plenty of moral support and credit for networking, sending out résumés, making cold calls, and pounding the pavement even without immediate results. Here, as everywhere, balance caring with respect for emerging adults' growing maturity, and hold your counsel if they have made it clear they want to get their job on their own.

From Launching to Landing in the Workplace

During the years from 18 to 29, most emerging adults define a career focus, explore and discard several jobs in that field (or possibly a different one), and eventually settle into something more or less secure. It's a crucial decade of discovery and decision with—for most—a hopeful arc from uncertainty to some degree of fulfillment and stability. There are marked differences between the tentative early job forays of an 18- to 22-year-old who's just launching, a 23- to 26-year-old who's exploring options and trying jobs on for fit, and a 27- to 29-year-old who lands in a steady job that's sustainable for many years to come.

These three portraits of young people at work illustrate the challenges and rewards of each phase.

Otis, age 21: Launching. At 21, Otis still lives at home in a three-generation family that includes his grandparents and his mother, Naima, 43, who has raised him on her own with only marginal help from Otis's father. Naima has a steady job in the human relations department of a large company, but she never made it to college (a bad car accident and her pregnancy derailed her). She desperately wanted her only child to fulfill the dream of college both for his sake and for hers, but he wasn't interested. "At his age, I was more mature," she reflects. "I was like a sharpened pencil; he's a little dull."

Otis is handsome and sensitive, extra close to the single mother about whom he once wrote, "We were like two halves of a moon. Without the other, we wouldn't be whole." Now, instead of college, Otis has had a series of low-paying, starter jobs that Naima helped him secure and handle—at Target (where his mom submitted his résumé) and at a bagel store. Without his own car and commuting from an unsafe part of town, Otis needed his mother's help to keep the jobs. Remembers Naima, "I was getting up at 2 or 4 a.m. to drive him there or pick him up at 11 p.m. He had me spinning." The hours, the poor pay, the distance from home—it wasn't sustainable.

Most recently, Naima found out about the Year Up program and steered Otis to this one year of intensive training at a nonprofit that provides inner-city youth with technical and professional skills, an educational stipend, and a corporate internship. Otis was accepted and placed in a large corporate office, and he has done well. "The program has been a great learning experience," Naima says. "He's wearing slacks and a tie and has learned about teamwork and getting along with people from different racial backgrounds." Glowing, she adds, "I met his teachers who know him. They talk about his character. That makes me feel proud as a parent."

The launching period is full of leaps as well as struggles, and so it's been for Otis, periods of growth and independence alternating with setbacks and continued dependence on Mom. Many parents of launching-age kids will agree with Otis's mother that "this learning stage is trial and error." Young workers at this stage still rely on parental support to meet their responsibilities. As Naima explains, "I take Otis to work. He's very slow in the bathroom, especially for a guy. He takes an hour and fifteen

Q: *Our 24-year-old daughter has just finished college and is ready to look for her first real job. She has a couple of missing years on her résumé caused by drug abuse and emotional problems and then rehab and therapy. Although she is back on her feet now, we're concerned that her history, if it's known, will be an obstacle to her getting hired. How should we advise her to present herself?*

A: There are a couple of different approaches your daughter can take regarding her history of drug problems, suggests New York City career counselor Marianne Rugierro. One is to make this issue the focus of her career and look for jobs working with other young people who have substance abuse problems. At some point, she'll probably need to get additional training (e.g., an MSW), but she'll be able to turn her own experience "into a badge of courage instead of a scarlet letter," says Rugierro.

The other approach is to low-key her past experience with a potential employer—while staying honest. If asked about gaps in her résumé, your daughter can say, "I had some health issues, but they're now under control, and I'm grateful for coming through it." She'll need to tailor her tone and the amount of information she is willing to share to the environment of each potential job. Some fields are less conservative than others: In TV production, for instance, substance abuse is not seen the same way as it would be in an accounting firm.

Your daughter may feel as if she's the only one having to cope with this set of circumstances, but they're more common than she might imagine; it's possible that her interviewer's son has just returned from rehab himself. Your daughter may be thinking, "Everyone is judging me," but her biggest judge may be herself. Remind her that she has a success story to tell. After all, she made it through her rough patch.

---

minutes! He hasn't preplanned his day. I'm part of the equation. [I tell him,] 'You can't tell me things at the eleventh hour.'"

Otis recently graduated from Year Up, and though his options may still be limited without a college degree, he has more skills, confidence, and contacts to set him up for his next job. Right now, Naima has one

dream for him: "My main goal is for Otis to get a job with health insurance. I also want to buy him a car because I don't like him on the bus. He's
been robbed twice, once at gunpoint." She sighs, adding that she's already
told him her conditions. "I'll take care of the car but you do insurance.
I don't cosign for anyone."

Josh, age 25: Exploring. At 25, Josh is pursuing his dream, which is one
version of the dream of many of today's 20-somethings—he's an entre-
preneur with his own small cookie-baking business. A bright, wiry, edgy
young man, Josh, in his father's words, is "extraordinarily smart but still
trying to figure out the world." He sailed through college in three years
with a double major and took a first job as an analyst in the tech field with
a $60,000 starting salary. But he was restless chained to an office com-
puter and, as he puts it, "wanted something that was mine. Now everyone I know is doing this."

In the local foodie world and the monthly Underground Market that
he's part of, there are eighty vendors selling their homemade goods—
jams, cheeses, breads—and many of them are in their twenties like Josh.
It's a coast-to-coast community of young people with more passion than
profits, trying to parlay a vision into a viable venture. Some will survive
the first rocky years. Others will flounder, fail, and need to move on, for
as career coach Littlestone points out, most entrepreneurs will have several failed businesses before the one that succeeds.

Like many young people trying to get a start-up off the ground, after
one year in the game, Josh has had some terrific highs and some distress-
ing and unforeseen lows. His original business plan involved spreading
word of mouth by giving away one thousand cookies for free and then
setting out to sell the next thousand. No surprise, the free cookies turned
out to be an easier "sell" than the cookies that cost. But snickerdoodle by
gingersnap, he's selling enough cookies now to move his baking operation
from his own small apartment to a space he shares with a local bakery.
And he's gotten a ton of glowing local press as a "baking evangelist."

His parents, Leslie and Sam, both professionals in their late sixties, invested in Josh's company at the outset and are also volunteering
sweat equity to support him. More than a baker's dozen of friends and

neighbors have offered to help out with the fledgling business. Leslie is his volunteer coordinator, but, Josh admits, she hasn't figured out how to use her list yet, how to communicate with the people who are attracted to his enterprise and want to pitch in. He's too busy keeping other balls in the air to give her much guidance. Both parents admit in private that they're becoming more dubious about the bakery's success after the unstable start-up year. Remarks his dad drily, "He has lots of press despite the fact that he can't pay the rent."

The stresses of launching a company have taken Josh by surprise. "I wanted to start a business," he confesses, "but cookies were arbitrary. Business things are massive. So many tasks are involved: baking, delivery, supplies, new relationships with potential customers, researching markets, branding, logos, how to manage other people."

Financing is by far the biggest strain. He wishes that he'd lined up more funding before quitting his well-paying job. "People told me but I didn't listen," he says now. Josh knows it can take two to three years to start a small business, and he's trying to think longer term. But projecting too far ahead, like five years, is "a whole lifetime away for me," he admits. His original seed money is gone, and sales haven't picked up enough to cover all the bakery's expenses, so he's applying for a small, no-interest loan. "This has taught me about patience," he reflects about his first year in business. "I thought things would happen faster. I've never planned more than two weeks or months ahead."

It's typical of the exploring phase to pick up and put down passions and projects, and it's still hard to predict whether or not Josh's brainchild is just pie (or cookies) in the sky, a stepping-stone to another venture. But whether or not the cookie company has staying power, Josh will have learned crucial business skills, from planning and money management to building out an organization from the ground up.

Leslie is still willing to help out with the bakery when she has the time, but Sam is more hardheaded. "We're not giving him any more money. He's got to make the business work or fail and get a job."

Kelly, age 29: Landing. At 18, Kelly did not seem like the type of young woman who'd ever land in a predictable way. She was quirky and rebellious with a mind of her own. She graduated from a large public high school and went off to a demanding college, sure that she'd never find a niche there. But she fell in love with it despite herself, worked hard, made many good friends, got excellent training in global affairs and writing, and graduated hoping to make a career in radio reporting. She got an internship at NPR right off the bat and did so well, she was hired as a producer on one of the daily shows. But those first good breaks didn't lead anywhere fully satisfying and secure. For several years, she was barely getting by. One short-term production assistant radio job in a tiny market segued into the next. To manage, she lived in a shared house or, once, in her older sister's basement. After a few years of this hand-to-mouth existence, she dropped off the grid entirely, questioned her direction, and headed to Ethiopia for a stint of adventure (her parents had worked there in the Peace Corps and encouraged her exploration).

But if anything, traveling in Ethiopia reaffirmed her dedication to her global worldview and her desire to continue reporting. She was 27 when she returned, and whether it was experience, good timing, or the luck she'd created, she landed the most stable job she'd ever had, this time as a reporter and one who could afford her own apartment. Working this job, she also found a serious boyfriend, and when she got an even better job offer in another, bigger city, he picked up, came along with her, and found work there, too. At 29, she feels securely landed in a job and location she loves. She and her boyfriend bought a car and a house together, and now they're planning their wedding. In her mother's proud words, "Kelly has created her adult persona."

Onward and (Eventually) Upward

These three profiles should give some encouragement to parents of grown-up kids, especially those whose children are in the launching or exploring phases of emerging adulthood. Most young people in their twenties begin like Otis, without much of a clue to the future, unsure of which path to take among those open to them. Then they often enter the phase that Josh experienced, of exploring more clearly defined options— but the options they choose may or may not work out. Finally, by their late twenties, they navigate their way through both opportunities and setbacks, as Kelly did, and land in a more stable career. It may be a direction they had known all along, or it may be one they never would have imagined at age 20 or 22. It may be just what they wanted, or it may be just enough to survive on for now. But it is usually a job they will have for at least five years, and probably more.

Of course, Otis, Josh, and Kelly are different in ways other than their ages. Education, class, race, and opportunities all play a role. Otis is not only age 21 but African American, and male, and the child of a single mom. His obstacles as he makes his way into the work world include not just his age but also his ethnicity, which some employers will count against him, and his origins at the low end of the socioeconomic scale. Despite his mom's desire that he go to college, there may be less of an expectation for higher education among his peers than in Josh's or Kelly's circles, where almost all their friends were college educated. Similarly, Kelly's success by age 30 is not just the result of development, of outgrowing the uncertainty and instability of emerging adulthood's launching and exploring phases. The invaluable college education she received, supported both by her parents and by loans, opened up attractive options for work. Finding a decent, stable, acceptable long-term job by age 30 is likely but not inevitable for emerging adults, and it is made a lot more likely by the kind of resources Kelly's parents, her education, and her valuable network of contacts provided.

Yet all parents can contribute to their children's success in the work world, as Otis's experience shows. His mother does not have a lot of money, but she made connections for him, even handed in a job application for him. She found a training program for him that resulted in valuable skills and credentials. It was not financial help that she provided to him; it was not even personal connections. It was her involvement, her engagement; it was that she cared enough, at the end of her own long workday, to summon the extra energy and focus to help him find his path.

Of course, Otis was willing to accept her help, and he appreciated it. Other emerging adults may need more assistance, and some may be reluctant to accept any help at all, insisting on doing it their own way and learning to stand on their own. Here, as elsewhere, the wise parent seeks the elusive ideal balance between nurturing, guiding, and standing aside.

10

The Bank of Mom and Dad

My daughter left school for a boy, buys toys with her
little cash, then needs help with her rent and food.

FATHER OF A DAUGHTER, 22

hen parents of grown-up kids get together, the talk often turns
to money matters, as in who pays for what and for how long.
Midlife economic pressures and emerging adults' extended
timetable for becoming self-sufficient can make both generations edgy.
A newly retired couple in their early sixties, for instance, anxiously
watches their 28-year-old daughter who is not yet fully self-supporting.
The former nurse and her businessman husband are plenty concerned
about taking care of their own futures, never mind their daughter's. "She
thinks she's financially solvent, but she isn't," laments this mother. "We
still pay for all her shoes and underwear!" And, she adds, "We gave her
our old car, and we cover the car insurance."

Yes, when it comes to paying for grown kids' things, where to draw
the line is something each family must decide based on its priorities
and resources. But shoes, underwear, and cars, even old ones, do add
up. Another parent has done the math: "I'd guess I add $5,000 a year to
our 24-year-old daughter's salary," says this mother, a divorced lawyer.
Without Mom's subsidy, her daughter's annual income at a nonprofit
wouldn't sustain her lifestyle.

This mom's not alone: According to a 2011 survey done by Vibrant Nation, a website for women over 50, more than half of all moms in the United States spend more than $5,000 per year on each of their 18- to 30-year-old children to help cover everyday expenses (not including tuition, room, and board). And 84 percent of respondents—you won't be shocked by this—also reported that they are paying more of their adult children's expenses than their mothers (or fathers) paid for them. This discrepancy means, among other things, that today's parents have no role models to show them when to sever financial ties. Should it happen when kids turn 21, 25, get a solid job . . . get married?

When boomers came of age, their parents typically stretched to pay for their college tuition and expenses for four years, and then the check writing stopped. But today's lengthened road to adulthood and challenging economic realities are pressuring the Bank of Mom and Dad to stay open much longer. For young people in the twenty-first century, becoming financially independent, like finding lasting love, solid employment, and a permanent separate address, is taking much of the twenties to accomplish.

A torrent of economic trends is to blame:

• *Student debt.* In 2011, the average student debt was close to $27,000, with 10 percent owing more than $54,000 and 3 percent more than $100,000, the Federal Reserve Bank of New York reports.

• *Unemployment.* According to a 2011 study by the John J. Heldrich Center for Workforce Development at Rutgers University, among the members of the college class of 2010, just 56 percent had held at least one job a year after they graduated. That compares with 90 percent of graduates from the classes of 2006 and 2007 who had jobs a year later. And what's more, only half of recent college graduates said that the first job they found required a college degree. For young people without a B.A., the job prospects are even worse; their unemployment rate is twice as high as for college grads.

• *The high cost of housing.* Rents are soaring through the roof for many young people, especially in major urban areas. Among the reasons the rental market has been swamped, sending rents into overdrive: Homeowners displaced from foreclosures are now looking to rent; potential home buyers are not willing or able to buy a home because of the ongoing slump in the housing market and tight lending conditions; and there's a dearth of new construction.

These can be unsettling times. You well may wonder if your emerging adult will *ever* be able to find a job and make it independently. Young people are haunted by the same worries. Meanwhile, there's no cultural script to tell you how best to handle money matters in a changing and challenging economic climate. Everything is up for negotiation. And it's hard to have a hard line about money in hard times.

The Money Talk

The Money Talk is often a defining moment for this generation of emerging adults and their loving but losing-patience parents. Indeed, the narrative of *Girls,* the HBO series about 20-somethings, turns on this very conversation. In the opening episode, the show's 24-year-old heroine, Hannah, is struggling to make it as a writer living in Brooklyn with three girlfriends (one of whom is employed as a gallerist and pays Hannah's rent). Over dinner out, Hannah's parents drop the bombshell: They won't support her any longer, and she has to get a job. Devastated, she comes back at them: "How about just eleven hundred a month?" she begs. No go, they say, standing their ground. And much of the plot then cascades from exactly what she'll do to survive.

Most parents will relate, and many will be in her parents' corner, not Hannah's. Some parents may even go so far as to blame themselves for their kids' lack of financial independence, asking themselves what they did wrong, going all the way back to early child-raising days. Why are their grown kids still so needy, why do some even feel entitled to be supported? Should they have made their kids do more chores, save part of their weekly allowance, practice self-sufficiency by paying for their own clothes? Mostly they hope it's not too late to instill good money habits now.

Every family needs to crunch its own numbers, taking into account both tangibles (like how much they can afford to help, if at all) and intangibles (like the attitudes or ideals they wish to pass along with their dollars). Emerging adults may feel the tension between still wanting to be taken care of, as in childhood, and wanting to know they can take care of themselves. Finally becoming financially self-sufficient is a major game-changer, a huge boost toward adulthood, and a source of confidence, self-esteem, and self-reliance. Despite the belly-aching and backsliding that shows like *Girls* reflect, most 20-somethings are just as eager to be self-supporting as their parents are to stop funding them.

In the national Clark University poll Jeff directed, 75 percent of 18- to 29-year-olds agreed that "I would prefer to live independently of my parents even if it means living on a tight budget." As the twenties-decade continues, more and more young people do fulfill this dream. It's true that, according to the Clark poll, 80 percent of 18- to 21-year-olds receive at least occasional financial help from their parents, and even at ages 26 to 29, 40 percent do. But only 28 percent of 18- to 21-year-olds receive "regular support for living expenses" from Mom and Dad, and this drops to 13 percent at ages 22 to 25 and to just 6 percent by ages 26 to 29. On the life path between staying connected and stepping back, between dependence and independence, closing the parental purse strings used to equal the final cut of the cord between parents and their grown children. But today the cord is more likely to be snipped a little at a time than to be cut cleanly.

The emotional subtext of money between the generations may be unvoiced but it can create considerable static. In every family, unspoken as well as shared-aloud messages are passed along with monetary support—or expressed through its withholding. Money is, indeed, "emotional currency," in the coinage of California psychotherapist Kate Levinson, and the title of her recent book. Families can use it in numerous ways, both beneficial and harmful, as she explains: "to express love, to manipulate, to support, to reward, to punish, to show favoritism, to control, to foster dependency."

Money can represent power and provide the freedom to choose. A well-timed gift can set grown children on the path to fulfill their potential, but monetary assistance can also keep a child tied to a parent, creating dependence, ambivalence, and resentment. Financial help often comes with strings attached, with conscious or unconscious expectations of what that help will buy. That's why, as the Clark poll shows, emerging adults would usually prefer not to take money from parents if they can scrape by without it. Money that's used to manipulate especially strains the bond, like parents who will pay their students' tuition only at the colleges on a preapproved list or only if their kids choose certain "get-ahead" majors like business or prelaw, not "how will you ever find a job?" majors like philosophy or folklore. Other parents' largesse comes with ulterior motives, like agreeing to contribute to housing costs—but only if the place is within ten miles of the old homestead, and no cohabiting allowed.

When Mom and Dad still hold the purse strings, it's natural to feel you should have a say in how your money's spent: "Hmmm, nice new outfit you got there; how much did that cost?" But be careful about using money to control grown children and their life choices—that tactic will create ill will. On the other hand, if children won't take your money, don't take it personally. Your grown kids' decision is part of a healthy desire to run their own lives without parental control.

Money is not an easy topic to discuss with grown children—perhaps only sex is more awkward—but it's important to talk about what you can and can't provide. Whether from discretion, reticence, or how their own families talked about money (or didn't), the older generation often pulls a curtain of secrecy around the family's bottom line—parents' salaries, household expenses, monthly rent or mortgage payments, savings and retirement funds—as well as debt, loans, or obligations to other family members.

How much you want to tell your children about your own financial situation is a personal decision. But even if talking about money matters is uncomfortable, it should be an essential part of your family's agenda when your kids reach emerging adulthood. It makes sense to open up a good-faith money talk on the occasion of (at least) two major turning points in your emerging adults' lives and then follow up as time goes on: first, as high school comes to an end and students start making college and other life choices, and again, after college, when young people consider graduate or professional school, look for jobs, and start figuring out how to fund their adult lives. It's better for you to be up front about family finances than to wait for a crisis to arise and then have to make a snap (and perhaps regrettable) decision.

First, set out the parameters. Be clear about what you can or can't offer to pay during the college and postcollege years. With college tuition costs so high, how will your family handle those costs? Perhaps parents will make whatever contribution they can afford and then the student will close the doughnut hole with financial aid, scholarships, student loans, work/study, or outside jobs. And for students who want to pursue graduate study, parents may well require that they'll have to pay for it on their own with another round of student loans or income from their own jobs.

College costs have gone up five times faster than family income since 1981, the College Board reports. So just as higher education has become more necessary to succeed in a complex, global economy, it's become more expensive. Most parents are no longer able to shoulder these rising higher education costs on their own, so it often makes more sense for students to take out loans for college than it does for parents to assume the heavy load of debt. Students are able to get lower interest rates, have the flexibility of income-based repayment (not available to parents), and have longer to pay off the loans.

Today 40 percent of four-year college students and almost 75 percent of part-time students work to contribute to their tuition and living expenses, according to the National Center for Education Statistics. In 1970, when many boomer parents went to college, only 10 percent of full-time students worked twenty to thirty-four hours a week; today, that number is up to 17 percent. And although working during college may be the only way that many students can afford their education today, students who carry two loads—a job and studies—are also more likely to drop out and never get that sought-after degree. For some, the stress of the double shifts is just too much to sustain.

But many emerging adults are doing the heavy lifting to make college affordable. They're stepping up by combining their studies with a job, or dropping out for a semester or a year to work and pay for the next year of their education. While some parents are bewailing their grown kids' roller-coaster ride to financial security, others are rightly proud of their college students who are making huge efforts to pay their way.

Emerging adults from divorced families may face extra strains over how to pay for college. Divorced parents often have trouble agreeing about who will take on the college costs, and their kids lose out. Especially if one or both of the former partners has a new spouse—and more children from a new marriage—things can get heated, and the aspiring college-bound children may get caught in the middle. Young people with divorced parents have lower college enrollment and graduation rates, because the mom may not have enough money to contribute and the dad often won't pay. If it's not too late, consider negotiating college costs in a divorce settlement.

After college, you and your grown kids should revisit the money talk once again. Can grown children move back home while they're looking

---

Q: *Our son has fallen in love with a college that doesn't offer a good scholarship package, and he has also been accepted by an institution that does. Our family does not have deep pockets, and the better tuition aid would certainly help our bottom line. Still, we hate to disappoint our son and crush his dream. How to navigate?*

A: Much as you wish you had that magic wand to make all your son's dreams come true, when it comes to major financial questions sometimes tough kitchen table talk is necessary. You need to be up front with your son and make it clear how much help you can give him, or if you can't or don't want to cover the difference in costs between the two colleges by going into your savings or taking out your own loans. Does he want that first-choice institution enough to take on the additional financial commitment? He may want to do whatever it takes to attend Dream U. But once he faces the math, the better aid package may start to make a more affordable second-choice school look more appealing. In any case, he'll gain the experience of making the kind of difficult choice all adults have to make.

for work, applying to graduate school, or working only part-time? Are you able or willing to offer monetary help at this point, and if so, in what ways? Besides education, some of the areas where you may (or may not) wish to offer monetary help are daily living expenses, the security deposit on an apartment, a car and car insurance, and travel home to see the family. In our interviews, cell phone plans and health care were the last bastions of parental help, as no parents want to drop out of contact or risk their grown kid's health, if they can help it. Besides, sometimes it's possible to get "family plans" where adding another phone costs little or nothing per month.

Number One Hot Topic

Couples may argue about sex, money, and how best to raise the kids, but between parents and their emerging adults the number one hot-button issue is money. Almost half of the parents in our survey called it the top source of conflict between them and their grown-up kids—ranking it above arguments about school, work, and substance use. Few topics are as emotionally charged, deeply personal, overlaid with family traditions, or culturally complex as money.

For most parents, their grown children's financial independence—along with accepting responsibility for themselves—is a major marker of becoming an adult. The two goals—financial self-reliance and personal responsibility—are intertwined, and in many parents' opinion, they seem to be slipping farther and farther out of reach.

Scenarios like these spell sleepless nights for parents: A new freshman heads off in September with a $1,200 check from Mom and Dad to cover three months of college expenses and blasts through the entire sum in the first three weeks. A sophomore is unaware of roaming charges on a cell phone plan and racks up a $3,000 bill long-distance calling his hometown girlfriend. A jobless college grad scrimps on car or health insurance and is one collision or broken ankle away from disaster. A first job-hunter buys pricey outfits to look sharp for interviews, or a newly employed young person lavishly furnishes a first apartment, and both rack up credit card debt that will dog them—and their credit score—for years.

Is it possible to head off these mishaps or is learning as they go the best way young people figure out how to handle money? Answer: a mixture of both. Giving grown kids a sensible survival kit of money strategies, being honest about your own financial situation and past money mistakes, and believing in your children's ability to become self-supporting—these guidelines will help create a solid footing for the younger generation's financial independence.

Your Money Squeeze

Timing often adds to the tension about money matters between boomer parents and their grown-up kids. Emerging adults' financial needs tend to collide with midlife parents' own money worries and constraints. Parents' job uncertainties, or worse, their unemployment, may undermine their security. Dwindling savings, shrinking 401Ks, falling home values, or foreclosures, as well as postponed plans for retirement, may add to parents' stress. As life spans get longer, midlife couples worry about covering their own expenses into an unknowable future. Meanwhile, their elderly parents are also living longer and often need financial support as well. Taking on the extended financial needs of their grown children can quickly become one burden too many. Saving for retirement versus paying for children's college tuition or post-college living expenses has become an increasingly perplexing calculus for many cash-strapped families. One father of five kids in their twen-

> Our son depends mostly on his father, who should cut him off, in my opinion.
>
> MOTHER OF A SON, 28

ties had to make up a song to lighten his financial burdens. The chorus went, "My thoughts of retirement are over and done / I'm learning that forty is the new twenty-one . . ."

Most financial experts advocate the "buckle your own seat belt first" strategy: Before you decide to offer help to your kids, you must first assess and safeguard your own financial well-being. As much as you love your children and wish to assist them through these rocky years on the way to adulthood, don't prop up your children's bank accounts while risking your own. According to the Federal Reserve Bank of New York, the number of borrowers of student loans ages 60 and older has tripled since 2005, making them the fastest-growing age group for college debt. (Although the figure is not broken out, presumably most of this debt is for their kids' education, not their own.)

But Carmen Wong Ulrich, author of *Generation Debt* and an expert on millennial generation money issues, believes that parents taking on high college debt for their kids' education is not a good idea. "Parents shouldn't sacrifice everything to put their children through school," she says. She has seen parents mortgage their homes or take out six-figure loans to fund their students' college educations, and she thinks that's highly unwise. "When parents help their kids at the cost of their own retirement," she adds, "that money will become their kids' to pay back down the road." If parents haven't protected their own savings for the future, they may need to turn to their adult children for assistance just as those young adults are raising families, wanting to buy a house, and thinking about funding *their* children's college educations. In many families, that could turn out to be too high a price to pay for both generations.

"I have big arguments with my husband," admits one mother of an underemployed 25-year-old son who's struggling to survive in an expensive city, "because my husband's living his life to save for our *son's* retirement." At 68, she wisely wants to secure her and her husband's golden years first and then decide if they can afford to lend their son a hand.

Many boomer parents learned to be careful with money from parents who were bruised by the Great Depression. These Depression Era parents taught the value of going without and the virtue of making do. Lowering the thermostat, turning out lights, using powdered milk instead of premium grade—scrimping, saving, and "waste not, want not" were the lessons Depression Era parents passed along. Today's emerging adults, for the most part, grew up during a booming economy when spending was freewheeling and often turned into excessive "affluenza." But now, like the rest of society, young people face a slowed-down economy that calls for belt tightening and a new frugality.

With more limits comes the need to make more conscious decisions about spending priorities. There can be a certain contentment in having

Money-Management Strategies for Empty Nesters

Families with emerging adults vary greatly in their readiness for retirement. Some parents who are 45 to 50 have just started to save; among older parents in their fifties or sixties some may have built up a decent nest egg, others may not have. For parents juggling their own financial needs with those of their aging parents and grown children, consider these suggestions:

• Consider putting aside money for five, rather than four, years of supporting your grown kids who are college-bound. This will give you a potential cushion if your child's B.A. takes five years, or if she or he needs financial assistance during a getting-settled or boomerang year.

• Increase your annual retirement contribution to at least 15 percent of your income. If you've shortchanged your retirement to cover child-raising expenses, now's the time to up the ante for your own needs later in life.

• Be judicious about the amount you spend from your savings or investments on grown kids' necessities. Some financial counselors suggest spending no more than 5 percent of savings per year, but that number will vary, depending on your circumstances.

• As of 2012, federal law allows one individual to give a gift to another of up to $13,000 tax free. If you're fortunate enough to be able to give a monetary gift to your children one year, make sure to reassess each year to see if a gift is possible. Be clear to grown kids that they shouldn't count on the same cash windfall every year.

• Think twice before cosigning a college or car loan for a 20-something, and consider private college loans (which do need to be cosigned) only as a last option. Loans can be a risky business. Contrary to what you might think, the cosigner is not the borrower of last resort. If the primary borrower—for example, the emerging adult—doesn't make the payments, collection agencies can choose to come after the cosigner for payments as well as any fees that have accrued. Being the cosigner for a loan in default can harm your credit record—as well as family relationships.

All that said, it's difficult to turn down a child in need, albeit a grown one, and even financially sophisticated parents may find themselves extending the credit line on their house or sacrificing in other ways to help out their kids. At least talk through the consequences and responsibilities on all sides before you leap.

a smaller footprint and fewer distractions, a deepening of values and the inner life. Affluenza versus austerity? From a parent's point of view, austerity is not always such a bad thing. And when 20-somethings start taking on all their own bills, they may have the same epiphany.

Set Limits, Encourage a Plan

Back in the old days when parents and kids still wrote letters, this joke went around: If you want to hear from your kids fast, send them a letter and say you're enclosing a check. Then don't include the check. You'll be amazed at how quickly they get in touch.

But today, simply popping a check in the mail is not so simple. So much depends on what individual kids in a family need in the way of currency, emotional and otherwise—and it may be different for each grown child in a particular family. One may need the bedrock security of knowing he can fall back on parents' help if a plan fails or a job doesn't pan out. But for another, parental help may convey the message, even if it's unintended, that she can't make it on her own.

Since inequities in monetary gifts can cause upset in families like nothing else, it's important for parents to stay mindful of how and whom they help. In the ideal world all gifts to kids would be equal, but in the messy real world different grown children may need different amounts or kinds of help at different times in their lives. A policy of fairness and openness will go a long way toward easing potential resentments. An emerging adult coping with a long bout of unemployment, for example, may need more of a helping hand than one who's settled in a good job. The cash provided by parents in this case may be a godsend for the struggling child but resented by the sibling who is employed at a dreary job and working long hours. Monetary gifts, especially large ones, can be interpreted as favoritism even by siblings who don't need the financial assistance. It's best to be as forthright as possible and explain the reasons you've given the help you did.

How does a family with emerging adults find the balance and decide what's right for each of them? Even those families who can afford to help out still wonder if it's a good idea. Is offering financial help to grown children a disincentive to making their own way? Will cash support or a small loan in their twenties raise a lingering, long-term expectation?

Does financial support lead to lifetime dependence or help pave the way for independence?

Talking about their families' financial philosophies, two mothers we interviewed show the opposite sides of this coin. Alice and Vera both work; each has two daughters; both moms are married and comfortable enough so that they could offer financial help. But Alice and her husband, Al, have had a strict hands-off, no bailout, tough-love policy once their daughters graduated from college. Their attitude is that they figured out how to support themselves after college without parental help, and now their daughters should, too. Alice is downright dismissive of friends who coddle their kids with extended handouts: "In our family, once kids leave the nest they assume financial independence. We help them, but we feel they need to figure it out themselves. We feel it fosters individuation, whereas friends are always buying, doing, paying for."

Vera favors the Mother Bear approach—protect her cubs at all cost, even in their twenties. She wants to help support her daughters until they're fully able to cover their own needs, and she can't bear to see them go without. Not untypically of couples with grown kids, Vera admits that her husband has a different idea: "My husband says we have to cut them off, even if it means they live on the streets. I say, 'I'd rather live on the streets before my daughters!'"

Since each member of a couple brings different financial baggage into a marriage, it's not unusual for the two of them to disagree about how to handle money with their own kids. (It's worth keeping in mind that money is also at the top of any list of sources of marital conflict.) Maybe Mom's family was very generous (Dad would call it "overindulgent") and Dad's family was thrifty (verging on "cheap," according to Mom). Or Mom's family supported an adult child long past the age Dad approves of, and he doesn't want to repeat the pattern with their kids. Couples tend to get polarized around money issues, says *Emotional Currency*'s Levinson. It's crucial for partners to talk through their differences while doing their best to see the other person's point of view before reaching big financial decisions that will affect the whole family's future.

There's certainly a way to navigate between the extremes of hands-on versus hands-off, counsels Ulrich, the millennial money expert. "A lot of young people need a fire lit beneath them to become self-sufficient," she says. Meanwhile, there's nothing wrong with parents helping their grown kids, but it doesn't have to be an all-or-nothing proposition, and it's important to set limits. Kids moving back home? Offer six months of rent-free housing and then they either move—or contribute to the family's monthly costs. "It helps to set out dates and goals," she suggests, to keep that gentle pressure going toward self-sufficiency.

It's a lot easier to offer limited financial help to grown children—if parents can afford it—as long as their kids have a capital P Plan and are actively pursuing it. Their Plan could be a fascinating but unpaid internship with a nonprofit or a low-paying starter job in a career with potential. Seeing grown children make progress on a promising path into adult life is the highest priority, and sometimes the financial help parents offer in the twenties can be the crucial tide-over they need. Ask your emerging adult: Where do you want your life to be one year, five years, and ten years from now, and what help do you think you need from us in order to get there? Especially in the early twenties the answer may well be "I have no idea," but asking the question is a good way to get your grown kids thinking about their strategies.

Even after children are launched, living on their own, and becoming self-supporting, a limited financial gift from parents for a particular purpose—rather than ongoing, unlimited support—can be positive for both sides. Help paying for an unexpected doctor's bill, education, a trip, or contributing toward buying a house or condo can be a chance to give and receive love, be generous and receive gratitude, and make a difference in the course of a young person's life. What parents want to avoid is creating the expectation that they'll always be there to bail out grown-up kids when the rent is overdue, a credit card maxed out, or some other mishap occurs.

"In our family, making your way financially is a sign of manhood."

Ruth, a retired school psychologist and her husband, Marvin, an accountant, are hardworking, urban professionals who gave their sons a good education, a comfortable home, and what they thought was an example of living well and within their means. But they learned the hard way that they should have been more forthright about money issues (Remember: *Set limits, encourage a plan*) and not simply expected that their values would be picked up by example alone.

Financial independence is a huge marker in any family but especially charged in theirs. As Ruth explains, "In our family, making your way financially is a sign of manhood." In her husband's family, young men made their own way in the world. "My husband's parents helped his sisters but not him," she reflects. "We're still close to the generations that had nothing."

Despite his parents' prudence, their younger son, Ezra, now 26, is a risk taker, whose choices derailed his straight route to fiscal freedom. Ezra was diagnosed with ADHD as a young boy and was on Ritalin most of his childhood. "School is not his thing," says Ruth, and that difficulty was hard to bear in a family where academics came easily to everyone else.

Ezra became addicted to online gambling in college and went through a small inheritance that his grandfather had left him to pay for tuition. Unhappy and socially awkward, Ezra would sit for hours mesmerized by the computer—not venturing into the real world. College students with ADHD are especially at risk for developing a gambling addiction, according to a 2009 National Institutes of Health study of more than two hundred 18- to 24-year-olds. Twenty percent of ADHD students are problem gamblers, compared with 10 percent of other students. Researchers are still teasing out the connections, but poor impulse control is a hallmark of ADHD and also a hallmark of addiction.

Eventually Ezra stopped the gambling (with the help of a good therapist) and made an agreement with his parents that he would pay for the rest of college himself. He had to take out costly loans to do it—and they were cosigned not by his parents but by his older brother, who holds a well-paying job.

With the hindsight that's always twenty-twenty, Ruth sees what they coulda/shoulda done differently. She regrets that she and her husband weren't more explicit about their financial values and strategies before sending Ezra to college. She also wishes she had kept a closer eye on him freshman year and intervened earlier to get him help before his gambling spiraled out of control. And though an inheritance may be an enviable problem to have, their biggest mistake, she realizes now, was to give it to Ezra before graduation instead of putting it into a trust. Now he's one course shy of graduation, working at a job in marketing to pay for it, and living in his parents' basement. "Our hurdle now is to ease him into financial independence," says Ruth.

Money Basics 101

The goal for all emerging adults is financial autonomy, and parents may do better contributing to that goal with guidance rather than dollars. Before launching young people into the world of getting and spending, it's wise for parents to share their financial know-how: smart budgeting and financial planning; establishing credit and using it wisely; handling student loans; getting the necessary health insurance; and savvy saving.

Of course, many parents have hardly led exemplary financial lives themselves, and many were wounded deeply by the financial doldrums of the past decade-plus. But even here your advice and experience can be valuable. If you've suffered financial reversals in the course of your adult life—and who among us has not?—you can provide the benefit of your hard-won experience so your children will not repeat those mistakes.

Kate Levinson puts it simply: "Being clueless about money is no longer affordable." Here are our guidelines for turning money taboos into talking points:

Demonstrate wise budgeting and financial planning. Bringing up the *B* word may make young eyes glaze, but before children leave home, parents will do well to introduce some budgeting basics, particularly the most basic rule of all: Spend only what you can afford. Suggest a trial run of tracking expenses for a month or so to compare income and outflow and see which costs fall into which categories: steady costs like rent, utilities, insurance, food, clothes, and entertainment, and big-ticket items like tuition, a car, furniture, travel, and so on. Online banking sites provide an accessible way to make a habit of tracking expenses, as do websites (and apps) like mint.com, learnvest.com, and dailyworth.com.

Setting spending priorities is a crucial building block for future financial planning, and in the best-case scenario wise budgeting will lead in that direction. Tracking expenses will suddenly make trade-offs become clear: Spend $150 on dining out each month, or eat at home more often and sock away that money toward student loans (or a big splurge trip to Cancun)? Skip the daily coffee and doughnut before school or work and instead save for a good, warm pair of winter boots? For a young person who doesn't yet know about deferred gratification, this could be the time to introduce it.

While most grown-up kids do their banking and bill paying online, it's still not a bad idea to teach the ancient arts of check writing and checkbook balancing before they set off on their own. Also advise young people to shop around before selecting a bank and setting up a first bank account. Compare monthly checking and ATM fees along with overdraft or bounced-check charges and make sure that come-ons to get new student accounts are actually beneficial.

Treat credit and debit cards with caution. Not all that surprisingly, *Generation Debt* is the title of not one but two books about today's emerging adults, because this cohort is the most debt-burdened generation in history. According to Carmen Wong Ulrich, in 1970, the average credit card holder owed $158; today that number has skyrocketed to $7,500, and younger folks owe a large chunk of this debt. Particularly if their credit card debt is added to their student loan debt, by their twenties, young people may be drowning in it.

If used wisely, a credit card can be a convenience; if misused, it can turn into a sinkhole. Since the 2009 Credit Card Act, credit cards can be issued only to those age 21 and over. For parents who want to help teach responsible credit card use, some financial experts suggest opening a joint, low-limit credit card with their 18- to 21-year-olds to educate them to pay bills on time, help them build a good credit score, and get them ready for wise credit card use when they turn 21 or afterward. Especially during the launching years, when some emerging adults may not be at their most responsible, a debit card may be a smarter choice than a credit card. With a debit card, the funds are transferred immediately from a user's bank account, not deferred to be paid later on. And if there's not enough money to cover it, the transaction will be declined— another stop sign to spending what isn't there. Debit cards help enforce a simple but crucial rule of thumb: Don't spend money you don't have.

If your emerging adult insists on getting a credit card rather than a debit card, be sure he knows what a huge rip-off credit card interest rates can be—a staggering 17 percent (and punitive rates spiking from 25 to 30 percent for missed payments or charging beyond a credit limit).

> My mother said, "Money is not a big deal," but it becomes one if you don't have it. We traveled even though we couldn't afford it and spent what we didn't have. Our son reacted against it. He put together his financial profile on mint.com, has some stocks, and keeps his restaurant tips in a shoe box.
>
> **MOTHER OF A SON, 26**

Emphasize to your kids that the smart path to solvency is to pay each bill in full by the due date. Simply paying the minimum required each month can turn out to be very costly over the long haul.

For some young people, having a credit card is an open invitation to spend what they don't have. If they do run up a large debt, many parents can't afford to bail them out, and many, on principle, wouldn't want to, even if they could afford it. Make it clear to grown children when they get their first card whether or not they will be totally on their own with their credit card bills, as that awareness might put the brakes on overspending.

Be smart about student loans. Some 94 percent of college students currently graduate with debt—up from 45 percent in 1993, according to a *New York Times* analysis of data from the Department of Education. Some observers believe that the Occupy Movement was fueled, in part, by the frustration of 20-somethings over their staggering student loans and pervasive joblessness, red-flag issues for today's young people, just as the draft and the Vietnam War were for their parents.

While all student loans need to be paid back starting after graduation, government-backed loans (also known as federal education loan programs) have some distinct advantages over private loans. Government-backed loans (through the big federal loan companies, Nellie or Sallie

Mae) don't need to be cosigned by a parent, and they offer a short, post-graduation grace period before interest payments start. After four years of perfect repayment, the government will shave up to 1 percent off the interest rate (a good savings on a 6 or 8 percent rate). In contrast, private loans do need a cosigner, and interest charges kick in as soon as a student graduates.

Public Service Loan Forgiveness (PSLF) is a federal program, established in 2007, to encourage young people to go into public service. For emerging adults who enter government, nonprofit, and other public service jobs, this program cancels any student debt that started in 2007 or after and still remains after ten years of making qualifying payments. There are also federal loan forgiveness options available for teachers in inner-city schools, nurses, and AmeriCorps and Peace Corps volunteers.

Another important federal program to know about is the Income-Based Repayment program, available to student borrowers but not their parents. Updated in 2011 as "Pay as You Earn," it caps monthly loan payments at 15 percent of after-tax income each year (and will drop to 10 percent in 2014), and forgives any debt remaining after 20 years. This is a big deal for grown kids and their parents who may have feared that a big load of student debt would gobble up half the kids' income for years.

An unemployment deferment, granted for six months at a time, could also be the right choice for a young person having trouble finding work. For subsidized federal loans, interest does not accrue during the deferment period. Interest does accrue on private loans, but if asked, lenders may be willing to postpone charging interest and add it all to the loan principal after the deferment period is over.

Currently, student loan default after the first three years is at a high of 13 percent, according to the United States Department of Education. Borrowers beware: Federal loans can't be discharged in bankruptcy and, if unpaid, will continue to accumulate fees and ruin future credit.

It's never too early to start saving for retirement. When young people start making a steady income and are able to cover their own living expenses, they need to do several valuable things at once—pay off high-interest debt, build a rainy day fund, and save for retirement.

The top priority, all financial experts agree, is getting rid of any high-interest-rate debt they've built up, especially from credit cards. Put aside a certain amount of money each month to attack that debt and stay at it until it's paid in full. And if it's been a deep hole, cutting up the credit cards and paying for things by using debit cards or only cash may be the best long-term solution.

Although putting hard-earned money into savings may be a low priority for young people in their twenties, financial experts recommend they set aside at least 10 percent of income to build a three- to six-month emergency fund. Though retirement may feel as distant as the moon to those in their twenties, do give newly employed children the "compound interest talk," and encourage them to start saving for their later years now. If they have a job with a company 401(k) plan, urge them to take advantage of it, especially if the company matches their contributions (usually half of every dollar they put in, up to a certain dollar amount). Although that money is not accessible without a 10 percent penalty until they're 59½, it will grow tax-free over the years—and be taxed only on withdrawal.

For those young people who can't access a retirement plan through work, it's still smart to establish an IRA (Individual Retirement Account) and make annual contributions to it—up to $2,000 per year can be invested tax-free. Even a smaller amount will accrue nicely over the decades, and it's also tax deductible right now. It helps to set up an automatic monthly deduction. Making these IRA contributions will instill the savings habit in young people and slowly start cushioning their old age. For parents who probably won't live to see their children's retirement, it's reassuring to know grown-up kids will have a good nest egg when their time comes.

If you find yourself grumbling about how the financial drain of parenting is lasting much longer than you expected, take heart. Most emerging adults are striving steadily to reach financial independence, and by age 30, most have at last emerged into stable employment with a higher income (often combined by then with a spouse's or partner's earnings). Like you, they look forward to the day when the Bank of Mom and Dad can close its doors for good. Until then, during these financially uncertain

Q: *We're feeling panicky because our part-time employed daughter will soon turn 26 and age out of our family health insurance coverage. Any suggestions?*

A: A healthy 20-something can get a decent, affordable policy through major insurers and state-run programs that will cover major medical setbacks and hospitalizations as well as a limited number of monthly doctors' visits. If you can afford to help your daughter cover this policy until (you hope) she finds a job that offers health insurance, this is money well spent. If you can't afford to contribute, make it clear to her that having health insurance should be a top priority, even if she feels healthy as a horse right now. Also, see if she might be eligible for your state's Medicaid program, which provides health care for low-income people. Without health coverage, one accident or serious illness could ruin her financial standing before she's even upright.

years, any judicious help that you're able to provide will enhance the likelihood that your emerging adults will flourish in their twenties and beyond. As young people become adults it's also good to be reminded of the interdependence of all stages of life. Right now, you may be stretching your resources both to assist your grown kids and to help out your elderly parents with medical expenses, housing, or more. But one day you'll be the elderly generation, and your children will have learned from you how to give a helping hand.

11

Keeping the Faith (or Not)

When our children were growing up we were
very active in church. I tried to instill
in them the idea that the spiritual component,
whatever form that takes, is part of us,
so I'm bothered by them turning their back on spirituality.

MOTHER OF A DAUGHTER, 25, AND A SON, 27

The twenties decade is a time for asking Big Questions, and this includes forming an ideology, a worldview, a way of making sense of the world. Deciding what matters most may or may not lead in a spiritual direction. But for most young people, their search means reaching at least tentative conclusions on some core questions about their religious beliefs: Do I believe in God? Do I believe in a life after death? Which parts of my parents' beliefs do I accept, and which parts do I reject? Am I more of a spiritual person than a religious person, and if so, what exactly does that mean?

Emerging adulthood is the crucial life stage for answering these soul-searching questions. Most 18-year-olds are still in the process of identifying a definite religious or spiritual perspective, but by the end of their twenties they usually have a well-defined sense of life's "ultimate concerns," in philosopher Paul Tillich's phrase, just as they usually have found a definite direction in love and work. Their decisions about what they believe and don't believe could land anywhere along a broad spectrum, from atheism to a vague belief in God to a devout traditional faith, from entirely embracing their parents' religious views to completely rejecting them and striking out on their own.

For some parents, their grown kids' religious choices are an emotional flashpoint; for others, the subject is almost a nonissue. Those whose questions about spirituality and religion have long been answered in the negative give scant weight to the topic. What their emerging adults believe is of little interest or concern to them; they may not even know. But when parents' religious beliefs are central to their worldview and daily lives, what their children come to believe by their twenties may be one of the most important measures of their success or failure as parents: success if their children accept and embrace the beliefs they were taught, and failure if they don't. For these parents, their responses to what their grown-up kids believe may be emotionally complex, fraught with meaning about their worthiness as parents.

Losing Faith? The Decline of Religion

Even parents who don't much care about religion may find it illuminating to learn just what emerging adults today believe. A number of recent studies show the same unmistakable pattern: that younger people are less religious than older people in every way, and that religiosity has declined with each successive generation.

For example, one of the most striking findings of the Pew Research Center's 2012 survey on Religion & Public Life is the high proportion of 18- to 29-year-olds who are classified as "unaffiliated," meaning that when asked what religion they are, they respond with some version of "none"—atheist, agnostic, spiritual but not religious, or just not religious. One-third of the 18- to 29-year-olds are unaffiliated in the Pew survey, a far higher proportion than among their parents (15 percent) or grandparents (9 percent). Even with this generational decline, emerging adults in the United States are more religious in both beliefs and practices than emerging adults in Canada or most of Europe. In northern Europe, especially, young people rarely enter a church or synagogue except for weddings or funerals.

Clearly religion is less important to today's emerging adults than to their parents or grandparents, and less relevant to their lives. In their comprehensive study, *Souls in Transition: The Religious Lives of Emerging Adults in America,* Christian Smith and Patricia Snell create a more nuanced portrait. Drawing on the National Study of Youth and Religion (NSYR) survey of over 2,500 young people and interviews with 230 of them, Smith and Snell conclude that for the majority of emerging adults, the beliefs they hold are most accurately described not as a form of Christianity, Judaism, or any other traditional faith.

> We're Catholic, and our sons did the first communion, confession, confirmation, went to C school. When my son made his confirmation, he was like, "Good-bye, church." I don't think it's anything against the religion, he just doesn't like the structure of it. But he believes in God.
>
> FATHER OF SONS, 19 AND 22

Instead, today's emerging adults adhere to an inclusive but vague belief in God. They believe God watches over the world and wants people to be good to one another, as taught by all the world religions, but they don't think there's much need for God in daily life, except when problems arise. They don't believe in sin, or redemption, or hell. They believe God wants us to feel good about ourselves, and that good people—that's nearly all of us except the Satanists and the murderers—go to heaven when they die, regardless of their religion.

To some parents with long-established beliefs, this view may seem a weak, diluted form of traditional religion. However, today's emerging adults mostly find traditional religion too rigid and not inclusive enough. The millennial generation's acceptance of diversity in religious beliefs is one part of their broader embrace of diversity, in areas including ethnic background, nationality, and sexual orientation. They believe, overwhelmingly, that religion is personal and people should be allowed to believe what they like. No one should persecute or even criticize others for believing something different. For religiously oriented parents, the implication of this big-tent acceptance is that your grown kids might get very prickly if you lean on them to attend religious services, even if those rituals are meaningful to you.

Religious Training and Its Limitations

Most American parents believe they should provide some religious training, whether or not it ultimately sticks. Parents in our survey described the religious training they gave their children this way:

- No religious training: 18 percent

- Occasional exposure to religion: 30 percent

- Regular participation in religious activities: 52 percent

What makes this pattern even more striking is that in our sample, when parents were asked "How important is religious faith in your daily life?" 42 percent responded, "Not at all important," a much higher proportion than other surveys have found among American adults. So even in our relatively nonreligious sample, the vast majority of parents provided their children with some degree of religious training, and many of those for whom faith was "Not at all important" nevertheless made sure their children received religious training.

Why would parents want their children to be exposed to religious beliefs the parents don't embrace themselves? The answer appears to be that many parents see religious training as morality training. Exposing children to religion is part of trying to ensure that they become good people, with a strong and clear sense of right and wrong and a commitment to seeing themselves as part of something larger than themselves— with responsibilities to care for others in their community, their society, and the world.

Does this strategy work? If parents provide their children with religious training, does this make it more likely that the children will grow up to be "good people"? Yes, says a large body of research. In both adolescence and emerging adulthood, religious beliefs and participation are associated with lower rates of substance use, illegal activities, and sexual

Q: *My wife and I are agnostics, but to our surprise, our daughter has become seriously involved with a young man who is deeply religious and from a very traditional and conservative religious denomination. She sounds more and more like she is inclined to convert to his religion. We are trying to respect her independence, but at the same time there is a lot in his religion that we find objectionable, especially in what we see as the subordinate status of women. Should we speak up or keep quiet?*

A: Go ahead and speak up. Your daughter probably already knows what you think, and she's unlikely to be surprised that you don't approve of the conservative views of her boyfriend's religion. So speak your piece, but do it respectfully, recognizing her right as an adult to believe what she wishes. Make your views known in a time and place where you are sure you can do so without becoming angry, resentful, or critical. And don't just talk; listen, too. Ask her what she finds appealing about his religion. (It could be that she's having some doubts, too.) Tell her how you see the religion's view of women, and ask her if she sees it that way or not. You can't expect to change her views, and you shouldn't expect to divide her from someone she loves because of his religious views, but like her, you have a right to your beliefs and a right to express them to her.

---

risk behavior (such as multiple partners). Religiosity in adolescence and emerging adulthood is also associated with a lower likelihood of depression and better relations with parents. And being religious predicts adolescents' and emerging adults' involvement in volunteer work, which might be seen as one reflection of being a "good person."

The Belief Disconnect

Overall, then, parents' goal of promoting the moral development of their children by involving them in religious training seems justified. But does the religious training that parents provide "stick," so that emerging adults continue to believe what they were taught as children?

Here the connection is cloudier. Most emerging adults depart from the religious training they received, sometimes a short distance, sometimes light-years away. Given what we have already seen about development in emerging adulthood, this should not be surprising. Religious questioning is part of the *identity explorations* that are woven into this life stage. This questioning sometimes leads young people to a confirmation of what they were taught as children, but more often it leads to at least some modification of their childhood beliefs and sometimes to a wholesale rejection.

Keep in mind that making independent decisions is one of the top criteria stated by young people when asked what they think makes a person an adult. This declaration of independence includes religious beliefs. Emerging adults generally hold the view that it would be wrong for them simply to accept what their parents and others have taught them about religious issues. A crucial part of growing up and becoming an adult is learning to think for yourself, including about what you believe.

That's why religious beliefs and practices decline from adolescence to the launching phase and even further in the exploring phase. In the landing phase there is a modest swing of the pendulum back the other way. According to Kara Powell and Chap Clark, authors of *Sticky Faith,* about half of the emerging adults who drifted away from their parents' religion do return in the late twenties, as they marry and have children and decide they want their children to have moral-religious training, as they did. But the other half has left for good.

In general, according to the National Study of Youth and Religion, parents from the most conservative religions are most likely to have grown kids who also share their religion. This includes Mormons, Orthodox Jews, and evangelical Christians. For example, Paul and his wife, Sheila, are evangelicals who raised their two boys in their faith, including sending them to a conservative religious primary school where Bible study was part of the daily curriculum. Now that one boy is in his late teens and the other in his early twenties, both have continued to believe much as their parents did. "Our boys are very different, and they even like different kinds of church services," says Paul, "but they both seem to be deeply committed to their Christian faith."

"I don't know what to believe now."

In contrast, the NSYR reports that Catholics are among the least suc-cessful denominations in keeping their lambs within the fold. Charles and Anna are devout Catholics, but their son David, 22, is questioning his faith in ways his parents find troubling. As David and his brother were growing up, Charles recalls, the family went to church not only once a week but other times. The parents still do. In fact, Anna has served as director of religious education at the church for the past ten years, a demanding but unpaid volunteer position. However, David, a junior in college, no longer holds his parents' Catholic beliefs. "I don't know what to believe now," he says.

It was going to college that began to turn him away from his child-hood faith. "I took a class on Christianity at school and it was kind of bad, how corrupt it was," he recalls. But it also seems that being away from the routine of going to church and participating in church activities has led him to see the religion differently on the occasions when he returns. As a child, he never really questioned it, but now he's been removed from it for a while, and going back to the old traditions is a shock. Beliefs and rituals he once took for granted now strike him as strange. He recalls tak-ing his younger sister to a Catholic summer camp and seeing it through different eyes. "It's kind of weird," he says, "because I used to go to that camp myself, and I just dropped my sister off and I was thinking, these people are crazy! Really extreme."

His parents, whose Catholicism is a vital part of their lives, are deeply disappointed by his rejection of his childhood faith. Anna tries to keep him connected to the church by requiring him to attend mass when he comes home to visit. "When he's home, he goes. It's the rule of the house." However, she admits, "He'll go only if we force him." Charles takes the long view, remembering that "I also went away from the church at that age, then came back." Perhaps, he thinks, David will go through a process of questioning his faith and exploring alternatives, then come back to it later. But, at least for now, David has turned his back on his family's beliefs.

Parents who are not especially religious themselves can usually toler-ate their grown children's drift away from conventional religious views and practices. Some share their emerging adults' all-inclusive approach to religion, and as long as their children are honest, kind, morally serious, and believe in God, whatever else they believe is fine. "If you are a good person, it doesn't matter" what you believe, says one such mother of two sons and a daughter in their twenties. Some parents took their young children to church only out of a feeling of parental duty, and when their children stop going, they stop going, too . . . and with a sense of relief.

There are also parents who are surprised to find that their children grow up to be more religious in emerging adulthood than they were at younger ages—and more devout than their parents are. The National Study of Youth and Religion found that about a quarter of 13- to 17-year-olds who were classified as nonreligious became Christians by the time they were 18- to 23-year-olds. This switch can be as hard for nonreligious parents as the change from believer to nonbeliever is for devout parents. In both cases, it is jarring for parents to realize that their children have adopted a way of seeing the world that is radically different from their own. But for nonreligious parents, it may be helpful to see this as a measure of their belief in the value of encouraging their children to think for themselves. If you believed they should make their own decisions about matters of faith, it makes sense that you should respect what they have decided upon, even if their choice is different from yours.

In Jewish families, too, emerging adults may become more observant than their parents. "They're both more religious than we are," one Jewish mother says with some astonishment at her daughter, 24, and son, 27. True, she and her husband raised their children in "a Jewish home," with regular observance of the traditional holidays. They involved the children in Jewish day school, camps, and youth groups, and "a lot of that stuck" along the way. But now both grown children keep kosher, which their parents do not. Their son is training to be a rabbi and is currently spending the year studying in Israel. Occasionally when they have to prepare a special kosher meal for their kids or fear their criticism, these parents may find themselves thinking, "This is a good thing, I guess, but is it too much of a good thing?"

Still, having children who are more observant than their parents is a problem some Jewish parents would like to have. Overall, like young people in other religions, Jewish youth are also drifting away from their inherited traditions. Keeping children within the religious tradition is perhaps more of a concern for Jewish parents than for most other parents, because for many Jews, Judaism is not just a religion but an ethnic and cultural identity as well. Even if Jewish young people are not strictly observant temple-goers, many parents still hope they'll at least be "bagel Jews" who identify with Jewish customs and traditions. To many Jewish adults, if young people forget or reject their Jewish roots, the very survival of Jews as a people is at risk. And some see interfaith marriage as a threat. As anti-Semitism has waned in recent decades, one consequence has been that the proportion of Jews marrying non-Jews has grown from just 5 percent in 1950 to over 50 percent

> We're Jewish, and we had a Jewish household all along, but we didn't force it on our children. My daughter would not marry someone who is not Jewish, and she also wants to have a Jewish household. I think our son is probably an atheist.
>
> FATHER OF A SON, 25, AND A DAUGHTER, 29

today. The children of these intermarriages are less likely to have a strong Jewish identity themselves, according to numerous studies.

Even with two Jewish parents, many young people drift away from their parents' beliefs in their teens and twenties. In response to this pattern, a variety of American Jewish organizations, acutely aware that the twenties are a crucial decade to cement Jewish beliefs, now have programs that actively promote greater religious involvement during these years.

The best known and fastest-growing of these programs is the Birthright program, which offers a free trip to Israel for Jews who are 18 to 26 years old. Birthright began in the late 1990s, the brainchild of a small group of Jewish philanthropists who were deeply concerned by surveys showing there was a very low affiliation with Israel among Jewish emerging adults. They feared that succeeding generations would lose a connection to Israel and to their Jewish identity. When Jewish emerging adults travel to Israel with Birthright, they visit religious sites and learn about the history of both ancient and modern Israel. So far, 150,000 young people have taken part, and enrollment is rising every year. The goal is that eventually a majority of Jewish young people will have gone to Israel and will feel a personal connection with it that lasts into adulthood. According to Rabbi Scott Aaron, author of *Jewish U: A Contemporary Guide for the Jewish College Student,* there is some evidence that the program succeeds in promoting greater participation in Jewish practices, but it remains to be seen how long the effects last.

Although emerging adulthood is a time for defining beliefs, this does not mean that these beliefs are forever fixed by age 30. Parents, too, continue their religious and spiritual journeys into midlife and old age. Many of them become more religious with age. In the Gallup polls of religious beliefs, in 1975, 45 percent of 18- to 29-year-olds indicated that their religious beliefs were "very important" to them. Twenty-six years later, in 2001, 60 percent of this same group—now ages 44 to 55, and parents of today's emerging adults—responded that their religious beliefs were "very important" to them. The increase in religiosity continues into late adulthood. With age, adults tend to think more in terms of life's deeper meaning and purpose, and many of them find consolation in religious and spiritual answers.

What Can (and Can't) Parents Do?

Our research suggests that most parents accept their emerging adults' decisions about what to believe. They may be surprised and even dismayed to find that all the religious training they provided ultimately had little lasting effect on their children's beliefs, but they come to respect their emerging adults' choices.

But for some parents with deeply held traditional beliefs, emotions run especially strong on this topic. They may criticize or even reject their children, as punishment for not remaining in the fold. We sympathize with parents who find themselves in this situation, where children are straying from their family's core beliefs. However, keep in mind that a rejecting response is unlikely to be effective. Criticizing young people for their beliefs (or absence of beliefs) will not bring them back to your religion and make them accept what you believe. In fact, given the importance that emerging adults place on making their own decisions, trying to force them to believe anything is more likely to make them dig in their heels and become even more resistant. A reality of modern life is that people get to decide for themselves what to believe, and emerging adults today feel they have not just a right but an obligation to make that decision (among others) on their own. "Turn the other cheek" may be the wisest course for parents here. The best way to persuade children of the value of your faith is to show the fruits of it in your life, including your capacity to forgive your sons and daughters for not believing what you believe.

The most that deeply religious parents can do is to provide their children with religious training and hope it "takes," while realizing that in a pluralistic society, it may not. "I raised them both Catholic," says one mother of two emerging adult sons. That meant weekly mass, religious education programs throughout childhood, and confirmation at puberty. One of the boys even attended a Catholic university. Yet, as of their early twenties, both have declared themselves agnostics and refuse to participate in anything Catholic. Their mother would have preferred that they remain within the faith, but she accepts their choices: "Our philosophy was, we want to raise them in something, and when they're old enough, they can choose." Knowing how important it was to their mother for them to be Catholic, her younger son was concerned about how she would react upon hearing he was an agnostic. Now, she says, "He was surprised how well we took it. We were very accepting." This live-and-let-live response is more likely to make children return to their family's faith later in life than a response of anger and rejection would be.

We certainly don't mean to make it sound as if this is easy for parents to do. It's hard, and harder still if emerging adults not only reject their parents' religion but choose a different one. It can be disorienting and disheartening to see grown kids adopting a religious worldview that seems bizarre and foreign. It may be that your emerging adult will embrace a religion that seems to be too far out of the mainstream, such as Mormonism or Scientology. Giving grown kids the benefit of the doubt will go a long way to help keep communication open. At least learn something about their new beliefs and perhaps attend an event or service with them to show your interest. If the belief system seems too extreme for you, ask them if they are open to hearing your opinion, and if so, be clear about your reservations.

Interfaith marriage and wedding ceremonies bring any differences between the new couple's religions to center stage. Where will the wedding be held and who will officiate, if there are two different traditions to accommodate? Sometimes a compromise is reached with a clergyperson from each tradition present. Or, for example, an interfaith Hindu and Christian couple may have a traditional Hindu henna-painting ritual first and later a less formally religious ceremony. Sometimes the path of least resistance is a nondenominational ceremony with a judge or nonreligious officiant.

Whatever your own religious background, you may embrace these new traditions and openly welcome

> I wanted to give our daughter more exposure to religion, but my husband, who grew up in a family where you had to be at church every time the doors opened, did not want to force religion on our child. He wanted her to have enough knowledge to make her own decisions.
>
> MOTHER OF A DAUGHTER, 22

your child's partner's faith—or you may find the different customs strange or upsetting. And your feelings may get even more complicated when the interfaith couple has a baby and makes decisions about how this baby, your grandchild, will be raised. Jewish parents may find themselves having to grit their teeth through the baptism of a grandchild in the Catholic church of their daughter's husband. Evangelical Christian parents may find themselves wincing while witnessing the bris (infant circumcision) of the grandchild born to their son's Jewish wife. Welcome to the multicultural world of the twenty-first century, with all its rich diversity and all its social and psychological strains and challenges.

Of course you can express your own point of view on religious issues, and have a vigorous exchange, as you might with any other adult. If you

---

Q: *Our daughter is seriously involved with a young man whose religious background is very different from ours. We have tried to accept him, but worry that if she marries him she will no longer hold to our beliefs and their children will not be raised in our religious tradition, either. What can we do?*

A: Your concerns are not unreasonable. It's true, statistically, that people in interfaith marriages are less likely to practice any religion, and children of interfaith marriages tend to receive less religious training. However, there are exceptions, and your daughter and her future children may be among them. The key question is, how important is religion to her? If it's a valued part of her life and her identity, she'll probably find a way to keep practicing her faith and to introduce her children to it. If it's not, she won't. In any case, your job is done here. You did your best to raise her in the faith that is important to you. Rejecting her partner will not make him go away. Rejecting her for loving him may indeed make her go away, but we hope that is not what you want, and we doubt that it is. The more you express your faith through love, forgiveness, and generosity of heart, the more attractive the faith is likely to seem, to her and to her family-to-be.

---

find yourself wondering what your grown kids believe, this may be a good time to initiate a discussion. You'll find, as we have, that they are sure to have opinions on religious issues, even if they haven't expressed them to you. Just don't expect to convert them back to your worldview. Whatever you taught them in childhood, they have been influenced by the larger society, too, where the reigning ethic is that children have not just a right but a duty to depart from their parents' faith and make their own decisions about what faith to follow . . . or not.

A Reasonable Middle Ground

Even if older and younger generations no longer share religious practices, it is not unreasonable for parents to expect their children to take part in family traditions—Easter at Uncle Mike's or Passover at

Grandma's. Some young people may resist, because they will feel it would be hypocritical (not to mention boring) for them to take part in rituals they no longer believe in. In truth, it will be a sign of their maturity when they can go along with such family occasions out of respect for their parents, without feeling threatened or defensive. But if they're not willing, at this age they can't be forced to go.

Parents often face resistance when they lean on their grown-up kids to keep attending religious services regularly, not only because the children's beliefs have changed but because many young people find traditional religious services far too slow and quiet for a high-tech age. Growing up as "digital natives," today's emerging adults are connected to media of one kind or another almost constantly—recorded music, digital devices, and television are all a ubiquitous presence in their daily lives. The pace and peace of a typical religious service may feel to them like walking through the door to an earlier century, and it's a place where they may feel like strangers in a strange land. Everything about it, from the music to the collectively chanted doctrine to the formal dress, seems centuries old, a relic of an ancient (and much less entertaining) era.

To many of the older people at religious services, the whole value of the experience is in maintaining the ancient traditions, in stepping away from the relentless technological barrage of today's world and savoring an hour each week of quiet contemplation. Consequently, the older congregants may be reluctant to update the format to appeal to the young, says Mark "Marko" Ostreicher, a youth pastor and author of *Youth Ministry 3.0.* "It requires the older generations to have a willingness to compromise on the style of the church service. Some are willing and some are not." But that's what seems to work, he says, for keeping young people engaged as they move from adolescence to emerging adulthood. He finds that more churches are developing programs specifically for emerging adults, as they realize their congregations are shrinking and will expire if they can't attract young people and keep them involved. But it will be tough to reverse the growing trend away from religion among the young.

12

When Things Go Wrong

My daughter had a breakdown her last semester of college.
She was depressed, and she had anxiety attacks and trouble
sleeping. It was very hard to see her like that. She always
appeared so self-assured. It was as if an eggshell broke.

MOTHER OF A DAUGHTER, 23

Throughout this book, we've sought to offer reassurance to parents who are worried that their grown-up kid might never grow up. Although most emerging adults experience struggles and disappointments and dead ends in the course of their twenties, nearly all of them make a more-or-less successful transition to a self-sufficient adulthood by around age 30, with stable commitments in both love and work.

Nearly all, but not all. This chapter is about the rest, the ones whose crises are deeper, whose problems are more severe, and whose prospects for a successful adulthood are less sure. These are the young people who need extra support from both family and professionals during their twenties and may continue to need it for years—perhaps even decades—to come.

Emerging adulthood is a high-risk life stage in many ways. Seventy-five percent of adult mental health problems show up by age 24, including diverse problems such as depression, anxiety disorder, substance abuse, eating disorders, bipolar disorder, and schizophrenia. The launching phase is especially perilous. It is during the early twenties that all sorts of risky behaviors reach their zenith. Alcohol use and abuse is highest at age 21, just when it becomes legal in the United States to purchase alcohol. Not surprisingly, that's the peak age for drunk-driving accidents and fatalities as well. Use of marijuana and other drugs, too, is most prevalent in the early twenties. So is sexual risk-taking and consequently that's the peak time for sexually transmitted infections, abortions, and births to single mothers. By the exploring phase of the midtwenties, risky behaviors have declined substantially, and by the landing phase of the late twenties they have declined further, to about the level where they will be for the rest of adulthood.

Although the emerging adult years can be treacherous, most young people manage them without major problems. In fact, as we've seen, numerous studies have shown that for the majority of emerging

> A lot of college kids, you ask them how much they drink, and everyone says they don't drink much. Then you ask specifically, and it's two to three times a week, five to six drinks each time for the girls, six to eight for the boys, and they don't think that's a lot because it's so common. They don't think it's a problem, even when they admit to blackouts, and to drinking and driving.
>
> PEDIATRICIAN

adults, self-esteem, well-being, life satisfaction, and a lot of other good things increase from the teens through the twenties. But it's helpful to learn what can go wrong and how to spot the red flags, when to step back and when to get professional help (short answer: for all serious psychological difficulties). It's not always easy to tell the difference between slightly troublesome and serious. When does a lively social life with lots of "partying" morph into a substance use disorder? When does a struggle with normal identity issues about "what to do with my life" become clinical depression? When does a preoccupation with looking good and staying fit become an eating disorder? Our goal is to offer information and guidance, but there are no simple answers to these questions and no magical solutions to the challenging problems some young people face.

Alcohol and Drug Abuse

Alcohol is by far the most widely used and abused drug in emerging adulthood—as it is in all adult stages of life. According to the national Monitoring the Future survey, the launching phase of emerging adulthood is prime time for binge drinking (five or more drinks in a row for men, four or more for women). Basically, a binge drinking episode means getting drunk. After a steady rise through the late teens, binge drinking rates (one or more episodes in the past two weeks) peak at 46 percent at ages 21 to 22, then decline through the twenties to 28 percent by ages 29 to 30, 23 percent by age 35, and 20 percent by age 40.

Most of this drinking is woven into the active social lives of emerging adults. In their early twenties, they often gather with friends, going to parties, clubs, or out for dinner, and drinking is often on the evening's agenda. It's certainly a big part of college social life, something that adds to their fun with friends.

But there can be serious consequences, for an especially unlucky or unwise few. True, most of the nearly half of 21- to 22-year-olds who binge drink will experience no effects more severe than a hangover. However, being drunk increases the risk of just about every type of catastrophe for emerging adults. A young couple who find themselves coupling while drunk are less likely to use contraception, setting up the risk of an unwanted pregnancy or an STI. Young women who are drunk are more vulnerable to sexual coercion or even date rape. Young men who are drunk are more likely to start a fistfight. When drinking is excessive, alcohol poisoning can result, which is life threatening. Being drunk also makes all kinds of accidents more likely. How many parents of emerging adults have heard a story about a young person at a party who fell drunk from a balcony to a broken neck and immediate death below, and thought to themselves with a shiver, "That could have been my kid"?

But by far the biggest danger of binge drinking is the deadly combination of drinking and driving. Automobile accidents are the leading cause of death among 18- to 25-year-olds. Nothing else is even close.

Demand a Designated Driver!

So what can parents do? Most emerging adults don't live with their parents anymore. They could be out drinking any given night of the week, and their parents would never know. Nevertheless, parents' influence can still be substantial, even from a distance. The most important thing parents can do is to promote an ethic of responsible drinking, especially in relation to driving. Ideally this begins in high school, when adolescents are first beginning to drive. Parents should talk directly to their adolescents: "Absolutely no drinking and driving, period. If you're going out for the evening to a place where there is going to be drinking, be sure there is a 'designated driver' who agrees to drive but not drink. If the designated driver drinks anyway, and the others in your group are drunk as well, call me and I'll come get you (option A), or call a cab and I'll pay for it later (option B). If you violate this rule, you will be grounded for a long time, and you'll lose your driving privileges, too. Your life is too important to me to risk in a drunk-driving accident. You and your friends have got to take this seriously. It's the biggest danger to people your age."

It's not too late to send (or repeat) this message in emerging adulthood, although it has to take a somewhat different form. Parents no longer have the power they did when their children were adolescents; they can't just lay down the law. Still, even in the twenties this topic is important and serious enough to warrant the direct approach, something like this:

Parent: *What are you doing tonight?*

Grown-Up Kid: *A few of us are going to go out to dinner, maybe to a club after.*

Parent: *Great. Be sure to have a designated driver.*

Grown-Up Kid: *(Sighs.)* I know.

Parent: *Well, I hope you do know. You risk your life if you drink and drive, or if you let somebody else drive you while they're drunk. I love you, and I want you to be around for a long, long time.*

Emerging adults will almost certainly find this kind of direct advice irritating. Remember how important it is to them to make their own decisions as part of becoming an adult. They are sure to bristle when parents tell them what to do, whether it's on this topic or any other. Still, they'll hear it, and they'll remember it, and many of them will be influenced by it.

And this, too: You will have met your responsibility as a parent. It's a welcome transition when parents and grown kids can be more like friends and treat each other like near-equals. But there are still times, even in emerging adulthood, when parents have to step into their role as parents, not friends. The issue of drinking and driving is too important and too potentially lethal to ignore. Any parents who avoid speaking up because they don't want to disrupt the cozy friendship are doing their child no favors. Being a good parent sometimes means being something other than a friend.

"He couldn't juggle the balls anymore."

Although most young people who binge drink during their emerging adult years mature into a less-alcohol-soaked phase by age 30, alcohol is a potentially addictive drug, and some fall prey to that addiction. Andrea, 48, and her husband have lived a nightmare for the past five years watching alcohol destroy the life of their son Connor—and their lives as well. The problems began in his senior year of high school. "That's when it started to go downhill," Andrea recalls. Connor's parents knew he was getting drunk frequently, but he was drinking only on the weekends. His parents thought, well, maybe he's getting it out of his system. He kept up his grades, too, taking all Advanced Placement classes and acing them. So how could there be a serious problem?

Connor got into several good colleges and decided to go to a university in the Southwest to study finance. There, too, he did well academically, but the problems with his alcohol use began to intensify. He was arrested for driving while intoxicated (DWI) once, then twice. "I kept hoping, hoping, hoping it was normal college drinking, but I knew it wasn't," Andrea remembers. "It kept escalating. After the second DWI, we all knew he had a problem that was beyond normal." He, too, seemed to realize he had a problem. He began attending Alcoholics Anonymous meetings, but only occasionally.

Nevertheless, he made it through his first three years of college and seemed on track to finish. In fact, the family was all scheduled to fly out west for his graduation. But with just three weeks to go, he suddenly dropped out and left school. "I think at the end he started falling apart and couldn't get it together to look for a job and finish all his classes—that's when he couldn't juggle the balls anymore," Andrea says now. His downward slide began when he applied for a job at a prestigious investment bank and didn't get it. "I think he was depressed that he didn't get picked for the job, when he's been the Golden Boy his whole life. He felt like he was heading into the abyss: 'I don't have a job, I'm a failure.'"

Connor entered a rehab program, briefly, but left because he didn't like the restrictions. Now he is homeless, living on the streets and getting by from one day to another, his mother knows not how. Andrea and her husband are in touch with him every day via phone or texting, but every

---

Q: *My son goes out drinking a lot, usually three to four times a week, and although he hasn't said so, I suspect that marijuana and other drugs are often part of the evening. Where is the line between a "partying lifestyle" and substance abuse?*

A: The main sign of a substance abuse disorder is that the substance abuse interferes with normal functioning. If emerging adults party with their friends and still pass their classes, still make it to work, still have healthy relationships, it's not defined as a disorder, according to the criteria established by the American Psychiatric Association. When a person has a substance abuse disorder, usually other people can see the problems it causes.

Of course, friends may not see, if they also have similar substance abuse problems, but others will. And the consequences will be evident in DWIs or accidents and lost jobs and relationships.

---

contact with him is agony. "I'm completely devastated by it," his mom says. "He calls to tell me he's going to get killed if I don't send him money. He texts my husband about his living situation, 'It's dangerous, I can't live here.' Last night, he said to me, 'If you don't give me any money I'm going to be dead.' It just killed me to tell him no, but that's what everybody tells me to do. But what if he's walking through a bad part of town and he gets killed? What if he does something desperate? You wait for the phone call to arrive in the middle of the night—your son has been arrested, your son is in the hospital."

This is a disturbing story to any parent of an emerging adult. Andrea and her husband seem as if they've done everything good parents should do, providing love and guidance to their child throughout his youth, and yet his life went horribly offtrack anyway in emerging adulthood. Many other emerging adults get drunk frequently during their college years and don't drop out of school or become alcoholics. Andrea herself admits that she and her husband were "huge partiers" when they were college students. Why didn't they become alcoholics and Connor did? "That's the million-dollar question," Andrea sighs.

It is worth noting that Connor's grandfather was an alcoholic as well, suggesting the likelihood of a genetic vulnerability to alcoholism. But is there anything Connor's parents could have done, should have done, to change the course of his life so that it did not come to this disastrous dead end? No doubt they ask themselves this question every day, and there is no easy answer. Maybe they could have more consistently promoted an ethic of responsible drinking. Maybe there should have been some kind of consequences, especially after the second DWI, but what? Take away his tuition money? Would that have helped, or would that have made things worse more quickly? Who can say?

Parents who have struggled with addiction themselves may feel especially helpless as they see their emerging adults sliding toward the same fate. They may feel guilty about having provided a destructive model that their child is now following. They may think, "What right do I have to tell my kid to stop drinking/smoking/using when I can't stop myself?" But this may be a chance for grown kids and parents to support one another in the effort to avoid, confront, or shake the addiction. Also, emerging adults like Connor, with a family history of addiction, need to be fore-warned if generational patterns indicate this risk.

One option for parents whose sons or daughters are facing a sub-stance abuse addiction or other severe crisis is simply to say, "Come home for a while, until you can get back on your feet. We'll help you find a way to straighten out your life and move forward again." For parents who choose this course, it would be best to make it clear from the start that it is not an open invitation, extending for years to come. It could be presented as a relatively brief transition, to allow for a consideration of options—perhaps entering a hospital or a rehab clinic, perhaps finding a job and living independently. Parents should also recognize that once troubled emerging adults move home, it might be difficult to get them to move on, even if you want them to. Still, parents like Connor's, whose grown-up kids are in what appears to be a life-threatening predicament, may feel that the door has to be opened, however reluctantly.

Marijuana and Other Drugs

Like binge drinking, marijuana use peaks in the early part of emerging adulthood and then declines through the twenties. According to the national Monitoring the Future survey, reported annual use of mari-juana rises through the late teens to a high of 32 percent at ages 19 to 20. By ages 29 to 30 it has declined to 18 percent, and further to about 10 percent at ages 35 and 40. Other illicit drug use also follows this pattern. According to the same survey, annual use of other illicit drugs (such as cocaine, Ecstasy, and methamphetamines) peaks at 20 percent at ages 21 to 22, declines to 13 percent by ages 29 to 30, and levels out at about 10 percent at ages 35 and 40.

Most drug use in emerging adulthood is driven by the same kinds of motivations that make binge drinking attractive. It's part of the social life of some peer groups, and sometimes it's just one part of going out with friends to a party or a club. It relaxes people and may make it easier to strike up a conversation with a new person. Some of it is motivated by the exploratory impulse that is so prominent at the emerging adult life stage; "to see what it was like" is a common reason reported in studies that ask young people why they used a drug. And just as for binge drinking, other drug use is made possible by the fact that most emerging adults have more freedom and fewer responsibilities than people of other ages do.

Even though alcohol is legal and other drugs are not, alcohol causes far wider devastation than all other drugs put together, because it is so widely used and so deadly when combined with driving. Nevertheless, other drugs can be damaging, especially when used frequently. A large body of research on marijuana use points to the conclusion that regular use of marijuana disrupts problem-solving abilities, lowers motivation for other activities, damages sperm production, and is highly addictive. Other illicit drugs are illegal for good reasons: They cloud judgment, weaken restraints, and carry risks of permanent physical and psychological harm.

One good piece of news for today's parents is that rates of all kinds of substance use have dropped substantially since they were young. Overall, the children of the baby boomers are much less likely to use or abuse substances than boomers were during their own youth.

Of course, this may complicate the message parents now send to their kids and create another opportunity for "Do as I say, not as I did." But just because parents may have used substances in their youth doesn't mean they can't persuasively urge their own children against following the same path. It's probably best to be honest and direct about a checkered past, something like: "I did some stupid things when I was your age that I regret now. I hope you don't take the risks I did. It could have ended very badly, and I might never have had the life I have now, including you. Believe me, it's not worth the risk."

Digging Out of Depression

Emerging adulthood is a time of high hopes, but it's also a time of struggle for most people. It can be exciting to be grappling with big identity questions about who you are and what you want to do with your life, but it can be confusing and overwhelming, too, especially if you have trouble coming up with any answers. It can be fun and fulfilling to try out a wide range of experiences—different educational paths, jobs, places to live, and love partners—but it can also be exhausting. Often the freedom of emerging adulthood is welcome—no one can tell you what to do and when to do it—but along with that freedom can come a sense of isolation, the chill of realizing you are on your own and have to swim constantly in order not to sink.

The result of these contradictory forces is this paradox of mental health during the emerging adult years: Overall, self-esteem and life satisfaction rise, but at the same time, rates of depression rise, too. Out on their own, most young people keep their heads above water, but more sink than when they had Mom's and Dad's daily support to hold them up.

As we've discussed earlier in the book, the college transition can be a rocky one, and depression sometimes first appears during the first year or two of college. Gloria Saito, a clinical psychologist who runs the counseling service at the University of California, Berkeley, says that she sees students with "a whole range of issues," everything from homesickness and roommate problems to eating disorders and bipolar disorder. But depression is one of the most common problems. At the campus drop-in clinic, she frequently meets students who are buckling under the academic and personal stresses of college life: "We often see students who can't focus, because they feel hopeless and they're having suicidal thoughts." Her first priority is to reduce their current distress. "We help them make a structured plan for how to relieve stress that day: eat a good meal, talk to a friend outside of the counseling center, come back in a couple days." If major depression is diagnosed, she refers them to someone who can provide more extensive mental health services.

One issue that complicates parents' involvement during mental health crises is that for students who are age 18 or older—as nearly all of them are—college counseling services will not inform parents of the student's counseling visit or the nature of the student's problem. The only way this confidentiality can be breached is if the student signs a release form or if the student is believed to be suicidal. If students decline to sign the release, they may be having any of a wide range of serious problems and parents would never know. This underscores the importance of regular contact between students and parents, especially during that first year of college, when risks are highest. Texting, phoning, emailing, and Skyping are key ways for parents to keep informed of how their emerging adults are faring. If you can, attend the parents' weekend most colleges offer during freshman fall.

In college and beyond, it's not unusual for grown-up kids to experience periods of frustration, disappointment, and distress. So how do parents tell when their child's problem is simply a normal part of development in this life stage, unpleasant but nothing to worry about, and when the problem is major depression or another psychological disorder that requires intervention and treatment? Here again, there is no clean line separating normal development from psychopathology. However, it may help parents to know the symptoms of major depression, as specified by the American Psychiatric Association:

- Depressed or irritable mood for most of the day, nearly every day.

- Reduced interest or pleasure in all or almost all activities, nearly every day.

- Significant weight loss or gain, or decrease in appetite.

- Insomnia or oversleeping.

- Unusually agitated or sluggish movements, observable by others.

- Low energy or fatigue.

- Feelings of worthlessness or inappropriate guilt.

- Diminished ability to think or concentrate.

- Recurrent thoughts of death, or recurrent suicidal thoughts.

For a diagnosis of major depression, five or more of these symptoms must be present during a two-week period and must represent a change from previous functioning. At least one of the symptoms must be "depressed mood" or "reduced interest/pleasure." According to a national study, about 8 percent of 18- to 25-year-olds fit this diagnosis.

Knowing the symptoms may be helpful, but the diagnosis of depression is a long way from being an exact science. "Depressed or irritable mood for most of the day," but how depressed or irritable? "Reduced interest or pleasure," but reduced by how much? How much of a weight

Q: *My daughter has been depressed for some time, and lately she has taken to saying that she doesn't really want to live anymore and that she'd be better off dead. I am terrified she may be thinking about killing herself. What can I do?*

A: This kind of talk often precedes a suicide attempt and you are right to be alarmed. You certainly want to urge your daughter to receive mental health treatment immediately, if she is not already. If you feel suicide may be an immediate danger, the best option is to contact the crisis hotline at your local hospital. Every hospital has a crisis hotline, and it is primarily for suicide. If you do not live near your child, there's also a national suicide hotline, and it is excellent (1-800-SUICIDE). They'll let you know the closest hospital that has a crisis intervention team, and they'll give you the number to call. Once you call, the crisis intervention team can provide immediate help. If your child is already in therapy, the therapist should be contacted immediately.

---

gain or loss is "significant"? Still, when parents recognize these symptoms in their emerging adults, it would be wise to urge them to see a mental health professional for a complete evaluation.

A key symptom in distinguishing between clinical depression and the normal identity struggles of emerging adults is loss of interest in their own lives. Say, your son used to love to hang out with friends, now he doesn't return their calls or texts. Or, you and your daughter used to go shopping together all the time, now she has no interest. A red flag is when they become noticeably disengaged from things they used to enjoy.

When major depression has been diagnosed, the recommended approach to treatment is a combination of psychotherapy and antidepressant medications. Research has consistently found that this combination works better than either therapy or antidepressants alone. A wide range of antidepressants has been developed in recent decades, and many of them are highly effective. However, the drugs can only raise mood; it takes therapy to address the underlying problems that may have also contributed to depression.

Bipolar Disorder and Schizophrenia

Among the most serious and challenging problems of the emerging adulthood stage are the severe mental health disorders, especially bipolar disorder and schizophrenia. For both these disorders, nearly all cases are first diagnosed at some time during the period from the late teens through the twenties. According to scientists, this is a biological, genetically based pattern. Both disorders have genetic origins and run strongly in biological families. People who have a close biological relative with bipolar disorder or schizophrenia are at much higher risk of developing the problem themselves. And for most people, the genetic trigger appears to be timed to go off in the late teens or the twenties.

Bipolar disorder, also known as manic depression, involves swings of mood from a manic extreme to a depressed extreme. Sometimes people go directly from one extreme to the other, and sometimes the extremes are separated by periods of relatively normal moods.

Manic moods involve more than simply being very happy. These are the criteria for a manic episode:

- elevated mood

- decreased need for sleep

- goal-directed activity

- increased energy and visible hyperactivity

- impulsive activity, such as spending sprees, sexual indiscretion, and alcohol abuse

- grandiosity

- accelerated speech

- racing thoughts

For a manic episode to be diagnosed, a person must experience at least three of these symptoms every day for several days. Similarly, for a depressive episode, the person must have at least three of the following symptoms for several days:

- unhappiness

- worry

- self-reproach/guilt

- negative evaluation of self

- hopelessness

- suicidal thinking or behavior

- fatigue

- slow and sluggish movements

Bipolar disorder has definite genetic origins, but there is some evidence that there may be environmental triggers as well, such as stress or child abuse. Fortunately, there are many effective drug treatments, and experts recommend combining medications with therapy to treat people with bipolar disorder. Unfortunately, many of the medications have unpleasant side effects, such as weight gain, hair loss, acne, and hand tremors. These side effects often lead people with bipolar disorder to stop taking the medications, which starts the cycle again.

"When Derek has a manic episode, it's like watching a two-year-old run into a busy street."

Derek, now 26, was an intense young man, intellectually sharp but never "well regulated," in the words of his mother, Joyce, 53. His high school years were unstable, and he developed an eating disorder for which he was almost hospitalized. The family found a residential program for him with a reputation for success with challenging kids, but Derek left as soon as he turned 18 and could not be required to stay. He worked as a retail clerk for a year and then felt ready for college in another part of the state where he'd grown up. It was in his first year there that he had his first manic episode, which involved, among other things, buying an expensive motorcycle that was eventually repossessed.

He came home, was diagnosed with bipolar disorder, and started psychiatric treatment and medication. A year or so later he returned to college, this time nearby so he could continue to live at home with Joyce and her second husband, his stepfather. Joyce and Derek's biological father divorced when Derek was 8. His father has also struggled with bipolar disorder but went through electric shock therapy and is now more stable. Still, he and Derek are not close.

Living at home has been good for Derek, providing him with stability and support, but it has been hard on Joyce's marriage. "There's angst getting Derek to function well daily," she admits. "It causes friction with

---

Q: *We saved for years and socked away a lot of money in our son's college fund. Now he's 20, and he's just been diagnosed with bipolar disorder. He's never even applied to college, and, frankly, it looks unlikely that he ever will. Should we spend his college money to get him the best possible treatment?*

A: The first step should be to see what mental health coverage your insurance provides. In addition to the 2010 federal law that requires health insurers to allow parents to keep children on their policy until age 26, a 2008 law requires insurers to cover mental health problems at the same rate as they would cover medical or surgical problems. The next step: the National Institute of Mental Health recommends that people with bipolar disorder keep a daily record of: (1) mood symptoms, (2) treatment, (3) sleep patterns, and (4) life events. This record will help your son's doctor treat him more effectively. Encourage him to keep this record; if he can't or won't, help him out or do it for him.

Don't give up on college yet. With the right medication at the right dosage, along with a good therapist, a person with bipolar disorder has the potential to succeed in college and beyond. If nothing else seems to be working, and you have the opportunity for a promising but costly therapy, it might be worth spending the money if you believe it has the potential to set your son on a healthier path. But check out all your options first, and keep in mind that a more expensive treatment will not necessarily be better for your son than what he can get through your health insurance.

[my husband]. He says I coddle Derek too much and I think he pushes him too much."

Moving in and out of schools and jobs, his friendships and love life often in turmoil, Derek remains highly volatile. His drug regime needs frequent adjustment, and sometimes he'll refuse to take his meds altogether. Also, he hasn't stopped using alcohol and marijuana, which only worsen his symptoms. Even during his infrequent calm periods Joyce finds herself on edge, wondering when the next upheaval will occur. The manic episodes are especially stressful. "When Derek has a manic episode, it's like watching a two-year-old run into a busy street."

Despite Derek's troubled twenties, Joyce remains hopeful that he will make a good life for himself. Yet she realizes that he will need her help for a long time to come, maybe her whole life. "I hope Derek can learn to manage all his ups and downs in work and relationships," she says. "We know he's going to require ongoing support, financial and emotional. I think he has to hit bumps in the road. And the hardest thing is to lay down the line."

"He spiraled down."

Like bipolar disorder, schizophrenia usually appears for the first time in the late teens or the twenties. Schizophrenia is a severe mental disorder that affects thought processes, emotional responsiveness, and social behavior. The main symptoms are:

- hallucinations, such as hearing voices

- delusions, which are false beliefs, such as the belief that someone is trying to poison the person's food or that the television is broadcasting the person's thoughts

- disorganized thinking and language; schizophrenics often jump from one topic to another, and their train of thought does not follow a straight path

- social withdrawal, a lack of interest in other people

- emotional difficulties, for example, sudden bursts of anger and hostility, or a lack of emotional responsiveness

Although the diagnosis of schizophrenia usually is not made until the late teens or the twenties, problems are often evident in childhood.

When Mollie, 55, married Stephen, 54, she became a mother as well to his three children from his first marriage. His first wife had been hospitalized with severe mental illness after the birth of the third child. Curt, the middle son, was the closest to his biological mother and felt her loss most deeply after Stephen's divorce and remarriage. When Mollie entered the family, Curt was just starting middle school. He was having a hard time keeping up with his classmates, and was already showing a host of problems. Over the next couple years he was diagnosed with obsessive-compulsive disorder, oppositional defiance disorder, learning disabilities, and ADHD , for which he tried medication that "didn't agree with him." High school was marked by constant frustration and anger outbursts, and eventually he dropped out.

Afterward, Curt lived at home and worked at a series of low-paying retail jobs. A troubling pattern developed, Mollie recalls, in which "he would work but then sabotage his jobs. Whatever he wasn't allowed, he'd do it. Then he'd get fired, and it was always everyone else's fault." However, he seemed to be settling down in his early twenties. He held a retail job in a pharmacy that lasted three years, by far his longest period of employment. But then, about two years ago, he got fired from that job for insisting on reading a book at the checkout counter while he was working. After that, Mollie says, "He spiraled down." He couldn't find another job, and soon the first definite symptoms of schizophrenia appeared in paranoid delusions.

Difficult as it was, Mollie had to tell him he couldn't live at home any longer, because his outbursts scared the young son she and Stephen had together. He moved into cheap housing with several other guys. Problems with the roommates arose when Curt became fearful that they were trying to inject him with HIV. Recognizing that he needed serious medical help, his parents sought to have him hospitalized, but he refused. Because he was legally an adult, they had to go through a long legal process to show he was potentially a danger to himself or others. They finally got the legal issues settled, and Curt was hospitalized. But the forced hospitalization sent him into a rage, and in the scuffle that followed, his foot was broken, adding to his problems. Since then he has been in and out of the hospital. At times when he is out of the hospital, he has been extremely paranoid and fearful; he has lived months at a time on the streets.

After more than a year of trying, his parents recently succeeded in placing him in a residential care facility for psychotics, which they regard as a much better environment for him than the psychiatric hospital, with a higher standard of care. Mollie has also managed to obtain financial assistance by getting Curt on Supplemental Security Income (SSI), a government program (through Social Security) that provides help to people with disabilities. Exhaling after so many difficult years, Mollie says now, "Curt has calmed down a lot."

Things may have improved for Curt, but the years of problems have taken a toll on Mollie. "This has been the hardest time of my life," she says wearily. "I can't imagine worse. There's no area where I can settle down and relax. I went through a meltdown last month, a mini–nervous breakdown." Her marriage has also suffered. All the stresses of dealing with Curt's problems nearly caused the couple to separate. She hopes their troubles will ease with Curt's new living situation, but she knows that his problems are not over. There is no cure for schizophrenia. Antipsychotic medications, such as those Curt is now taking, can be effective in addressing some of the symptoms, but the challenges of dealing with the disorder will be lifelong for Curt—and for Mollie and her husband as well.

So, what steps can parents take if they believe their emerging adult has a serious mental health disorder? According to Jennifer Tanner, a research professor at Rutgers University and editor of the book *Developing Mental Health in Emerging Adulthood,* it's important to start by recognizing that you can't fix the problem by yourself. "Love is not enough," she says. "Mental health disorders usually require professional intervention. Try to see your role as parent as a connector between your emerging adult and a professional. That's how you can be most helpful."

Treatments for mental health problems are not cheap, and parents and emerging adults may fear that financial concerns will be piled upon the burden of the disorder. The national Affordable Care Act passed in 2010 helps greatly; under their parents' health plan, most emerging adults should be able to obtain access to mental health services until age 26. Of course, many parents lack health insurance themselves. In such cases, their children may be eligible for treatment under the Medicaid program, which serves low-income families and individuals.

Eating Disorders

Of all the problems that arise in emerging adulthood, perhaps the most mysterious are the eating disorders: anorexia nervosa, which is intentional self-starvation, and bulimia, which alternates bingeing (extreme episodes of overeating) and purging (intentional vomiting). Anorexia is the more serious of the two disorders, because self-starvation is extremely damaging to long-term health and can result in death. Both types of eating disorders occur predominantly among women, at a ratio of about 9 to 1, women to men.

For a diagnosis of anorexia nervosa, food intake must have been reduced so much that the person loses at least 15 percent of her body weight. As weight loss continues it eventually results in *amenorrhea,* which means that monthly menstruation ceases. Hair becomes brittle and may begin to fall out, and the skin develops an unhealthy, yellowish pallor. As anorexics become increasingly thin, they frequently develop physical problems that are symptoms of their self-starvation, such as constipation, high sensitivity to cold, and low blood pressure. Many women with anorexia are preoccupied with food, and they may cook elaborate meals—for others. Obsessive, solitary exercise is also a common part of the disorder.

One of the most striking symptoms of anorexia is that young women with this disorder do not see themselves as too thin and do not regard their eating habits as abnormal. They sincerely believe themselves to be too fat, even when they have become so thin that their lives are threatened. Standing in front of a mirror with them and pointing out how emaciated they look does no good—the anorexic looks in the mirror and sees a fat person, no matter how thin she is.

The denial of the problem and the resistance to change can be frustrating for parents, as Leo has learned. His daughter Janelle, who's now 25, has had anorexia for about five years. Like most anorexics, she never showed signs of future problems when she was a girl. In fact, she was a high achiever and seemed headed toward great things. She graduated from high school at the head of her class and went to a top university. But it was there, in her second year, that the eating disorder developed. Leo visited her after not seeing her for a few months and was shocked at her appearance. "It was one of the worst nightmares of my life," he recalls. "She looked gaunt, all skin and bones." She had been thin freshman year, too, but Leo had thought it was just part of the low-budget student life. "Her mother was concerned about her eating habits for a long time, but I didn't think it was a problem, because she was still normal weight. As a student she didn't have much money, so she didn't eat that well, but she looked great."

Now she didn't look great anymore, she looked ill, and Leo knew instantly that she had a serious problem. Not only was she thin but her skin had a sickly pallor and her hair was falling out. Leo could not hide his alarm. "I totally freaked out," he recalls. "I said to her, 'What's happened to my daughter?!' But she said to me, 'I don't think I have a problem.'" He persisted. "I asked her, 'Have you weighed yourself? You look awful.'" But she resisted, sometimes angrily. "The scary thing was, her view of it was so out of the range of any reality," Leo reflects now. During a few days with her, Leo noted other causes for concern. Janelle got up at 5 a.m. daily to work out at an exercise club for three hours. When Leo took her out to dinner at a restaurant, she ordered only a salad containing no protein—then ate just half of it.

Returning home with a heavy heart, he conferred with his ex-wife about what to do. "We don't have positive feelings about each other, but one thing we're proud of is, we've been good coparents," Leo says. "We both ask, 'What's the best thing for the kids?'" When Janelle came home a few weeks later, they urged her to discuss the problem openly with them. "We had serious sit-down meetings about what we thought was going on with her, getting her to look at how much weight she had lost. But she'd look at me and say, 'You know it's not that simple.' Telling an anorexic to eat more is like telling a depressive to cheer up."

Little changed after Janelle's parents confronted her about their concerns. Treatments for anorexia usually have little success, mainly because anorexics are reluctant to take part. As Leo observed, "You've got to think you need help in order for any treatment to do you any good." Janelle did agree to have individual therapy and group therapy in an eating disorders program, and Leo thinks these methods "raised her consciousness a bit" and moved her toward recognizing the problem. However, her eating habits didn't change, and her weight didn't change, either.

What finally triggered an improvement is that Janelle was accepted to a graduate program in bioengineering. The director of the program believed she was an excellent candidate, but he realized instantly when she came for the interview that she had anorexia. So, after consulting with his colleagues, they decided to admit her—under the condition that she would raise her weight to 110 pounds within her first year. She failed to do so, and they were about to drop her from the program, but they told

---

Q: *I have been through the wringer with my daughter's problems for the past seven years—anorexia, depression, drinking binges, bad-news boyfriends, and more. She's now 28 and still asks me for money on a regular basis, still calls or texts me daily to complain about something. I'm exhausted, financially and emotionally, but I don't feel like I can cut her off; I'm about all she's got.*

A: Don't cut her off, but don't go down with her, either. You don't have to cut her off in order to make some space to have a life of your own. Is she seeing a therapist? If so, it might be time for you to have a joint session with the therapist, where you can explain how you feel before someone who can serve as a mediator. If she's not, then try having an honest talk with your daughter. Tell her you love her and you want to support her, but that you're feeling like it's getting to be too much to bear her problems as well as your own. See if, together, you can lay out some guidelines for how much financial support you can (or can't) give her, as well as how many times a week you should be in contact, and whether it's important to get outside professional help. This may be the spark she needs to move ahead with her own life.

---

her she could come back in the fall if she entered an in-patient treatment facility during the summer, and she agreed.

She participated in the treatment for only thirty days, not the ninety days the treatment providers wanted, and she didn't like it and says now she would never go back. Still, the program brought her back from the brink. She gained some weight, her skin color became healthier, and her hair stopped falling out. Nevertheless, Leo knows that the disorder remains, lurking underneath the facade. "There's no question in my mind that the problem is still there. She's borderline where she can stay in her graduate program and not be kicked out. She's figured out what she has to do to avoid people telling her to shape up."

Leo remains distressed over her condition. "Every time I see her I feel sick," he says, thinking about her bright potential and how unhealthy she looks. Yet he has learned that it is futile for him to try to direct her toward a healthier path. "I used to insist she tell me how her treatment is going, but she'd get all defensive. So I just stopped asking." He has been forced to accept the hard truth that Janelle's problems are beyond his control:

> Sometimes I have to put it away and not think about it. You have to let your children grow up and have their independence. It's their life; you can't live it for them. I've learned that I need to back off. My tendency is to jump in, try to fix things, but that's not what's best for her. It's not my problem to solve. This is going to be her battle. The best I can do is to be as loving as possible.

Getting Help

Although parents' influence diminishes once their children reach emerging adulthood, they can still provide an essential boost by helping their children make connections to mental health services. One way for parents to find resources is to consult the National Alliance on Mental Illness (NAMI), whose website (nami.org) contains a wealth of information on a wide range of mental health disorders, including treatments. It also includes contact information for programs and services pertaining to specific mental health disorders. In addition, through the website parents can connect to local and state NAMI chapters, where they can make direct contact with other parents whose children have faced similar problems.

> One of the common issues for emerging adults with serious mental health conditions is how to engage them in the treatment program. You can't force them to be there, so this is the age when young people drop out of treatment faster than any other age group. Whether it's "I've decided I don't want to go," or "I can't get insurance," or "I've moved," that's often when they stop.
>
> **MENTAL HEALTH TREATMENT PROGRAM DIRECTOR**

The NAMI website has special sections for childhood and adolescent problems, but nothing specific to emerging adults, and this omission reflects a larger problem in the mental health system. Currently, there is no specialized mental health training for the distinctive problems and issues of the life stage between ages 18 and 29. There are specialties for childhood and adolescence, but once people reach age 18 they enter the adult mental health system, which does not distinguish whether the "adult" is 18 or 80.

Nevertheless, parents and emerging adults seeking a mental health professional may be able to find someone who has extensive experience with this age group. For example, Jane Malkiewich, a clinical social worker in Massachusetts, has seen a broad spectrum of problems and responses to treatment in her thirty years of working with people in their twenties. In the course of her work she sees young people who have schizophrenia, bipolar disorder, major depression, and substance abuse disorders, along with a wide range of other problems.

Many of the young people Malkiewich sees in her clinical work have already been in the mental health system for years as adolescents. When they reach emerging adulthood and can't be forced to receive treatment anymore, they often refuse treatment for a period. "You see them wanting to get away from the mental health system," Malkiewich observes. "They've been in group homes, and mental hospitals, and now they want to break away. Sometimes that means not taking their meds, not doing their treatment. Before 18, their parents and other adults make the decisions, but once they turn age 18, they're in charge."

When their children have serious emotional struggles, parents may find it frustrating that their influence diminishes as children move from adolescence to emerging adulthood. But for young people, this transition can be empowering, and ultimately it can improve their chances of dealing successfully with their problems, Malkiewich believes. Young people "are the experts about themselves," she says. "So, when they become emerging adults and they can legally make their own decisions, they can have more impact on their own treatment, and their parents don't have to agree with them. If they want to pursue something like education or their own apartment or a job, and their parents don't think they can do it, they can try it anyway. Parents are used to them being dependent, used to taking care of them, and they don't want them to fail, but sometimes remaining dependent is not the best thing."

When seeking a therapist for your grown kid, you may wish to consider choosing one who has skills in both individual and family therapy. Many therapists elect to see only the emerging adult. However, Jack Brunner, a psychotherapist in suburban Cleveland who specializes in treating emerging adults, believes that relying on individual therapy alone can limit its effectiveness. In his experience the parents are often a valuable source of information about the emerging adult, and he treats them as allies in the treatment process. He meets the parents at the beginning of treatment and takes a careful life history of his emerging adult client. Later, he may use family therapy sessions to resolve conflicts within the home.

"If you just meet with the emerging adult," he observes, "you can miss a lot of crucial facts about his life. When you talk with the parents, you learn all sorts of things, like the emerging adult being frequently irritable if not explosive, playing video games until 4 a.m. and waking up at 1 p.m., and expending little energy toward finding a job or continuing his education.

"Moreover, in family therapy, the presence of the parents triggers emotions in the emerging adult that you never see in individual therapy, such as anger, confusion, and fear. Working through these emotions in the family system can be helpful to both the parents and emerging adult."

The purpose of family therapy is to provide a setting for constructive parent-child communications that may be unlikely to occur otherwise. This approach can help parents and their grown kid know which limits are fair to set, and understand which responsibilities are the parents' and which belong to the emerging adult.

Jesse Viner includes this method in his *Yellowbrick* program, a residential treatment program in Evanston, Illinois, for emerging adults with serious mental health problems. "We invite parents to come each week to what we call Family Rounds, which are like strategic planning meetings for the treatment." An important part of Family Rounds is providing a structure for grown kids to talk openly to their parents. "We don't speak for the emerging adults," says Dr. Viner. "They speak for themselves, and we encourage that. In fact, we require it. So much of what has gone wrong is that the emerging adults have lost their sense of agency, their belief that they can do things effectively, and we think it really has to come from them and be about them for it to work. Only they can really speak for who they are and what's going on inside them."

Yellowbrick is founded on a principle of what Viner calls *connected autonomy,* which is similar to the stepping back–staying connected balance we've emphasized throughout this book. Promoting autonomy usually includes trying to elevate the emerging adult's status within the parent-child relationship. "If emerging adults have been having mental health problems for a while, parents have taken more power," explains Dr. Viner. "We promote power-sharing, because we believe emerging adults need to have more of a sense of control over their own lives." He adds, "What we're *not* doing is digging up past family traumas, because we discovered that when families came in and talked about traumas it was like a hand grenade and knocked all the blocks down. We've found it's best to look forward."

Here again, our persistent theme: the challenge of stepping back while staying connected and offering support. It's even more acute for parents of emerging adults with mental health problems than for other parents. And it's especially difficult to step back when you have seen your child struggle, stumble, and fall so many times before. Likewise, it's especially difficult to stay connected when doing so often brings pain and frustration. Parents of emerging adults with mental health disorders often need to stay more connected, for longer, than other parents do, because their grown-up kids need more help in order to make progress toward building an adult life. Most emerging adults make a more or less smooth landing into a stable adult life by age 30, but 30 is no magic number, and for those with mental health disorders it may take longer. The improvement may be intermittent, and there may be steps backward as well as forward. Yet for nearly all, progress is possible, with parents' support and with access to mental health treatment.

13

Emerging at Last

I knew my son had reached adulthood when
he bought a high school graduation card for a
family friend—and put his own money in it!

MOTHER OF A SON, 25

A lthough the road from adolescence to adulthood is longer today than ever before, the journey does eventually end—with nearly all emerging adults becoming full-fledged grown-ups, capable of handling the range of responsibilities that are part of adult life. Parents sometimes fear that the uncertainty and unsteadiness they see in their grown-up kids may be permanent traits. They grimly envision sons and daughters in their thirties, forties, and beyond, launched but never landed, still wandering . . . and still financially and emotionally dependent on their parents. But except in cases of severe physical or mental illness, this rarely happens.

Sometimes there's comfort to be had from literature as well as life and reassurance that the flip-flopping of the emerging adult years does come to an end. In Benjamin Kunkel's novel, *Indecision,* written when he was 33, we meet his 28-year-old hero, Dwight Wilmerding, who is "having a pathological crisis of indecision." Should he commit to his girlfriend or break up with her, find a new job (and if so, in what?), stay in New York City, move to Vermont . . . or travel? Kunkel defines Dwight's syndrome as "paralyzed with the maybes" and gives him a diagnosis that has not yet made it to the psychiatrists' manual: "Abulia . . . the impairment or loss of ability to make decisions." Then the novelist imagines— ah, if it were only this easy—a magic pill that he calls "abulinix" to cure this human condition.

Dwight enrolls in a double-blind study to test abulinix and dutifully takes his daily doses of the pill while stumbling forward with his life. He decides to travel to South America, parts company with his girlfriend, falls in love with a young woman he meets on his trip, and returns to the States with a more centered life and the ability to move forward. Only then does he find—spoiler alert!—that the drug he's been taking is the placebo; he has actually resolved his existential dilemma on his own.

So it goes for most abulia-riddled 20-somethings. Like Dwight, they muddle through this decade-plus with tentative steps, missteps, and sidesteps, and they do eventually create a path toward a life's work, a steady relationship, and financial stability.

The Gradual Emergence of Grown-Up Kids

Even given this hopeful prospect, it turns out that knowing exactly when emerging adults have emerged is rather subtle and complicated. How do you know when your child has reached adulthood? What does it mean to become an adult?

One reason Jeff first came up with the term "emerging adulthood" is that 18- to 29-year-olds he interviewed rarely gave a simple "yes" or "no" answer to the question, "Do you feel like you have reached adulthood?" Instead, they most often gave an ambiguous response: in some ways, yes; in other ways, no. By now this finding has been confirmed in many studies, by Jeff and others. It applies to both young men and young women, it applies across social classes and ethnic groups, and it applies around the world—from Argentina to Austria, from Israel to China. Emerging adults typically feel like they are on the way to adulthood, but not there yet.

Most of their parents see them that way, too. Research by Larry Nelson and his colleagues at Brigham Young University reports that two-thirds of parents of college students nationwide view their children as adults "in some ways yes, in some ways no." In our survey of parents for this book, 52 percent chose the "in some ways yes, in some ways no" response, 8 percent responded "no," and 40 percent chose the straight-forward "yes." Most "yes" responses applied to older children, in their late twenties. "At times she seems so accomplished, but at others so naive," observed one mom in a typical response. A dad described his daughter as "very intent on supporting herself financially, but is not yet able to have her car repaired herself or balance her checking account." "Still a kid in many ways," another mom wrote of her son.

This in-betweenness puts parents in a tricky position. On the one hand, their emerging adults are still emerging, and still need and want parental assistance—on their own terms. On the other hand, parents who offer to help—or try to take things over—may be resented and pushed away. "Our daughter wants to be more independent but doesn't exhibit some of the necessary traits to 'make it on her own,'" says one frustrated mom. "She hates my 'overmothering,' but also relies on us in ways that make me wonder if she can do it by herself." The safest strategy—and one we've advocated throughout this book, on issues from love to money—is to provide help only when requested, and only when you are able and willing to give it. But it can be difficult to hold back from rushing in when grown-up kids seem to be struggling or even sinking on their own. Some parents also acknowledge that they feel some ambivalence about their children becoming adults. "Part of it is that he is still in-between, and part of it is me not knowing how to stop being a full-time mother," admits one mom. For some parents, stepping back from being the full-time, go-to person can be as ongoing a challenge as becoming a self-sufficient adult is for their grown kids.

The Big Three Markers of Adulthood

One of the reasons the transition to adulthood is so gradual and ambiguous today is that the main criteria for adulthood are also gradual and ambiguous. Back in Grandma's and Grandpa's time, reaching adulthood was simple and straightforward, marked by specific events: You finished your education, you left home, you got married, and voilà, you were an adult. Then you had a kid, too, to seal the deal.

Today, however, none of these traditional markers remains an important signifier of adult status, not for emerging adults and not for their parents, either. When we asked parents in our survey, "What is important in reaching adulthood for your child, in your opinion?" these were the responses:

- Accepting responsibility for him/herself   89 percent

- Becoming financially independent   85 percent

- Making independent decisions   79 percent

- Finishing education   63 percent

- Moving out of parents' household   48 percent

- Becoming more considerate of others   33 percent

- Getting married   10 percent

- Having a child   6 percent

This list does not comprise the entire universe of markers that may be important to individual families. Parents can be very specific and sometimes droll about the eureka moment when they realized their particular child was a grown-up: He fills up the tank with gas after borrowing the car. She starts flossing. He starts paying into his retirement fund. She starts worrying about her parents traveling to dangerous places. Nevertheless, overall, most parents favor the Big Three markers of adulthood—*accepting responsibility for one's self, making independent decisions,* and *becoming financially independent.*

To researchers, the Big Three are familiar. The same basic pattern has been reported numerous times in the United States, across genders, regions, ethnic groups, and social classes, and in countries all over the world. It is still a truly remarkable pattern. None of the Big Three is one of the traditional events that have defined adulthood historically across cultures: leave home, get married, have a child. The Big Three are all processes, not events, taking place gradually over several years for most young people. This new pattern explains why so many emerging adults

My daughter takes full responsibility for her activities, obligations, and commitments, but she's a student and completely financially dependent on us. And she sometimes still leaves the table without clearing her dishes.

FATHER OF A DAUGHTER, 22

have that "in some ways yes, in some ways no" feeling about adulthood.

But what is most remarkable is the way the traditional signposts of adulthood have declined in importance. Finishing education still ranks pretty high, right after the Big Three. Moving away from home is also regarded as significant by about half of parents. But marriage, long regarded as the indisputable stamp of reaching adulthood, has faded to irrelevance. Nor is having a child any longer seen as a crucial indicator of adult status, much less a requirement for adulthood.

The demise of marriage and parenthood as markers of adulthood is surprising, but there are good reasons why they have faded in prominence. Think for a moment what marriage represented for your grandparents. For most of the men and nearly all the women, it was when they left home for the first time. Marriage was also the first time they ever lived with anyone but a family member. And upon marriage they often had their first sexual relationship. Furthermore, marriage in those days really did mean "'til death do us part." Divorce was extremely rare, so marriage was a permanent commitment. In light of these considerations, it is understandable that marriage was a life event with huge, multiple meanings, including the entry to adulthood.

Marriage remains a major milestone, of course. Most people still intend it to be a lifelong commitment, even though that now turns out to be true only about half the time. We still surround the event of marriage with a big celebration—bigger (and more expensive) than ever, in fact. But today most young people, women as well as men, have left home for many years before they enter marriage. They have lived with many other people, and about two-thirds have cohabited with a romantic partner, most likely the person they are now marrying. They have been sexually active for a decade or more by the time they choose to marry. So, marriage is still an important life transition, but it is nowhere near as momentous as it was for Grandma and Grandpa.

Similar observations could be made about parenthood. Having children used to follow in a predictable sequence after marriage; now 40 percent of American births take place outside marriage. Parenthood used to be inevitable for anyone who had a regular sexual relationship; now, with effective contraception widely available, people can choose when, where, and whether to have children, and can easily avoid becoming parents if they want, regardless of their sex lives. But some things *haven't* changed: Jeff's original research shows that young people who become parents at a relatively young age still see parenthood as a sudden thrust into adulthood, ready or not.

Early marriage and parenthood aside, the new Big Three markers of adulthood mean that the entrance to adulthood must be understood differently. Instead of a parent asking, "Why isn't she married yet?" it may be better to ask, "Is she learning to make her own decisions?" Instead of "Why is he still living at home with us?" it may be better to ask, "Is he learning to take responsibility for his actions?" Even emerging adults who still live at home or have moved back home can be making progress toward taking on responsibilities, making independent decisions, and becoming financially independent. As long as steps are being taken toward the Big Three, parents would be wise not to obsess over whether the traditional markers have been attained yet. If emerging adults are moving steadily toward the Big Three, then moving out, getting married or finding a long-term partner, and having children are likely to come in good time.

> When will she be an adult? When she stops getting pissy!!
>
> MOTHER OF A DAUGHTER, 20

"I Grew Up Faster"
Parents Reflect on Becoming Adults

You might think that boomer parents and those who followed— products of the same social revolutions that eventually produced the new life stage of emerging adulthood—would easily relate to this new way of becoming adult. But in our interviews, relatively few parents mentioned any of the Big Three when we asked what had marked the entry to adulthood for them. Instead, they tended to recall specific events that had been important signifiers of adult status. Marriage and parenthood were more important in the past than today, partly because these transitions often took place so early. "For me, getting married" signified adulthood, recalled one mom. "I got married at 22, right when I finished college." She contrasted her experience with her 23-year-old daughter's path: "My daughter is going back to school next year; she's not an adult yet." Another mother exemplified the sudden lurch into adulthood that takes place when young people become parents at a young age—for her, age 22: "I remember when we were driving home from the hospital when our first son was born, we were like, 'What do we do now?' We knew we had to grow up fast to take care of him."

Finishing education is another major event parents often cited as a marker of their adulthood. One dad recalled feeling adult "when I got out of college and got my first real job. Buying the suits, going to work every day."

Studies of emerging adults today have found that they often feel adult earlier than their peers if they have experienced tough times growing up, and we found this to be true of parents as well. A mom in our study, who grew up as the oldest daughter of a single mom, felt fully adult already at age 16, when she started working part-time to help support the family: "I got my first job, at a department store, and we had to contribute back to the household, even if it was five or ten dollars. I wanted to do anything I could to help my mother." Another mom also remembered feeling the pressure to help her poor family financially from a young age, and had the additional responsibility of helping care for her aging, ailing grandmother. "I have felt like an adult from very early on," she recalls. "My friends were out partying and this and that, and I never did. My nanna was living with us and she was dying, and I had to help care for her. I was working from the time I was twelve, helping provide for the family, because my parents didn't have much money."

Because the timing of the entry to adulthood has changed so much in just a generation, parents have to be careful not to apply the norms of their generation to their own children and conclude that their children are falling short. It's a great temptation to indulge in the many judgments that begin, *"When I was your age . . ."* Just because parents got married at 21 and had a first child at 22 doesn't mean that's the timetable their children should follow, even if it worked out fine for the parents. Just because the parents finished their education by age 22 and have worked full-time ever since doesn't mean that the same strategy would be successful for their children and end in long-term happiness. Research indicates that people who wait until their late twenties or thirties to marry and have children are generally happier in their marriage and more patient as parents than their peers who entered those roles earlier. As for education, yes, it takes longer than in the past, but that's not because young people are lazier. It's mainly because they are employed more hours while in school in order to pay the high costs of college expenses. Young people need support in their twenties to pursue their Plans and reach their goals.

The Pros and Cons of a Later Adulthood: Parents' Perspectives

We've made a case throughout the book for the upside of the new life stage of emerging adulthood, partly to give consolation to parents who worry their children are taking too long to grow up and partly to dispel the many negative stereotypes about young people in their twenties. But how do parents see the upsides and the downsides of the lengthened road to adulthood? When we asked parents in our survey whether they saw the later entry to adulthood today as positive, negative, or both, few parents responded with either a straight "positive" (10 percent) or a simple "negative" (20 percent). Most (70 percent) chose the ambivalent "both positive and negative" response.

Parents were usually positive about the opportunity for explorations that a later entry to adulthood allows, but negative about the problems that some emerging adults have in making progress toward building an adult life: "Positive because adulthood is not forced on them and they are allowed to develop at their own pace," stated one mom, but "negative because it causes some to never grow up." "Positive because they have longer to get to know themselves to make better informed choices," explained another mom, but "negative because we seem to have lowered our expectations for them." A dad observed, "It gives them time not to rush their choices, but since they don't feel the rush, they might delay doing certain things they should be doing."

Many parents expressed concern that their help might actually be hindering their emerging adults' transition to adulthood. "My son still lives at home," said a dad. "In one way this is positive because he is trying to become more financially stable in order to move out. On the other hand, it's negative because we (his parents and the comforts of home) are like a crutch. It may be too easy to stay home." Some parents noted how their grown kids' later entry to adulthood affects their lives, too. This mom was both succinct and sardonic: "Positive: They see parents as resources; negative: They see parents as resources."

Parents also sometimes made generational comparisons, noting how they entered adulthood earlier than their children did because, as one dad said, "It was simply expected." However, other parents observed that their earlier transition to adulthood was not such a great thing. One mother expressed regret that "our generation rushed into adulthood without thinking about what we really wanted to do or who we really wanted to be." Another mom went back one more generation for the comparison: "Families today have the luxury of allowing their children to grow up more slowly, and to take the time to pursue higher education. In this way it's a positive. I think that the World War II generation would have liked to have taken longer to grow up, but they didn't have the same opportunities for higher education that we have today. Their faster entry into adulthood was a necessity."

So how *should* parents regard their emerging adults' longer-than-in-the-past transition to adulthood? Bonanza or burden? Delightful or deplorable? Like many of the questions we've addressed in this book, no one answer fits every family. The answer depends on the personalities, relationships, and life circumstances of the people involved. What we *can* tell you is that research strongly indicates that when parents are able and willing to provide financial and emotional support during their grown-up kids' twenties, the kids are more likely to emerge successfully into a

The Parents' Do and Don't List

DO:

- Support grown kids' pursuit of higher education and job training in every way you can. Remember that education is the key to success in the modern economy.

- Provide contacts for possible jobs when your emerging adult is looking for one.

- Offer a shoulder to cry on when love goes bad—and remember that shoulders don't talk, they listen.

- Be willing to open up the bedroom-now-guestroom/ exercise room to a returning child for a clearly defined transition period.

- Be willing to provide financial support, if you are able without compromising your own financial health, especially if it's for a worthy purpose.

- *If* asked, talk about the pros and cons of having children at the ages you did.

- Talk about your own experiences in your twenties and what you learned from them, good and bad.

DON'T:

- Make snide comments about the job prospects in the field your son or daughter is studying in college or graduate school.

- Urge your emerging adults to take a job in a field that pays well but that they hate.

- Confide how you "never liked" that ex-boyfriend/girlfriend, then detail why. Remember, that was a person your grown kid once loved, and exes sometimes come back into the picture.

- Do all the housework and laundry and make all the meals for grown-up kids living in your home. They are capable of contributing to household duties as an adult, so sit down and agree on who will do what.

- Use financial support as a way to control the decisions your grown kids make in love and work.

- Mention repeatedly that all your friends have grandchildren already and you sure wish you did, too.

- Expect your emerging adults to make the same choices you would have made as they construct their own adult lives.

stable and self-sufficient adulthood in their thirties. True, you may not love it when you see your 20-somethings changing jobs yet again, or asking for money to try still another educational track. But for most young people, the explorations of their twenties will help prepare them for a steady and fulfilling adulthood. As long as young people are working on what we've called the capital P Plan—this is crucial—their parents' assistance will make them less rather than more dependent in the long run.

And what if they do *not* have this Plan? What if they seem listless and aimless, passive in the face of the challenges of building a life? What if their "exploring" phase seems more like floundering, and their landing is nowhere in sight, even in their late twenties? Parents can talk to their emerging adults, if the emerging adults are willing, and see if they can help them sort through their options and define goals. But the goals themselves, and the motivation to get there, are not something parents can give to their children at this life stage, much as they might wish to. Consider whether depression or other emotional issues might be involved. Even if a diagnosis of major depression may not fit, it may be a good idea to involve a therapist who can help emerging adults talk through their lives in an objective but caring way.

The Best and the Worst of Times

In the course of this book we've talked repeatedly about the dance of stepping back while staying connected. When we asked parents about the best and worst parts of parenting during these years, this theme came up once again.

Staying connected is prized by the parents of grown-up kids, but they emphasize that the nature of the connection changes during this decade-plus. As we have described, parents and children make a transition sometime in the late teens or early twenties from a parent-child relationship to something that is more like a friendship. This is a change that most parents find gratifying. According to one mom, "The best part is starting to develop an adult relationship with them, a friendship—which I don't think you *should* do when they're younger. When you get to the point when you can have that friendship, it's fun!" Another mom says that the mutual support she gets from her relationship with her son is especially important to her as a single parent. For her, the best part of parenting in this life stage is that "I have a best friend! I have support. When I'm falling he picks me up, and when he falls I pick him up."

But why is stepping back so often mentioned as both the best *and* the worst part of parenting emerging adults? Stepping back is "best" in the sense that parents take great satisfaction in the progress of their emerging adults toward building a life; but it's "worst" in the sense of losing the power to protect them from life's slings and arrows. When children succeed in beginning to establish an adult life for themselves, it feels like parents have succeeded, too. A dad of a daughter and son in their twenties says he takes great pleasure in "seeing my kids go out on their own and making it in the world. It makes me feel that whatever I did when they were growing up must be working."

Yet this life stage can be agonizingly the "worst," too, since it means sending children out into a world that can be hard on youthful dreams. For one mother of two sons in their twenties, the most difficult part of parenting now is "not to be able to make everything OK. You want to fix everything." For another mom, this one of an 18-year-old daughter, the biggest challenge is "Letting her go! Definitely the hardest part. Letting her make her own decisions. Letting her fail!" Many parents have learned by now not to offer unsolicited advice, no matter how wise and well intended it might be. But holding back isn't always easy. "The hardest part is when I see them doing something I know is not the best way to do it, and they're not open to any advice," says a dad. "I've had to learn that I can't tell them what to do anymore."

The other "worst" part of parenting emerging adults is that it often means being less close to them than at earlier life stages. Yes, it's wonderful to discover how a grown child can become a friend, but often your new friend is someone you don't see nearly as much as you'd like to. "The hardest part, I guess, is that we're very close to the end of the story," reflects a mom, speaking of her two 20-something sons. "They're almost grown up." A mom of two girls is delighted to see their capabilities growing daily, yet she can't help but regret that "it will never be the same again! And that's really hard, because I have just loved it." A mom of one son has to remind herself that times have changed in a way she misses.

> Our son possesses a spectacular work ethic, knows that gratification and rewards come from hard work, and is rather independent. On occasion, though, he likes to be taken care of. He just runs out of steam.
>
> **MOTHER OF A SON, 26**

"We used to cuddle a lot, but now I try to be careful not to kiss him on the cheek in public. He doesn't want me to do that anymore. But I'll text him and tell him I love him. I think it's important to let him know."

And what advice would these parents give to other parents whose children are about to reach the 18-to-29-age period? Step back, hard as that may be. But stay connected, to the extent you can. Not that it's easy, attaining this delicate balance. One mom recommends that parents "try to be there for them, try to guide them," but she also acknowledges, "you can't make them do anything! Try to hold on, it can be a rough ride!" Give your grown-up kids the room to build a life according to their own dreams. One wise mom advises parents: "Really take a great deep breath away from all of your expectations for how your children should live their lives and what you should expect of them as adults so that they can become themselves."

What Now?

My, how quiet it is after the kids have left home. No one coming in the door noisily in the wee hours after a night out partying with friends. No gang of kids gathering in the kitchen and bantering and laughing loudly as they devour everything in sight. No mile-a-minute dinner table conversations where everyone wants to talk at once on a hot topic.

It's pleasant, in a way. You probably won't miss lying awake waiting for your child to return from that late night out with friends. Your grocery bill will diminish dramatically, along with your bills for pretty much everything else (except college tuition, but that's another topic). Dinner table conversations may be less lively, but now you and your spouse or partner will actually be able to hear each other and get a word in edgewise. If you were a single parent, a huge responsibility will lift from your shoulders and you'll turn back to your own life with more freedom. Still, once your last emerging adult leaves home, a big question looms: Now that the parenting part of my life is over, what should I do? How will my life change?

Of course, in one sense the "parenting part" of life never ends for people who have children, because they maintain the connection throughout life. Still, there's no doubt that the day their youngest child leaves home is a major milestone in the lives of parents. This is true today more than ever. It used to be that most people's entire adult life centered around raising children. Two hundred years ago, the average American woman gave birth to eight children! Often, some of them died in infancy or early childhood, but most would live to adulthood. And most adults died much younger. At the start of the twentieth century, few people lived past their sixties. There was no post-parenthood stage of life for most people. You got married, you had kids, you raised them (if you were lucky to live long enough), and you died.

Thanks to the medical and contraceptive revolutions of the twentieth century, all this has changed. Most parents have only one or two kids, and few have more than three. Life expectancy has increased astoundingly. It is now close to 80 years, and rising steadily with each medical advancement. People who reach age 65 are likely to live at least another twenty years, on average. Parents typically have their kids in their late twenties or early thirties, so most are only in their forties or fifties by the time their youngest child reaches age 18. That means there is a lot of life left ahead of them.

Fortunately, life satisfaction typically rises during the fifties, as we have discussed earlier, and it continues to rise through the sixties and seventies for most people. Meanwhile, stress, worry, and anger all decline from midlife onward. Divorce rates plummet; couples who have stayed married for twenty or more years are less likely than ever to split. Work satisfaction peaks in the forties and fifties, as most people reach a level of authority, expertise, and income higher than at earlier periods of their work lives.

Midlife, then, is no dismal slough of despondency for most people, but the prime of life, the sweet spot. Entering the post-parenting stage of life does not mean a slope-shouldered slide toward oblivion but new opportunities for self-development and reinvention. After about two decades when so much of life was structured around providing for children and running them here and there and keeping them safe and happy, at last it's time for parents to turn their attention back to their own lives. Identity questions, long shunted aside in the press of parenting duties, now reemerge. Emerging adults ask, "Who am I?" In the post-parenting stage, midlife adults ask, "Who am I *now*?"

This rosy portrait of post-parenting midlife does not apply to everyone. For people who lose their jobs, experience a midlife divorce, suffer financial reversals, or encounter serious health problems, this stage of life is a struggle. They do not have the luxury of entertaining identity questions, because they are desperately trying to make it through each day.

Overall, however, the post-parenting stage holds potential as a time of great promise. It marks an end, but also a new chapter. For those who can avoid serious health problems and financial difficulties, it can be a time of flourishing like never before, with many of the same freedoms as emerging adulthood but with more self-knowledge about what you do best and what you really enjoy (and don't enjoy). Will this be a time when you finally do that thing with your life you've always wanted to do? For parents who are single, will this be the time to strengthen your circle of friends or perhaps find a partner to share the second half of your life with? Why not go back to school to retrain yourself in a new field, or just to learn about something that has sparked your curiosity? Maybe the real "glory days" are not those footloose, expansive times of the emerging adult years, but the post-parenting years, when freedom returns, this time accompanied by greater wisdom, maturity, and self-knowledge.

Your grown kids will be part of your post-parenting life, too. Eventually grown-up kids do grow up, nearly all of them. They become self-sufficient, they become financially independent (yes, it will happen!), they finally stick with a job that lasts for many years. They find a beloved partner, and most will have kids of their own. That's a happy vision of their future lives, and your life, too, as you complete the shift from parent of an emerging adult to advisor, confidant, and friend of your fully grown kids.

ACKNOWLEDGMENTS

Above all our heartfelt thanks to the hundreds of parents who shared their stories in interviews and in our survey, as well as to many of their grown children who had their own versions to tell. We appreciate their honesty and openness about the exciting, unnerving, and transformative years between 18 and 29.

Our thanks as well to the experts in many fields who generously discussed their valuable ideas and insights, including Scott Aaron, Ellen Bader and Peter Pearson, David Blustein, James Cordova, Carolyn and Philip Cowan, Toni Littlestone, Monica McGoldrick, Mark "Marko" Ostreicher, Marianne Ruggiero, Jennifer Tanner, David Treadway, Carmen Wong Ulrich, Jesse Viner, the late Judith Wallerstein, and Sheri Glucoft Wong.

We're grateful to the friends and family members who kindly read drafts or gave important suggestions: Mike Arnett, Jack Brunner, Anne Fishel, Leah Fisher, Josie Gerst, Kirk Getsinger, Mona Halaby, Bob, Nate, and Will Houghteling, Regina Kelly, Dusky Pierce, Nancy Pietrafesa, Ray Quinlan, Mary Jane Ryan, Merry Selk, Antoinette Sheridan, David Skeel, Maya Tester, Susan Waisbren, and Alice Wilkins-Malloy.

Our appreciation, as ever, to our terrific agents, Joy Harris and Neil Salkind, who shepherded and supported this project from the beginning.

Huge thank-yous to our gifted editor, Suzie Bolotin, who brought us together, and whose vision, careful reading, and good spirits helped shape this book at every stage. It was a special bonus that she also had the expertise that comes from being the mother of two emerging adults.

We are impressed with the entire creative, hard-working Workman team: Peter Workman, Bob Miller, Page Edmunds, Avery Finch, Andrea Fleck-Nisbet, Courtney Greenhalgh, Amanda Hong, Raquel Jaramillo, Anne Kerman, Randall Lotowycz, Jenny Mandel, Claire McKean, Selina

Meere, Steven Pace, Kristina Peterson, Julie Primavera, David Schiller, Sarah Smith, James Wehrle, Walter Weintz, Jessica Wiener. Thanks to each of them for their expert help in launching this book.

Elizabeth gives a special shout-out to her beloved sons, Nate and Will, and her eight nieces and nephews, Sara, Charlotte, Sylvia, Pearl, Gabe, Joe, Sam, and Jack, who taught her so much of what she knows about 20-somethings. And finally, love and thanks to Bob who makes the solitary writing life less solitary and so much happier.

Jeff is grateful to his parents, Marjorie and Calvin Arnett, who somehow survived his all-too-eventful emerging-adult years. He also thanks his wife, Lene, always full of wise insights and counsel, and his twins, Miles and Paris, from whom he has learned volumes about being a dad and who promise to teach him even more when they reach emerging adulthood. No hurry, though, kids.

Finally, Jeff would like to thank Clark University, especially the president, David Angel, and the provost, Davis Baird, who arranged funding for the Clark University Poll of Emerging Adults that was an important contribution to the data for this book.

INDEX